The Twentieth Century
A Century of Wars and Revolutions?

The Twentieth Century
A Century of Wars and Revolutions?

Edited by Keith Flett and David Renton

Rivers Oram Press
London

Published in 2000
by Rivers Oram Press, an imprint of
Rivers Oram Publishers Ltd
144 Hemingford Road, London N1 1DE

Distributed in the USA by
New York University Press
838 Broadway
New York, NY 10003–4183

Distributed in Australia and New Zealand by
UNIReps
University of New South Wales
Sydney, NSW 2052

Set in Galliard by
NJ Design Associates
and printed in Great Britain by
T.J. Press International Ltd

British Library Cataloguing in Publication Data
A catalogue record for this publication is available from the British Library
ISBN 1 85489 127 8 (paper)
ISBN 1 85489 126 X (cloth)

Contents

Introduction   1
The Best of Times the Worst of Times?
The Twentieth Century in Retrospect
    Keith Flett and David Renton

1. **Globalisation in the Twentieth Century**   14
    Adrian Budd

2. **One Step Forwards, Two Steps Back**   33
    Progress German Style
        Esther Leslie

3. **Daughters of the Century**   54
    The Politics of Women's Liberation 1900–99
        Anne Alexander

4. **Reformism at the Polls**   80
    Workers in the United States 1918–24
        Andrew Strouthous

5. **John Reed and the United States of America**   99
    John Newsinger

6. **The Success and Failure of the Comintern**   117
    Ian Birchall

7. **'Revolutionary Gymnastics' and the**   133
Unemployed
    The Limits of the Spanish Anarchist Utopia 1931–37
        Chris Ealham

8. **Recent Trends in the Historiograpy of**   156
    Italian Fascism
    Tobias Abse

9. **Woodrow Wilson is Amongst Us**   172
    The Consequences of the Principle of Nationality in
    South Asia
    Barry Pavier

10. **The Long Boom and the Advanced World**   183
    1945–73
    Michael Haynes

11. **Socialists and Economic Growth**   204
    The Myth of Employers and Union Connivance in
    Explaining Relative Economic Decline
    Carlo Morelli

12. **The Twentieth Century**   220
    An Age of Extremes or an Age of Possibilities?
    Chris Harman

    Notes   234
    Index   273

The contributors

Keith Flett is an active socialist and trade unionist who convenes the socialist history seminar at the Institute of Historical Research, University of London. He has published numerous articles and pamphlets on nineteenth- and twentieth-century British labour history and is a well-known contributor to debates in journals and British newspapers.

David Renton has taught at Rhodes University, South Africa and is a history lecturer at Edge Hill College. His recent books are *Fascism: Theory and Practice* and *Fascism and Anti-Fascism in Britain in the 1940s*.

Tobias Abse is a lecturer in modern European history at Goldsmiths' College, University of London and author of *Sovversivi e fascisti a Livorno: Lotta politica e sociale (1918–1922)* and numerous articles on Italian twentieth-century history.

Anne Alexander is a low-paid worker in the National Health Service. Elsewhere she has written about the history of Egypt and the Sudan. She is a member of the Socialist Workers' Party.

Ian Birchall is an independent socialist historian and has written on Babeuf and Sartre (forthcoming), and translated Rosmer and Serge.

Adrian Budd teaches at South Bank University, London, and is on the editorial board of the journal *Contemporary Politics*.

Chris Ealham teaches Spanish history in the School of European Studies at Cardiff University. He is the author of several articles on labour and social protest in Spain.

Chris Harman is the editor of *Socialist Worker*. He has published several works of history and economic theory, the most recent of which was *A People's History of the World*.

Michael Haynes teaches economic history at the University of Wolverhampton. His published work includes a biography of Bukharin and several major articles on Eastern Europe for *International Socialism Journal*.

Esther Leslie lectures in English and Humanities at Birkbeck College, University of London. She has had articles published in *Historical Materialism*, *Revolutionary History* and *New Left Review*.

Carlo Morelli teaches economic history at the University of Dundee. He has published widely on economic theory and history.

John Newsinger lectures in history at Bath Spa University College. His most recent books are *Orwell's Politics* and *The Dredd Phenomenon*.

Barry Pavier is a lecturer at Bradford College. His next book, *South Asia in the Era of Capitalism*, will be published in 2000.

Andrew Strouthous is a lecturer in history at Colchester Institute and the Open University. He recently published *US Labor and Political Action 1918–24*.

Introduction
The Best of Times, the Worst of Times?
The Twentieth Century in Retrospect

Keith Flett and David Renton

At the close of the century, it is appropriate for historians to begin thinking and writing about these years to make sense of our past. But what is the best way to structure a history of the last one-hundred years? Some accounts of our century are chronological: Martin Gilbert's monumental *A History of the Twentieth Century* offers its readers around twenty-five pages for each year of our century, while Sheila Rowbotham's *A Century of Women* limits itself to a chapter on each decade.[1] The method in this book is different. In order to come to a coherent sense of the past, not just describing events but also interpreting them, the structure of this book is thematic. Chapters address issues such as the rise of women, ethnic cleansing, the development of globalisation and the post-war boom. So which themes matter? How should historians choose the themes which enable them to make most sense of the twentieth century? One difficulty is that there is no agreed hierarchy of meaning. Different writers, historians, various political traditions have each placed their own rival interpretations on the years which we have lived through.

In the US, *Time* magazine has summarised the past hundred years in three phrases, 'the century of freedom', 'the century of capitalism', 'the American century'. Why freedom? Because in this century mankind has turned decisively towards the ideas of Plato and Locke, Mill and Jefferson, bringing 'individual rights, civil liberties, personal freedoms'. Why capitalism? Because of the defeat of Russia in the cold war, 'Lenin laid the groundwork for a command economy, and his successor, Stalin, showed how brutal it could be.' With Russia defeated, the only possibility left open was a capitalist future. Why the USA? Not only says *Time* because the USA is a superpower, but also because the USA is just, 'Some countries base their foreign policy on realism or its Prussian-accented cousin, *realpolitik*...America is unique in that it is equally motivated by idealism.' Triumphalist, complacent and dishonest to the past, *Time* magazine tells us that the great story of the twentieth century is the history of the victory of the USA over the Soviet Union in the cold war.[2]

It is not difficult to show that most of *Time*'s arguments are false. The majority of the world's population are not living in freedom, do not receive economic justice, do not celebrate American 'idealism'. After Hitler, Stalin, Franco, Augusto Pinochet and Pol Pot, and with far less than half the world's population yet enjoying civil liberties or multi-party elections, it should be clear that this has not been a century of freedom. It would be just as accurate to say that this has been an age of dictators and tyrants. On a simple head-count, the twentieth century must be 'the most violent century in human history'.[3] Capitalism's economic success can also be questioned. This is the system which has brought the world to disaster, most famously in 1929, but also in four global recessions since 1973. At the end of the century, it is estimated that the world's three richest families possess as much wealth as 600 million people, or one-tenth of the world's entire population. The world's 200 richest people own a staggering one *trillion* dollars ($1,000,000,000,000), while 1.3 billion people live on less than a dollar a day.[4] Under any normal test, progress towards equality, economic justice or freedom, twentieth-century capitalism is no unambiguous success. Even the image of the USA the victor is vulnerable. Trapped and defeated in its bloody colonial war in Vietnam, the American empire remains marked by fear and self-doubt. Muddling through against the threat of Japan and the instability of the New World Order, through the murder of one million civilians in Iraq and the possibility of global recession, the US has passed each of its recent tests, but none with conviction.

If not a century of the USA, then whose century has it been? Another magazine, *New Internationalist*, has christened this the 'radical' century, maintaining that the great social and political achievements of the past hundred years have been the product of protest and resistance movements, anti-colonialism, feminism, the labour movement, peace campaigns and environmentalism.[5] Such an approach is more optimistic, but remains one-sided. Those of us who have taken an active part in these campaigns are only too aware of how difficult it has been to transform the world in the direction of greater justice. In most countries, workers do not have noticeably more rights now than they did one-hundred years ago. The average working day is hardly shorter. The income gap between workers and managers is about the same, while the gap between workers and owners has grown enormously. The cold war may have ended—but the goals of the peace movement have not been realised.[6] Environmental campaigners have not secured a new era in which production is planned and considered in terms of human need. There have been some changes, certainly, but the underlying dynamic of the system is no different. And while we continue to live in a society where production is for profit, then any popular change will be partial and contested, and will need constant renewal.

As historians differentiate between the competing claims of success made on behalf of different radical movements, it may be that the twentieth century is remembered as the time in which the countries of the Third World won their national liberation. While profit, capital and war remain, the oppression of nations does seem to be on the decline. At the start of the twentieth century, there were just two independent states in the continent of Africa: the Ethiopian empire, and Liberia (itself a semi-colony of the USA). The century ended with the defeat of apartheid in South Africa and the victory of the ANC over white minority rule. There are no more colonies, the British, French, German and Portuguese empires have been consigned to history. And yet the defeat of colonial rule has not brought with it an era of general prosperity. From the 1970s onwards, Africa's share of world production has been in decline; in countries such as Somalia, Ethiopia and the Congo, progress towards social equality seems to have been reversed. In the 1980s, most African countries on average witnessed a 10 to 25 per cent drop in incomes, a 50 per cent reduction in per capita spending on education and a 25 per cent reduction in per capita spending on health.[7] The unequal balance of power between states continues.

One alternative description would be to name the 1900s as 'The Century of Women'. As Sheila Rowbotham points out, women have increased access to education, are more likely to own property, are overcoming legal obstacles and barriers against promotion in the workplace. The language and ideology of inequality are in retreat, and the claim that women should remain within the 'separate sphere' of domestic life has fewer defenders. Thus for Rowbotham, the twentieth century has witnessed 'the long trek into (almost) equal citizenship in the public sphere.'[8] Yet even in this context, the judgement is one of gain and loss, victory and defeat. 'The story that unfolds when we look at this century as a whole is neither a straightforward march of progress, nor one in which débâcle is ever absent.'[9] In every country in the world, women still do more work than men for less reward. In this book, Anne Alexander develops Sheila Rowbotham's argument, agreeing that this century has witnessed real advance in women's rights, but also stressing that for the majority much still needs to be done. Alexander concentrates on the politics of feminism, arguing that at the century's end many feminists offer a limited vision of what change is possible, and one that is a step backwards from the emancipatory demands of the women's liberation movement of the 1960s.

One theme which recurs across several chapters is that of

progress. For much of the century, the word has conveyed possibilities of peaceful change, of a more equal society, of slow but definite improvement. Science and medical technology have expressed themselves in major scientific advances: Einstein's theory of relativity, the discovery of penicillin, the invention of the electronic computer, the green revolution in agricultural productivity, Crick and Watson's discovery of DNA, the space programme. Descending from the world of science to the realm of politics, the dominant force within socialism, feminism and radicalism for most of the past hundred years has been Social Democracy. Labour and Social Democratic parties have both promised this limited progress. But how much has Social Democracy actually delivered, and how can historians test its achievements?

The key period is the 1950s and 1960s, when the world economy did grow at a steady rate. According to Eric Hobsbawm, 'Just how and why capitalism after the Second World War found itself, to everyone's surprise including its own, surging forward into the unprecedented and possibly anomalous Golden Age of 1973, are perhaps the major questions which face historians of the twentieth century.'[10] The increase in ownership of televisions, fridges, washing-machines and cars seemed to open an era of affluence; and many believed that the abuses of capitalism were being transformed and people enjoyed better access to travel, technology and proper medical care. The rapid rise in working-class living standards seemed to disprove Marx's theory of the rising rate of exploitation. Greater access to education, in particular, offered the hope of a classless future which could be achieved without conflict or struggle.

In this collection, Michael Haynes takes up the theme of economic convergence, asking why different capitalist economies prospered or declined between 1945 and 1973. He explains the success of the boom in terms of the high general levels of arms spending. The cold-war economy temporarily limited pressure towards overproduction and high levels of arms expenditure created a boom. Yet the countries which spent least on weapons, Japan and Germany, prospered most. Meanwhile the states which contributed most to the cold war (notably Britain, but also the Soviet Union and the USA) were the ones who saw their economies grow at the slowest rates. In a similar vein, Carlo Morelli explains the economic growth which did take place, rejecting the common view that growth was a product of consensus on the shop floor, he shows that it was possible only under accidental and unique circumstances.

If the twentieth century was a century of progress then a fundamental question is: who were the agents of change? Often change, particularly scientific advance, is seen as something impersonal. At other times change is described as if it were implemented by governments, the Clement Attlee Labour government of 1945–51, or Mitterrand's socialist administration in France after 1981. The chapters in this book take as their starting point the notion that change in society comes from below, and is shaped and led by working people and their political movements. There is often an engagement with forces from above, as the dialectic of change works itself through. Reforming governments succeed or fail depending—to a considerable extent—on the pressure from below for such reform. At other times, as the chapters on the theme of progress make clear, the economic prospects may be such that limited reforms from above can be used to control this pressure for change and progress.

However, it would be absurd to write only of the progress. Although this has been a century of increasing wealth and production, it has also been an age of brutality and dictatorship, in Samuel Totten's phrase, a 'Century of Genocide'.[11] The mass killings have included the murders in South-West Africa in 1904, in Armenia in 1915–23, in the Ukraine following collectivisation in 1932–3, and in Bangladesh in 1971. Millions were killed during the US war in Vietnam, and in Laos and Cambodia, and further by Pol Pot in Cambodia following the bombings in 1975–9. There have been genocidal killings in East Timor, Rwanda and the former Yugoslavia. Six million Jews were murdered in the Holocaust, and at some 50 million people died in the Second World War. In his history of the twentieth century, Clive Ponting takes an example of the generation born in Eastern Europe around 1900, 'People born in the Ukraine at the beginning of the century experienced the First World War and the German occupation, followed by civil war, mass killings and widespread starvation by the time they were in their twenties. If they survived they would have faced the imposition of Soviet rule, the ruthless anti-kulak and collectivisation drives, mass starvation...and the Stalinist terror.' After German invasion and Russian counter-invasion, Ponting writes, 'Anybody who survived until old age would have suffered from the consequences of the Chernobyl nuclear disaster.'[12] It follows from this dismal list that historians have a role, in cataloguing and explaining the brutality of the past. Writing the history of racism, nationalism or similar forces, historians should explains how it was that these ideas could hold such a powerful influence over the minds of millions. In this book, Toby Abse takes issue with recent trends in the historiography of Italian fascism, describing such figures as Renzo de Felice and Ernst Nolte as revisionists, whose work would minimise the destructive impact of fascism. Addressing the issue of genocide, Barry Pavier examines one notorious example of ethnic cleansing, the partition of India and Pakistan in 1948, and the victory of communalism in South Asia.

'The twentieth century', according to Francis Fukuyama, 'has made all of us into deep historical pessimists'. Hannah Arendt expressed a similar sentiment nearly fifty years ago: writing in 1953, Arendt described this as a century of violence and decay, mass politics, the defeat of liberal governments and the rise of totalitarianism: 'We no longer hope for an eventual restoration of the old world order with all its traditions, or for the reintegration of the masses of five continents who have been thrown into a chaos produced by the violence of wars and revolution and the growing decay of all that has still been spared.'[13] Yet not all of us are pessimists. The most satisfying descriptions are those which capture instead the contradictory nature of the past one-hundred years. While the world is richer, and human beings have far better access to education, a majority still live in poverty. While the past years have witnessed the most terrible wars and man-made famines, they have also seen an enormous advance in medical science, and human life-expectancy. The best histories are those that remark on the disparities in recent human development. In this way, Clive Ponting labels this the era of 'Progress and Barbarism', while Eric Hobsbawm names it the 'Age of Extremes'. According to Martin Gilbert, 'the twentieth century has witnessed some of humanity's greatest achievements and some of its worst excesses.'[14]

Such insights are not original. One of the earliest of its formulations appeared in the work of the Russian revolutionary Vladimir Lenin, who predicted that the twentieth century would be an age of wars and revolutions. For Lenin, a now deeply unfashionable thinker, popular revolutions were a source of hope! A similar perspective was developed by Rosa Luxemburg, the Polish Marxist murdered in Germany at the end of the failed Spartacus uprising of 1919. She predicted that this would be a century in which there would be one defining choice, 'socialism or barbarism'. One possibility was that the forces and values of capital would dominate, in which case the world would experience years of colonial plunder, misery and war. The alternative was that a different system would emerge, based on planning and collective discussion, human needs instead of profit. The perspective which informs the chapters in this book is that Rosa Luxemburg's choice has not yet been decided, and the last hundred years have witnessed both human progress and human retreat, an uneasy combination of reaction and reform.

The role of socialist historians is to show how it was that reform and reaction were connected, how it could be that the same processes of capitalism lead to such different results. One such trend has been the transition from peasant-based to industrial economies. At the start of the century, the dominant relations of profit and trade were clearly capitalist, yet a majority of the world's population lived on the land, and many were able to live with only a marginal relationship to the market. These one-hundred years have seen an enormous transition in the way that the majority of people work. Over half of the world's population now live in towns and cities and only now do a majority of people work in Marx's phrase, 'doubly free'—legally free to choose where they work, but free of capital and unable to control the conditions of their employment. The major trend in economic thinking now is to see the 1980s and 1990s as a period when global capital achieved a decisive advantage over the state.[15] A critical look at the way the world economy has developed over this century is given here by Adrian Budd who argues that the processes of globalisation have been with us since at least 1900.

Since this has been the first century in which a majority of people have produced for profit, it follows that class matters explain the events of the century. Our claim is not just that there have been movements of the oppressed: the authors of the chapters in this book also argue that the success of such movements helps to explain events in the high political arena. For example, it is impossible to understand the sheer brutality of Nazi Germany without looking at the rise and fall of German labour. As Donny Gluckstein has argued, it was because the German workers' movement was so strong, that capital required a mass movement to crush it; and it was because the German workers' movement was defeated, that the Nazis had the strength to move on and defeat their other enemies as well.[16] As socialist historians, the authors argue that it is economic changes: Marx's 'base', that have shaped events in both politics and culture: Marx's 'superstructure'. Thus there is a connection between history from above and history from below.

In terms of high politics, one of the most striking features of the twentieth century has been the relative decline of Britain, the nearest thing the world enjoyed to a superpower in 1900, and now barely a player on the second rank. Part of the reason for this decline has been economic stagnation, and on one estimate, the United Kingdom's share of world manufacturing has fallen from 18.5 per cent in 1900 to 4.1 per cent in 1980.[17] One explanation for this decline lies with the rise of colonial movements. National liberation movements in Asia and Africa have succeeded in winning their independence and 'The empires which dominated the world when the century began have all dissolved.'[18] Meanwhile the industries of empire, coal, iron, ship-building, have been deprived of their markets, and have withered and decayed. Elsewhere John Saville has examined the role of British foreign policy, as it has developed through empire and decolonisation, and has demonstrated the reactionary role of British policy in shoring up American imperialism (in Vietnam, the one war where Britain appeared to be aloof, the British government supplied arms and sent support troops).

As the British state has declined, other powers have prospered, including Germany, Russia and more recently Japan, but above all the USA. Ever since Werner Sombart's famous essay of 1906, radical historians have asked 'Why was there no socialism in the United States?'[19] This question has been broadened out, and historians have asked 'Why was there no Marxism, no environmentalism, no peace movement, in some formulations, no struggle?' In the process, the movements which did exist have been marginalised, until the ascendancy of US capital is treated as something unchallenged and unquestionable. Two chapters in this book question this notion of US exceptionalism. Andrew Strouthous describes the US labour movement and the attempts of socialists and trade unionists to found a broad-based labour party in the 1920s. He focuses on the arguments within the American Federation of Labor, leading to the 1924 election, where an independent candidate backed by the trade unions won five-million votes. John Newsinger examines the life of John Reed, the author of *Ten Days that Shook the World*, and one of the USA's best-known revolutionaries.

The most powerful challenges to the ascendancy of capital in the twentieth century have come from the workers' movement. The threat of the working class has been constant throughout this century, from 1905, the first Russian Revolution which followed the war with Japan, to 1989, when revolts toppled the governments of Eastern Europe like dominoes. In the most important cases, moments of upheaval have led to the formation of workers' councils, or soviets. Across Europe in 1919, France and Spain in 1936, Budapest in 1956, Portugal in 1974, Iran in 1979 and in Poland in 1980, workers' councils have represented the agency and potential for change. Through them, workers have been able to seize and control the direction in which society was going. George Orwell's famous description of workers' Barcelona in 1936, or Colin Barker's assessment of Solidarity in Poland both underline the importance of workers' control.[20] In these popular movements, change has not come about as a gradual accumulation of knowledge and material advance. Instead progress itself has been a series of sharp movements, of sudden advances and ponderous defeats. Such a conception of historical change runs counter to the traditional way of looking at the past, which has been in Ramsay MacDonald's phrase a straight line, running 'Up and Up and Up and On and On and On'.[21] By contrast, the approach of this book is to describe the twentieth century as having been simultaneously the best and worst years of human development. This dialectical way of thinking about the past is discussed by Esther Leslie in her chapter on Walter Benjamin's theory of progress. Although Benjamin lived through the darkest years of the century, he retained an optimistic voice, seeing hope for change in the future rise of the workers' movement.

The twentieth century has been a century of revolutions, but real progress has often been frustrated. It is a history not so much of failed revolutions, but rather of revolutions that succeeded, and yet did not lead to a transformation of society. Political change has taken place, but greater democracy has been deferred. A number of the chapters here suggest reasons for this: the betrayal of 1914, when socialist parties across the world supported the First World War, and which left the workers' side divided in two between Social Democracy and Communism. Drawing on Pierre Broué's recent history of the Communist International (the Comintern), and on the work of left critics of Stalinism, including Victor Serge and Alfred Rosmer, Ian Birchall analyses the success and failure of the Comintern. He argues that the degeneration of the International predates the rise of Stalin, and began under Zinoviev's presidency. In Victor Serge's phrase, Zinoviev was 'Lenin's biggest mistake'. Certainly, in Hobsbawm's phrase, 'the state interests of the Soviet Union prevailed over the world revolutionary interests of the Communist International.'[22] Thus by the end of the 1920s, there was little hope of profound change to be found from the official communist movement. Meanwhile, Chris Ealham looks at one alternative to Russian Stalinism, Spanish anarchism. This alternative 'anti-politics' was an inadequate solution to real problems. The anarchists claimed to provide a libertarian alternative to the degeneration of the October Revolution, but proved incapable of defending their own movement from the threat of Franco's forces outside the labour movement and from the challenge of Stalinism from within.

In the last chapter of this book, Chris Harman compares Eric Hobsbawm and Rosa Luxemburg's notions of historical change. Hobsbawm is one of the best-known Marxist historian of the century, yet Harman finds his account undermined by fatalism and nostalgia. The late twentieth-century world according to Eric Hobsbawm is less European, more integrated, less shaped by old patterns of human social relationship, less aware of its own history. Chris Harman challenges what Hobsbawm has called elsewhere a 'sense growing *fin-de-siècle* gloom, and returns to the points raised in this introduction: that this has been a century of both progress and reaction, of victory and decay, and of defeat but also hope. Harman describes the movements which grew across the world following May 1968 in France. 'The workers' movements of the last quarter of the twentieth century', he writes, 'were also a foretaste of what we should expect from the larger than ever, more universal than ever, working class of the new millennium.'

The chapters here were delivered at a conference organised by the London Socialist Historians Group (LSHG) which was held at the Institute of Historical Research in May 1999. The LSHG was set up in 1993 to promote discussion of new approaches to history, developing an understanding of the working class both 'from above' and 'from below'. Its members include trade unionists and socialist activists, as well as professional historians. The editors of this book are aware that the chapters here do not offer a complete picture of the twentieth century, nor address such important themes as the changing nature of work, the world wars, or the nuclear arms race. These tasks must fall to others. Our hope is that in describing some of the last century's contradictions, the way can be opened for a fuller historical understanding of the past. In this process of developing historical knowledge, socialist historians have an important role to play.

1. Globalisation in the Twentieth Century

Adrian Budd

Foreign holidays, access to the web, satellite transmissions, commodities from all over the world—all add up to a rapid shrinking of our world. A chorus of academics, politicians, journalists and business people have argued that the world economy, culture and politics are undergoing profound changes.[1] These arguments are not value free and frequently conceal threats to established structures and institutions. Germany's SPD chancellor Gerhard Schröder, for example, argues that globalisation has occurred not only in product and service markets 'but has also subjected labour markets to unprecedented international competition. Using national policies to protect these markets has become largely impossible...the only open path is comprehensive economic and social modernisation'.[2]

Anthony Giddens, echoing David Harvey's concept of 'time-space compression', provides a widely used definition of globalisation—'the intensification of worldwide social relations which link distant localities together in such a way that local happenings are shaped by events occurring many miles away and vice versa'.[3] Giddens is right, but his choice of 'worldwide' rather than 'capitalist' social relations conceals the uneven and antagonistic nature of globalisation.[4] This definition appeals to defenders of capitalism but a political counter-current has emerged, frequently drawing on Paul Hirst and Grahame Thompson's *Globalization in Question*.[5] But where these sceptics argue that millions, perhaps billions, are excluded from globalisation (they prefer the term 'regionalisation'), it would be more accurate to say that they are excluded by globalisation. The globalisation of capitalism as a world system is a reality, and its processes are deeper and have greater consequences than sceptics acknowledge. National institutional structures, especially in the advanced countries, are not going to be dissolved rapidly and as we enter the twenty-first century it is already clear that the antagonisms of capitalist social relations are beginning to be expressed in the context of globalisation.

The New Imperialism

Localised human societies have always made connections with others, but capitalism, slowly evolving as a world system since the fifteenth century, has given a particular impetus to this interconnectedness.[6] In *The Communist Manifesto* of 1848, Marx and Engels wrote that 'the need of a constantly expanding market for its products chases the bourgeoisie over the whole surface of the globe. It must nestle everywhere, settle everywhere, establish connections everywhere'.[7] From the second half of the nineteenth century, under pressure of competitive accumulation, capitalism increasingly broke up the relationships of pre-capitalist world society and incorporated them, albeit unevenly, within social relations based on exchange and the law of value.

Capitalism created a world that was for the first time, in Eric Hobsbawm's words, 'now genuinely global'.[8] This was so in two senses. First, remote parts of the world were increasingly integrated into the international circuits of capital either as production sites, destinations of financial loans, or, more often, the source of commodities, chiefly raw materials and food for new industrial processes and the rapidly expanding working class. To transport these commodities the world's merchant shipping tonnage, which remained more or less constant between 1860 and 1890, doubled over the next 24 years.[9] Second, the development of new means of communication and transport reduced the handicap of distance. As the Russian marxist Nikolai Bukharin noted seventy-odd years before 'globalisation' entered the vocabulary 'there grows an extremely flexible economic structure of world capitalism, all parts of which are mutually inter-dependent. The slightest change in one part is immediately reflected in all'.[10]

Second, global society was transformed. As rival states stripped away the feudal barriers to capitalism (Germany, Japan), and/or reached a level of development that impelled capital to expand overseas, so Britain's international industrial pre-dominance was challenged. Its chief rivals were the USA, gradually recovering from the civil war, and Germany whose exports, after unification in 1871, grew from half Britain's to overtake them in the 30 years to 1913.[11] Rival capitals now enlisted their home states in a quest for colonial territories. Competition produced a mob mentality, what in Germany was called the *Torschlusspanik*, fear of the door being closed by partition by rival powers.

Between 1870 and 1914 much of the world was partitioned between the imperial powers. In mid-century Britain, certain ruling-class voices had questioned the necessity of empire, at least in the form of dominion/colonisation, yet Britain's empire had expanded by nearly 5 million square miles in the last three decades of the century. The French empire expanded from 700,000 to 6 million square miles. Germany had no empire in 1871 but one of 1 million square miles and 14 million people in 1900. Where only 10 per cent of Africa was under European control in 1870, by 1900 less than 10 per cent was not. The scramble for Africa was followed, briefly, by a scramble for China. Japan soon emulated the European drive to empire, defeating China in 1894 and gaining major concessions which were then moderated under Russian, French and German pressure. Theorists of imperialism, such as the British liberal J.A. Hobson, Bukharin and another Russian Marxist Vladimir Lenin, now argued that monopoly capital, finding profitable investment opportunities reduced at home by an overaccumulation looked increasingly to overseas markets. According to the German Social Democrat, Rudolf Hilferding, banking capital now aggregated surplus-value in its hands, creating 'finance capital', which transferred surplus funds abroad.

The interpenetration of bank and industrial capital never really developed in Britain. Capital exports were frequently not to the new colonies, but to states where capitalism was more established. Between 1870 and 1914, 68 per cent of British investment went to the older white colonies (Canada, Australia, and South Africa) and European settler states (Argentina and the USA).[12] Belgian capital exports to the USA dwarfed those to any other destination, including its colonies, while German investments in Africa in the decades before the First World War were only two-thirds of those in Austria. Furthermore, the bulk went not as FDI, but as loans for railway and public utility construction (76 per cent of British capital exports in 1913).[13] Bukharin's figures for French capital exports in 1902 show only 12.5 per cent going into 'mining and industry' while over half went to 'state and commission loans'.[14] If, however, we locate imperialism not in one particular feature but in the totality of capitalist relations of production, including competition for markets and raw materials, it is clear that the world was being rapidly drawn into an ever denser network of interconnections based on the law of value.

Monopolisation attenuated competition in domestic markets, but greatly intensified it internationally. At first, capitals formed international cartels and trusts to divide the world market between them (what are today called strategic alliances). Alliances, however, can be broken. National states can be called upon to break open colonial markets, provide insurance for investments in weaker states that could not guarantee those investments, property rights, etc., and also to provide protection from rivals. From the 1870s onwards there was a general shift from free trade to tariffs, which enabled monopolies to increase domestic profits and, in turn, encourage overseas dumping for greater market share.

Germany in 1879, Austria-Hungary 1878, France 1881, Spain 1877, USA 1883; all imposed industrial tariffs. Even in Britain, whose economic supremacy ensured a continued commitment to free trade, sections of ruling-class opinion began to campaign for tariffs. As Bukharin argued, internationalisation creates 'a reverse tendency towards the nationalisation of capitalist interests'.[15]

The dialectic of internationalisation and nationalisation (in the sense of greater state intervention in and regulation of national economies rather than state ownership) sharpened national rivalries and international instability. Via episodes of greater or lesser intensity, like the Fashoda incident in 1898, which brought Britain and France close to war, and the Russo-Japanese war of 1904–5 over Korea and Manchuria, these would lead ultimately to the First World War.

Nationalism and State Capitalism
Counter-tendencies to Internationalisation

The internal corollary of imperialist expansion a century ago was an intensification of nationalist ideology in preparation for economic and military competition, first in the imperialist countries themselves and then, in opposition to imperialism, in the colonised countries. This should caution us against one-sided or linear theories of globalisation today for, as Roland Robertson has argued, it entails both the universalisation of the particular and the particularisation of the universal. Nationalism was an international phenomenon, developing within the world as a single space but exacerbating its differentiations. Global and local processes remain in a contradictory tension today.[16]

D'Azeglio argued during the Italian *Risorgimento* that 'we have made Italy, now we must make Italians', i.e. break people (subjects) from localised identities and forge their identification with the Italian state. As international rivalry intensified before 1914, ruling classes in all the imperialist countries embarked upon attempts to simultaneously marshal their working classes behind them in what Benedict Anderson has called 'imagined communities' and distract them from their class grievances.[17] As one German imperialist remarked, 'we must gain power not only over the legs of the soldiers, but also over their minds and hearts'.[18] Education, expanding everywhere to provide the next generation of workers with the necessary skills for industrial work, was an obvious vehicle, while national holidays, pageantry and symbolism were introduced at this time.[19] The mass capitalist press sought to articulate populations to imperialist interests: in Britain the *Daily Mail*, founded in 1896, was violently and consistently imperialist. The *Daily Express*, founded in 1900, proclaimed in its first leader, 'our policy is patriotic: our policy is the British Empire'.[20] Additionally, to improve workers', and potential soldiers', health and secure their identification with their national states, welfare, initially to a minimal extent, began to develop across the advanced countries.

As internationalisation was 'eclipsed by the rise of nationalism, the nation-state, and primarily nation-centred ways of thought' so capitalist contradictions were exacerbated.[21] Internationalisation conforms to capitalism's central competitive dynamic, such that John Holloway has argued that 'capital, by its nature, knows no spatial bounds'.[22] The massive transnational movements of capital, people and commodities in the nineteenth century illustrate this dynamic, but as international production, trade and interconnectedness of all kinds produced new contradictions so national ruling classes were compelled by competitive pressure into measures that tended away from internationalisation. Spatialisation was forced onto the system, in the form, for example, of protectionism and, by the turn of the century, immigration controls.

The First World War gave the sharpest expression to the antagonistic interpenetration of internationalisation and nationalisation while the 1917 Russian Revolution did the same for class antagonisms. But the tension between internationalisation and nationalisation was not resolved by the war, neither tendency emerging unequivocally dominant. The most powerful victors, Britain and the USA, sought to assert their relative power via the re-establishment of an open international order based on the Gold Standard. World trade recovered in the 1920s but in response to the Wall Street crash and the depression both Britain and the US came off the Gold Standard in the early 1930s.[23] International trade and investment collapsed and in Latin America there was widespread defaulting on debt, as ruling classes attempted to insulate their national economies behind state boundaries and increased regulation. Yet, state capitalism was a contradictory expression of the international law of value not an alternative to it. As Trotsky wrote in 1930, against the Stalinist 'logic' of 'socialism in one country':

> Marxism takes its point of departure from the world economy, not as a sum of national parts but as a mighty and independent reality which has been created by the international division of labour and the world market, and which in our epoch imperiously dominates the national markets.[24]

Competition within the world economy, intensified by crisis, ensured that when the world's major capitalist powers returned to the unfinished business of war, the renewed conflict would be fought out over the whole globe.

Postwar

The Second World War saw the decisive reshaping of the balance of economic power in favour of the US. By 1944 aircraft production, which had been 6,000 in 1939, was 96,000 (more than Japan and Germany, or the USSR and Britain combined) and by the end of the war the US produced nearly half the world's arms, half its goods and coal and over half its electricity. America's rulers were determined to use, project and protect this power via new institutional arrangements for global politics and the global economy.[25] Seeking to break open the markets of the European imperial powers, free trade became an ideological justification for US power, as it had once been for Britain.

Free trade and anti-colonialism were circumscribed by US interests. Where its interests predominated it guarded them jealously: regarding Latin America, Secretary of War Stimson argued in 1945 'that it's not asking too much to have our little region over here which has never bothered anybody'.[26] And where, once the cold war had started, anti-colonial movements threatened destabilisation that might benefit the USSR, the US supported the Europeans: in Indo-China, for example, it was paying 80 per cent of French costs by 1954. Nevertheless, over the first three postwar decades the institutions established at the 1944 Bretton Woods conference— the International Monetary Fund, World Bank, General Agreement on Tariffs and Trade—alongside the orchestrating think-tank of the richest countries—the Organisation for Economic Cooperation and Development (OECD)— became vehicles for integrating the western economies.

At Bretton Woods the US was forced to compromise with the European powers. The path towards international trade liberalisation under GATT's regulatory auspices would have to be smoothed via US loans, and IMF support for countries experiencing balance of payments problems, if weaker countries which had recently experienced massive destruction were to be encouraged to participate. As Alan Milward has shown, Europe used the developing superpower rivalry of the cold war as a bargaining counter.[27] Marshall Aid was extracted from the US, while in the face of the 'Soviet threat', the US accepted that 'the European and Japanese states would rebuild their economies in relative isolation and at a more rapid pace than would have been possible under a true international free trade system'.[28] Thus, currency convertibility was tried and rapidly abandoned in the late 1940s.

Nevertheless, trade expanded more rapidly than output as the OECD countries became increasingly interdependent and by 1958 even the nationalist governments of de Gaulle and Franco returned to convertibility. A host of Transatlantic rivalries re-emerged once the European states had fully reconstructed; but the US undertook the bulk of the defence of western interests in the cold war and while the long post-war boom lasted the general increase in prosperity reinforced the cold-war alliance and together ensured a relatively easy massaging of intra-bloc antagonisms.

When the long boom gave way to crisis in the early 1970s the tension between internationalisation and nationalisation became more acute. But where the 1930s crisis saw the rise of state protectionism, this time round, while competition did intensify, a renewal of Keynesian demand expansion was short lived. The intertwining of the OECD economies over a quarter of a century and cross-national capital movements already exerted their pressure on national economies. Keynesianism gave theoretical expression to the state capitalism developing from the 1930s and appeared to fit the needs of capitalism in the boom.[29] But, when first the Callaghan government bowed to IMF pressure and retreated from the goal of full employment to fight inflation, and then the Thatcher government of 1979 announced the arrival of neo-liberalism, a trail was blazed that the rest of the world economies would soon follow.

Globalisation Today

The world has clearly become a smaller single space within which economic, cultural, political and other interconnections have intensified and reshaped social institutions, structures and practices.[30] But globalisation theory too often mistakenly extrapolates from these developments in a linear fashion, presenting one-sided accounts of a contradiction-free process. Thus, far from simply homogenising world culture along western lines and obliterating local traditions and cultures, globalisation can provoke particularistic responses, illustrated by the revival of nationalism or religious activism, as people struggle to assert some measure of control (often imagined or symbolic) over more powerful global forces.

The processes of globalisation are clearly uneven and differentiations in the thickness of international interconnections are extremely marked: the chair of Citicorp, one of the world's largest banks, has argued that 80 per cent of the world is 'not bankable'; 80 per cent of the world's people have never used a telephone (Tanzania having just three lines per 1000 people); and 88 per cent of internet users are concentrated in the advanced industrial countries containing just 15 per cent of the world's population.[31]

Sceptical views of globalisation highlight such unevenness and emphasise that world FDI and trade are increasingly concentrated within a triad of advanced regions—the EU, Japan and its neighbours, and North America. They thus prefer 'regionalisation' or 'triadisation' to 'globalisation'. Hirst and Thompson's figures show that 28 per cent of the world's population took 91 per cent of its FDI in the early-1990s.[32] The world's MNCs are based in just 25 states and, although MNCs in mining and low-tech sectors, for example, do invest in the Third World, this orientation on the triad regions indicates that low wages and welfare costs are neither the overriding concern in location decisions nor the cause of deindustrialisation in the advanced countries as much globalisation orthodoxy suggests.[33] Within the EU Britain has both lower overall labour costs and lower manufacturing employment than France or Germany, despite receiving roughly half the FDI into the EU, of which low-wage Portugal and Greece receive a negligible amount. MNCs are concerned not just with labour costs (accounting for only 20 per cent of total costs), but overall costs relative to output, and therefore profits and productivity. These rest on factors like workers' health and flexibility, high quality supplier networks, patent and property protection, market size for rapid turnover of costs and profit realisation, modern and efficient infrastructure, the concentration of research institutions, knowledge and expertise. Such factors are concentrated in the most advanced regions, providing firms with dynamic external economies, and few states today have the resources to emulate Singapore over the last three decades and break into this near monopoly via huge expenditure on education and training.[34] MNCs continue to concentrate investment in a small part of the world.[35]

It is within the triad regions that, as Ankie Hoogvelt puts it, 'cross-national economic activity is being whipped up into a frenzy'.[36] But this intra-triadic frenzy also points to a major weakness in the sceptics' case. For, while the impact of the law of value has been most dramatic in the previously heavily protected state capitalisms of the Soviet bloc, China, etc., and the structurally adjusted poorer countries, it is a social not a geographical law.

The pre-1914 world was highly integrated, but trade flowed chiefly within rival imperialist blocs (save for the special case of Britain) but in the slump after the First World War, it disintegrated into trading blocs. After the Second World War, by contrast, world trade expansion consistently outstripped output growth, and slowly bound the developed countries together in a deepening international division of labour. The corollary was a decline in the poorer countries' share of world trade, from a relatively stable 45 per cent between 1870 and 1960 to 27 per cent in 1990, and it remains precarious in the face of the development of synthetic substitutes for raw materials, miniaturisation, and increasing agricultural self-sufficiency in the advanced countries.[37] The international exchange of complementary products (food and raw materials for manufactures) has been gradually replaced by that of competitive industrial products. To argue then, as Hirst and Thompson do, that trade as a proportion of world output only reached its 1913 level in 1973 obscures these structural changes. Since the crisis in the mid-1970s world capitalism has become more integrated or a reversal of the 1930s.

Hirst and Thompson show average export-GDP ratios of 10 per cent for the US, Japan and the EU (but 32 per cent for Germany and 25 per cent for Britain), concluding that 'a key issue for domestic prosperity and welfare is the productivity of the remaining 90 per cent, which is domestic productivity *per se* and not relative to other nations'.[38] Ruigrok and van Tulder argue that of the world's 100 largest firms 'only eighteen' keep over half their assets abroad and that the top 100 firms in terms of assets abroad hold, on average, 'only 37 per cent of their assets abroad'.[39] Even the most internationalised MNCs, from small states like Switzerland and the Netherlands, among others, concentrate R&D and management control within their home states or regions. Hirst and Thompson's figures show a similar home concentration of MNC assets. Others have highlighted a tendency towards Toyotism—the location of major firms, usually MNCs, within networks of primary, secondary, etc. suppliers in a just-in-time supply chain—implying not so much globalisation as 'glocalisation' within what economic geographers have called industrial complexes, and Ruigrok and van Tulder 'industrial systems'. The relative locational immobility of MNCs leads sceptics to assert the continuing viability of state regulation: Allen argues that 'the world is still one of national economies and protected markets'; Hirst and Thompson that 'success in the international economy has national sources' and that 'it is not beyond the powers of national governments to regulate these companies'.[40]

Both the sceptics' figures and their interpretations, however, are problematic. In the advanced countries many manufacturing sectors have a high trade dependency (imports of materials or components, export of output), reflected in the fact that intra-firm trade is up to a third of total world trade according to recent UN estimates.[41] Stephen Cohen's figures, showing that 70 per cent of US home production is subject to international competition compared with 4 per cent in the early-1960s, illustrate that it is the *possibility* of imports (the market principle), not just actual imports (the market place), that influences domestic producers.[42] Possibilities are not always actualised, as Britain's inflated consumer goods' prices indicate, but even firms producing non-traded goods and services for local markets, whose production is not easily shunted off-shore, such as water, sewage and refuse collection after privatisation in Britain, are subject to international competition and possible hostile takeovers. On MNCs' home-centredness, Hirst and Thompson's figures are from the late 1980s and early 1990s, that is, around only half-way through the current restructuring race. Even then, however, it was possible to capture the scale of restructuring, intra-EC FDI growing at an annual average of 38 per cent between 1980 and 1987 and European FDI in the US growing more rapidly still such that European firms built up a greater investment stock in the US than in other European countries.[43] Certainly Japanese MNCs have been much more deeply embedded in domestic industrial groups (*Keiretsu*), but Hirst and Thompson's figure of 97 per cent of their assets held at home is simply wrong: one-fifth of Japanese production is now overseas and companies plan to increase this to one-third.[44] Ruigrok and van Tulder's own figures for the percentage of assets held abroad in 1990 reinforce this. Available figures for Japanese MNCs range from 'low', i.e. less than 10 per cent, through 23 per cent for Toyota, 37 per cent for Honda, 40 per cent for Bridgestone, up to 49 per cent for Sony.[45] Sony, a late-comer to Japanese industry, was less integrated into a *Keiretsu* than others, but the degree of internationalisation of this relatively young firm suggests that it is a prime indicator of the developing trend. Internationalisation has been further strengthened via strategic alliances, in fields such as research and marketing, by which firms link to wider circuits of capital to reduce costs, gain access to best practice and markets, etc. Recent change has again been dramatic: the vast majority of strategic alliances have been concluded since 1980, most of these between firms from different triad regions.[46]

Given the recent history of state capitalism the national base of international success is hardly surprising. After all, international restructuring on the scale we have seen in the last two decades is of recent origin: FDI between 1980 and 1987 was greater than the entire accumulated stock before

1980. Investment may still be predominantly local/national, and perhaps 80 per cent of the world's final industrial output is produced by domestic firms, but against Ruigrok and van Tulder's 'only eighteen' of top 100 firms holding over half their assets abroad, 'fully eighteen' would be more appropriate.[47] In any case, there is no reason why half of assets should be the yardstick of internationalisation. Their figures show 49 of the 89 firms providing data holding more than a quarter of assets abroad in 1990, a remarkable degree of internationalisation. In the words of the then chief executive of Thomson SA, Alain Gomez, 'you do not choose to become global. The market chooses for you; it forces your hand'.[48] It is also forcing the hand of states.

Globalisation and the State Today

A key issue in the globalisation debate concerns the future roles of nation-states, which have shaped the political, economic and cultural landscape of the twentieth century. There is no simple polarity between, on the one hand, globalisers arguing that states face fundamental restructuring (or, *in extremis*, transcendence) and, on the other, sceptics arguing that states retain regulatory/controlling powers over capital within their territories. Giddens, for example, while accepting the globalisation of economic activity, argues that the nation-state is not becoming a 'fiction' in a 'borderless world' and government obsolete, 'but their shape is being altered'.[49] Indeed, globalisation necessitates expanded governance, a view shared by the sceptics Hirst and Thompson. Both propose a renewal of governance via international institutions such as the G3, WTO, IMF, WB, UN, etc., operating alongside states. Giddens uses the EU institutions (parliament, council, and court of justice) as a model for this renewal: 'it isn't difficult to see how they could be reformed in this direction'.[50] In reality, the antagonistic relations between firms, between firms and states, and between states themselves make such a scenario very difficult to envisage.

Neither states nor firms are things, but social relations: capitalism subjects all its differentiated parts to the same law of value. As capital has restructured over the last two decades so too have states.[51] That structural interdependence is, however, both internally contradictory and articulated with a further contradiction, that between capital and its states and the working class.

Across the advanced countries between the late 1960s, and early 1980s states tended to expand under working-class pressure—extending welfare, increasing taxes, entrenching union rights, etc. But, faced with the first major postwar crisis of profitability, when the Callaghan, Schmidt and, most famously, Mitterrand governments sought to continue or even intensify state economic management, capital forced retrenchment and began to dismantle postwar class compromises. Capitalist restructuring has depended on generalised defeats inflicted on the working class by the combined powers of individual capitals and states, just as it did in Japan, whence many restructuring strategies emanate, in an earlier period.[52] As capital has internationalised so, for example, public policy in the EU states (and its neighbours) has been Europeanised and, more generally, what James Petras has referred to as the internationalisation of the state, whereby parts of the state executive promote and protect the international expansion and interests of capital, has been intensified.[53] Pierre Bourdieu argues that it is the left hand of the state (the trace of earlier struggles) that has been in retreat while the right hand (those parts of the state most directly articulated to ruling-class interests) has been relatively impervious.[54]

State capacities are clearly unequal, yet even weaker states remain not external to but a constitutive element of economic transactions. The imposition of structural adjustment across the Third World has not been uniform, depending on local states' bargaining strength and negotiation of IMF demands, and has, in Ankie Hoogvelt's words, 'had to uphold the state and destroy it at the same time'.[55]

Potentially profitable state enterprises have been privatised and welfare programmes, food subsidies, etc. cut, while debt has been nationalised as a guarantee of repayment. Stronger states, for example those of the Newly Industrialising Countries (NICs), have more room for manoeuvre. So, in 1998, a year after the Asian crisis and conventional neoliberal World Bank 'remedies', Hong Kong's government bought 10 per cent by value of its stock market and Malaysia imposed exchange controls. These states remain central to their national economies and the fortunes of their enterprises in the way that Bukharin suggested in 1916. Thus, as I wrote in 1993:

> regional players such as China, South Korea, and Taiwan are integrated in a deepening network of trade, investment and diplomacy. But regional integration serves to sharpen competition and historical antipathies, and today the region is one of the growth areas for world arms sales. China, for example, has recently engaged in a rapid build-up of arms acquired cheaply from the CIS and Russia while in September 1992 the planned sale of 150 American F–16 fighters to Taiwan was announced. This added to regional tension which has already seen armed clashes between China and Vietnam over the mineral-rich Spratly islands, to which all the regional actors lay claim.[56]

All states, however, have been restructured over the last two decades when, in Robert Cox words, they 'willy nilly became more effectively accountable to a *nebuleuse* personified as the global economy.'[57] The transnational class interests involved in restructuring are clear: while, for example, 'by 1989 the amount of assets held abroad by Latin American residents *exceeded* their countries' outstanding debt to commercial banks', the burden of Third World debt has been shifted from those private interests that contracted it and placed on the shoulders of whole national societies, including the poor.[58] Where in the long boom postcolonial states were a source of stability and jobs, today they have become agents, in Robert

Cox's words, of 'global poor relief and riot control'.[59]

According to Immanual Wallerstein, 'pervasive anti-statism, by delegitimating the state structures, has undermined an essential pillar of the modern world system, the states system, a pillar without which the endless accumulation of capital is not possible. The ideological celebration of so-called globalisation is in reality the swan song of our historical system. We have entered into the crisis of this system. The loss of hope and the accompanying fear are both part of the cause and the major symptom of this crisis'.[60] This is most dramatically exemplified in the poorest parts of the world where 'the patrimonial glue that holds society together is dissolved'.[61] The combination of crisis and restructuring has impacted on the NICs almost as dramatically: 'prior to the crisis there were 30m people living on less than $1 a day in Indonesia, Malaysia, the Philippines and Thailand. By 2000 that number could easily double to 60m'.[62]

Legitimacy has also been undermined, albeit less dramatically, in the advanced states too. International restructuring, tax cuts, and the shift in taxation onto the poor has produced immediate gains for capital. But it has also produced new contradictions such as the decay in state services for capital and deficient demand, reinforced by downward pressure on wages. The Blair government's education policies give expression to the contradiction between the interests of individual capitals and the requirements of national capitalisms within a global system. Blair recognises the contribution of education to competitive advantage, yet his attempts to expand education without increasing taxes have exacerbated the tensions within the system.

Social democracy thus faces a crisis of political agency and ideology more generally. Historically committed to capitalist regulation it has been severely disoriented by capitalist restructuring and internationalisation since the end of the long boom and has moved, sometimes quite dramatically as in the case of the now-defunct Italian Socialist Party, towards openly pro-market policies. Rather than highlight the fault-lines of capitalism which have destabilised and disrupted established patterns of social life, social democrats emphasise the faults in others. Ex-prime minister of France Edith Cresson blames the Japanese, 'staying up all night thinking of ways to screw the Americans and Europeans'; The EU, now dominated by centre-left governments, far from inhabiting a 'borderless world' has erected new anti-immigrant borders around 'Schengenland'.[63]

Interwar capitalist instability spawned, alongside violent authoritarianism, theorists like Keynes and Polanyi and a new interest in regulation. Today's instability has produced signs of confusion in international ruling-class circles and a hesitant reassessment of the destructive powers of free markets, even by spectacular beneficiaries like George Soros.[64] World Bank chief Joseph Stiglitz has argued that the poorer parts of the world experiencing financial crises since 1997 require state-led reflation to boost demand and profitability rather than interest rate hikes to satisfy international capital. Minimal responses to global turmoil have begun to be voiced (a 'Tobin' tax on international speculation, a stronger international financial authority and UN, a global central bank, a powerful international environment agency, TNC supervision, etc.).[65]

Conclusion

The idea of globalisation captures important trends. Since the end of the long boom, intensified international competition has produced a frenetic pace of technological innovation and business reorganisation. But as capitalist social relations have intensified global interconnections so the contradictions between the interests of the most internationalised capitals, states and the mass of humanity have deepened, producing a repetition of the instability and antagonisms that accompanied the interpenetration of internationalisation and nationalisation 100 years ago. Recent events in the former Yugoslavia, Kurdistan, Iraq, parts of Africa and the former

Soviet Union, give a compelling quality to Bukharin's assessment that international competition inevitably leads to war, i.e. is in the long run 'solved by the interrelation of "real forces"...the force of arms'.[66] Events in the 1990s since the victory of western liberal capitalism in the cold war make claims of a 'new world order' of peace and prosperity, rather hollow. In the words of the chief economist at Kemper Financial Services, Chicago, 'the world could drift towards a cold peace more akin to the troubled years that followed the Treaty of Versailles rather than the prosperity which followed Bretton Woods'.[67]

Globalising tendencies are the contemporary expression of capitalism's history of combined and uneven development, of anarchic international competition, of the sundering of fixed and fast social relations in the pursuit of profit. The attendant global instability is not new and it is worth remembering that a period of similar instability lasted from the final quarter of the nineteenth century, through two world wars, fascism, the holocaust, and economic depression, to the middle of this century. But while the law of value imposes structural imperatives on economic and political actors to behave in certain ways, it also clashes with the interests of the vast majority of humanity. Real people, living within real social relations and real communities, possess interests, aspirations, memories and intentions which can impel them towards resistance to capital's imperatives. Within the last epoch of instability the Russian Revolution of 1917 stood out as the high point of that resistance. The demonstrations against the World Trade Organisation meeting in Seattle at the very end of the twentieth century give cause for optimism today. When human value has become so subordinate to the accountant's rulebook and the competition between capitals and states that deprivation, insecurity and misery stalk the globe, the choice facing humanity is the same as it was then: socialism or barbarism.

2. One Step Forwards, Two Steps Back
Progress German Style

Esther Leslie

Walter Benjamin: Culture and Barbarism

On several occasions in the late 1930s Walter Benjamin voices the sentiment that 'there is not one document of culture that is not at the same time a document of barbarism'.[1] Benjamin looks back over history to witness the parallel lines of cultural advancement and social destruction. He insists that those who enjoyed, perpetrated and made their own the former were also the proponents of the latter. Any document of culture was made under conditions that occasioned suffering. It is not just that someone happened to suffer while culture was being made, but that—because of the fact of class society, with its need for surplus and markers of status—suffering is a necessary correlative of culture's existence. In the light of this dialectical recognition, Benjamin attacks conventional notions of culture which fetishise culture, abstracting it from its location within living, historical relations as they have developed through time. Benjamin observes that the various elements which form a general history of human achievement must not be regarded as abstractions, separate from the day-to-day business of living. Culture should not be seen as apart from everyday life, distinct from and above the barbarous. Culture is not pure, clean and autonomous. Such an opinion is an abstraction. The historical materialist:

> approaches this abstraction with reserve. He would be justified in this reserve by the mere inspection of the actual

past: whatever he surveys in art and science has a descent
that cannot be contemplated without horror. It owes its
existence not just to the efforts of the great geniuses who
fashioned it, but also in greater or lesser degree to the
anonymous drudgery of their contemporaries.[2]

It is a question of culture's descent—how it could come into
being, how it came to be here and how it exists now. That is
to say, Benjamin raises questions of class: the special function
of art, patterns of ownership and modes of access to culture
must be grasped in order to understand its full meaning.[3]

A sustained examination of this idea appears in his study of
the revolutionary Eduard Fuchs from 1937. Fuchs was a
member of the illegal Socialist Party of Germany (SPD) in
the late 1880s. After opposing the war, he founded the
Spartakusbund and the Communist Party of Germany
(KPD). Later he joined the KPD-Opposition. Fuchs wrote
various cultural histories between 1905 and 1923, based on
his own passions and collections. He was a collector of cari-
cature and erotica. Fuchs was also the editor of a socialist
newspaper devoted to political satire. These facts are important to Benjamin's argument, for he uses Fuchs's 'practical'
engagement with reproduced and mass culture to assault culture's place and cultural value on the part of many other
Social Democrats (such as the 'scholarly' Franz Mehring[4]).
Fuchs is peerless because he was quick to derive implications
from the constellation of 'the mass' and technologically
reproduced culture. This is a practical critique of the idea of
an effortless—and untransformative—arrogation of bourgeois high cultural booty. Benjamin finds the Social
Democratic approach to culture enmeshed in inherited
notions of cultural value, which are more appropriate for the
bourgeois perspective on fetishised genius, and insistent only
on the wholesale appropriation of an existing cultural heritage. He notes the existence of dissenting views within the
movement, and these are views which claim authority from
reference to the 'fathers' of historical materialism:

It was the hopes, and even more the misgivings, of those few that found expression in a debate reflected in *Neue Zeit* [a German SPD journal]. The most important contribution was an essay by Korn entitled 'The Proletariat and the Classics'. It dealt with the notion of heritage, a concept which has again become important today. Lassalle saw in German idealism, Korn argued, a heritage of which the working class took possession. But Marx and Engels held a different view. 'They did not derive the social priority of the working class from an inheritance, but rather from its decisive position in the production process itself. Besides, what need is there to talk of possessions, even cultural possessions, on the part of a *parvenu* class, like the modern proletariat, that daily and hourly demonstrates its *right* through...its work that is constantly reproducing the entire apparatus of culture?'[5]

A materialist approach to culture places an artefact within the complex of social relations, rather than abstracting it as a supra-class ideal. And regards it historically, considering questions of ownership, access and reception over time. These relations are what constitute its barbaric aspect.

Benjamin voices the bitter dialectic of culture and barbarism again in his final piece of writing now known as 'Theses on the Philosophy of History'.[6] This work, a series of theses, sometimes in the form of word-pictures, on politics and history writing, was begun in 1939. Just before the line 'There is not one document of culture that is not at the same time a document of barbarism', Benjamin notes:

Whoever has emerged victorious participates, to this day, in the triumphal procession in which the present rulers step over those who are lying prostrate. According to traditional practice, the spoils are carried along in the procession. They are called cultural treasures, and a historical materialist views them with cautious detachment. For without exception the cultural treasures he surveys have an origin which he cannot contemplate without horror.[7]

The argument concerns the appropriate relation to cultural treasures from the past. This debate had been raging on the literary revolutionary left for a while, with positions ranging from the Futurist-proletcultist demand to demolish cultural treasures and invent new forms to Lukács's recommendation to usurp the highpoints of pre-1848 bourgeois culture. For Benjamin, aware that the question of heritage has a new political topicality, it is not only the case that culture and barbarism are two sides of the same coin of class society, and so each document of culture is at the same time a document of barbarism. In addition, 'barbarism taints also the manner in which it was transmitted from one owner to another'.[8] Benjamin is speaking of the booty that is handed on, that material which is the canon of valuable items, owned privately or stored in museums. But more than that, he was mindful, at that moment, of the destruction of culture that was being carried out by one of the most 'advanced' industrial civilisations, Germany.[9] Indeed Benjamin notes that so-called 'cultured states', here he means precisely Germany, 'are fashioning themselves as artworks'[10] and with this statement he invokes his vision of fascism as an aestheticisation of politics, a system of illusion, of spectacular representation (mass rallies, uniforms, tightly directed cultural forms, and so on). This is representation but without political enfranchisement.[11] Benjamin's argument is general—and polemical: all culture stems of barbarism, and is passed on within a system of ownership whose very existence is barbaric. But the relevance of the argument is heightened by developments in Germany in the 1930s. Where theorists—such as Max's brother Alfred Weber—had proclaimed in 1912 the existence of culture to be evidence of social progress, emergent only when 'life has become a form which rises above its necessities and utilities',[12] the historical victory of the Nazis is proof that progress is a chimera or, that this type of 'progress' has benefits only for the few. Perhaps, Benjamin reckons, it is progress itself that is the problem.

In the late 1930s, Benjamin came across the tract, *L'Eternité par les astres* by Auguste Blanqui, the putschist. Blanqui had been present at many uprisings since his student days in Paris and in 1824 he joined a branch of the Carbonari, a revolutionary secret society. He had spent more than half his life behind bars for his activism, and having watched revolutionary wave after wave founder he ended up doubting any possibility of progress. After the Paris Commune had been smashed all Blanqui could see was repetition. The number of our duplicates is measureless in time and space, writes Blanqui, and these *doppelgänger* are flesh and bone, sporting our breeches and jackets, crinolines and chignons. They are the people of the present eternalised, 'vulgar re-editions, redundant reproductions'.[13] They are condemned to repetition ad infinitum. This is revolution not as a forward movement but circular. It returns to the same place again and again. The repeated revolutionary efforts of the nineteenth century came to signify this for Blanqui. Benjamin did not concur with these pessimistic political conclusions, but he did see Blanqui's tract as a remarkable critique of the 'ideology of progress'. The tract's blindspots are evident—the tract is just as ideological as the ideology it claims to counter. Its pessimism is rooted in economic and political crises that are historical and not eternal, not part of the human condition. Blanqui is unable to perceive that. What Benjamin means is that the tract is unable to locate the cause of its chastising view—and yet it is still valuable, because it does raise the question of progress as a problem. Understanding that problem could be of use, Benjamin decides, in grasping and counteracting the failure of the left in more recent times.

Progress, Benjamin declares, is a nineteenth-century phantasm. The belief in progress affected bourgeois industrialists and philosophers as much as Social Democratic reformists. Benjamin's 'Theses on the Philosophy of History' present a critique of progress in history as inherited from nineteenth-century historiography, produced by a bourgeoisie that, so he tells us, had reneged on a critical attitude, for which it no longer had any use. The concept of progress becomes a dogma at that moment when it is no longer a socially critical concept.[14] In addition to his suspicion of the concept of progress, Benjamin's theses on the philosophy of history and the study of Eduard Fuchs level a more specific criticism of the confusion of human progress with technological progress. The bourgeoisie imagined infinite expansion, with the production of endless commodities to be placed in untold markets. And the Social Democrats thought that such expansion could in the end benefit the working class, for it would allow eventually the enrichment of each and everyone, and the gradual evolution to socialism, without the need for violent revolution. Perhaps even without the need for socialism—as Marx noted in 1875 in his scathing criticism of the *Gotha Programme* of the German Social Democratic Party. They thought that changes could happen without too much, or too obviously, altering the status quo. Benjamin cites Marx's critique of the *Gotha Programme* in the 'Theses on the Philosophy of History', and notes a confusion that arose in Social Democracy at this time.[15] The confusion arises from a misguided understanding of the role of labour, which turned into a fetish of labour, and a belief in salvation through technology, rather than through altering the relations of production. Just as culture is abstracted and regarded as autonomous, so too is technology seen as an abstract, neutral entity.

> This vulgar-Marxist conception of the nature of labour bypasses the question of how its products might benefit the workers while still not being at their disposal. It recognises only the progress in the mastery of nature, not the retrogression of society; it already displays the technocratic features later encountered in Fascism.[16]

Benjamin's *Arcades Project* quotes a letter from early KPD leader Hermann Duncker to Grete Steffin. Duncker reports that Marx and Engels were ironic about any absolute belief in progress.[17] Marx's proscription of an undialectical fetishism of concepts led him to suspect and shun the word progress. Progress is regularly alleged to have value for the totality when, in fact, it is meaningful only for particularities. Benjamin, likewise, turns his attention to breaking up the notion of progress historically and politically, diagnosing its class inflections. In bourgeois terms, technological upgrading and technical mastery of nature effect intensified alienation and more energetic exploitation of the operators of technology and the raw products of nature. Any simple identification of technological evolvement with progress neglects questions of social form or production relations. In such a case, technology is disengaged from the circumstances of use and renovated as *per se* a sponsor of progress.

The Social Democratic reformists had been convinced that progress would occur, indeed was occurring, and also were so sure of the existence of their mass base, under any circumstance, that they had entered into bargains with the political establishment. Their bull-headed belief in progress and their faith in a mass base is pinpointed by Benjamin as the political will for 'servile inclusion in an uncontrollable apparatus'.[18] The Social Democrats' dogma holds faith with the permanently progressive yellow-brick road of history, flanked by ever-developing forces of production, interminable technical progress and the cheering crowds of a mobilisable mass base. Technological development, industrial production that 'outstrips human needs'[19] (most noticeably in the production of newspaper copy and armaments) and the swooning crowds, mobilised but not 'active', had brought about something quite other than socialism: world war. The nationalist-imperialist conflagration of 1914–18 was not opposed by the mainstream of German Social Democracy. On 3 August 1914, the SPD group in the Reichstag decided by 78 votes to 14 to approve the government's requested war loans. The next day war broke out and the SPD voted unanimously for the first War Loans Bill. On

2 December, Karl Liebknecht was the only one in the
Reichstag to vote against the second War Loans Bill. The disaster was occurring with barely any opposition from the left:
a scenario which was, by-and-large, repeated across Europe.

Benjamin was twenty-two years old when war was
declared, and it shocked him. Two of his close friends committed suicide and war caused Benjamin to re-evaluate his
political and philosophical allegiances. It caused him to break
with the liberal-anarchist Youth Movement whose leadership
supported the war, despite their appeals to 'ethics' and
'morals'. More than twenty years later Benjamin reflected on
the philosophical and political conditions that made war possible and so heartily received by those with influence. For
Benjamin the matter is philosophical—or metaphorical.
Modes of thinking made the unthinkable thinkable. An allegory in the preparatory notes for 'Theses on the Philosophy
of History' ponders the movement of history in terms contrary to any notion of assured revolutionary progression.

> Marx says that revolutions are the locomotive of world his-
> tory. But perhaps it is quite different. Perhaps revolutions
> are the grasp for the emergency brake by the human race
> travelling on the train.[20]

It is to the use of metaphor in the history of socialism and
locomotion that Benjamin refers. He uses the image of trains
and socialism in an unorthodox way, undercutting more conventional notions of progress guaranteed through technological development. Instead, in this image, revolution
appears as an obstruction or break, motivated by an act of
conscious intervention on the part of the travelling collective. The classless society is not the telos of progress, but
depends rather on the arrest of progress.[21] The language of
Benjamin's image implies a rejection of any concept of
progress, however 'Marxist' its expression, that does not
countenance interference or consciously enacted decision as,
for example, illustrated in Plekhanov's pledge: 'We, indeed,

know our way and are seated in that historical train which at full speed takes us to our goal'.[22] This contrasts with an image of class society in Engels's *Anti-Dühring* (1876–78). Here the bourgeoisie, powerless to direct the energies of the forces of production, comprise 'a class, under whose leadership society is racing to ruin like a locomotive whose jammed safety valve the machinist is too weak to open'.[23] Engels's image warns of the barbarism to come, if the status quo of production relations is not shattered. The issue is one of control, control of policy as much as control of technology.

There are various inflections of the ideology of progress in Social Democracy: Darwinist evolutionist determinism, blind optimism, and the dogma of the inevitable, iron-law victory of the party. The Social Democrats base their political practice on a notion that is continuous and unavoidable. Progress is irreversible. Benjamin draws an image in the theses on history: empty and homogenous time—moving steadily towards liberation—a spatial aspect, an antechamber where subjects anticipate the dawn of the revolutionary period, their existence directed towards the future. Benjamin's move challenges theories of history that assume better times need only be awaited, a world where today is always better than yesterday. Such an attitude, he remarks, cannot begin to address the meaning of fascism. The Social Democratic credulity in progress in history, warranted by technological advance, explains its 'later collapse' politically once it is contradicted by fascism. To be aghast that fascism can transpire in the 'more cultured' twentieth century is a result of a faith in linear and cumulative progress. But this faith in progress led to what Benjamin terms 'betrayal'.

At a moment when the politicians in whom the opponents of fascism had placed their hopes are prostrate and confirm their defeat by betraying their own cause, these observations are intended to disentangle the political worldlings from the snares in which the traitors have entrapped them....It seeks to convey an idea of the high price our accustomed thinking will have to pay for a conception of history that avoids any complicity with the thinking to which these politicians continue to adhere.[24]

Understanding the thinking that makes betrayal possible is one task of the theses. The acts of betrayal are several. It concerns not just the broader insistence on guaranteed progress through technological advance of Social Democracy, but also the more recent acts of policy on the part of the Communist movement. One of the motivating factors for ideas distilled in the theses was the signing of the Nazi-Soviet non-aggression pact, on 23 August 1939. The pact took effect immediately and had the following provisions: Germany and the Soviet Union resolved not to attack each other or aid any third-party assault on the other. Communication and consultation on common issues would be maintained. The two powers agreed not to align with powers that plan aggression against other signatory. The pact was to hold for ten years with an automatic five-year prolongation, unless one party gave the other a one-year notification of termination. These clauses were public. The pact also contained a private clause: Poland and Eastern areas were to be partitioned. The Soviets were to gain Bessarabia, Latvia, Estonia, Finland and Poland east of the Vistula and San rivers. Germany invaded western Poland on 1 September 1939. The Soviets invaded eastern Poland on 29 September. Non-aggression went hand in hand with a trade treaty and arrangements for large-scale exchange of raw materials and armaments. For Benjamin, the political worldlings are the proletarians of Europe and the betrayers are the politicians who acclaimed a reputed anti-fascist tactic. This tactic resulted in the Communist Party welcoming Hitler as Stalin's ally.

Benjamin's theses voice, essentially, a bitter critique of Social Democratic reformism, but they are also critical of the German Communist Party's political doctrine, which had likewise fallen victim to inevitabilism or a secular form of fatalism. For example, in the slogan, 'After Hitler Us'.

Nazism is presented as the actual historical beneficiary of such reasoning and (anti) practice. The theses were intended to be a formulation of 'a theory of history from which fascism can be viewed'. That this was necessary was a result, according to Benjamin, of the 'betrayal' of the European proletariat who now found themselves prostrated before a Nazi ruling class whose victory had been deemed impossible or short lived.

In a letter to Gretel Adorno, Benjamin explains the originary moment of the theses on the philosophy of history. The theses, he divulges, had been germinating for twenty years;[25] from 1919 to 1939—when, perhaps, the germ of the thoughts is planted by the calamitous struggle of the one political group enthusiastically cited in the theses, Rosa Luxemburg's and Karl Liebknecht's *Spartakus*, revolutionary challenger to Social Democracy. Both were cut down with its tacit approval:

> Not man or men but the struggling, oppressed class itself is the depository of historical knowledge. In Marx it appears as the last enslaved class, as the avenger that completes the task of liberation in the name of generations of the downtroddden. This conviction, which had a brief resurgence in the Sparticist group, has always been objectionable to Social Democrats. Within three decades they managed virtually to erase the name of Blanqui, though it had been the rallying sound that had reverberated through the preceding century. Social Democracy thought fit to assign to the working class the role of redeemer of future generations, in this way cutting the sinews of its greatest strength. This training made the working class forget both its hatred and its spirit of sacrifice, for both are nourished by the image of enslaved ancestors rather than liberated grandchildren.[26]

The motive for working-class rebellion is revenge. The reason for acting is hatred of the oppressor and an insistence on recompense, not simply begging for a place at the master's table. With his theses, Benjamin hopes to recast the philosophy of history (theory) in order to make space for action (practice) in the grisliest days of the twentieth century. For this key terms need new meanings; he writes in the theoretical section of his *Arcades Project*:

> Definitions of basic historical concepts: the catastrophe—to have missed the opportunity; the critical moment—the *status quo* threatens to remain in place; progress—the first revolutionary measure.[27]

Since his turn towards Marxism in the 1920s, having read Georg Lukács's *History and Class Consciousness* and, at the same time, meeting Asja Lacis, a Latvian Bolshevik, Benjamin had been defying any pollyannaist versions of social change. 'Fire Alarm' in the collection *One-Way Street* (begun in 1923, published in 1928) is one such example. Here Benjamin couples technology and the technological potential for liberation or destruction with the balance of class forces.[28] He contends that the bourgeoisie is inexorably fated to expire through its internal contradictions, irrespective of whether it succeeds in defeating the proletariat at any one particular moment. Capitalist decline is inescapable. The Communistic reorganisation of social relations is, however, not an inevitable outcome. And yet if the proletariat is not victorious, then not just the bourgeois class but all humanity is sentenced to death. Turning correct political actions into questions of deadlines, tactics and class-conscious organisation, Benjamin insists in 'Fire Alarm' that 'the burning ignition fuse must be severed before the spark reaches the dynamite'.[29] The elimination of the bourgeoisie and its relations of production, he asserts, must be achieved before an 'almost calculable' moment of economic and technical development, flagged up by inflation and gas warfare. Proletarian takeover is not a mechanical or necessary result of technological change, but a viable suspension of cataclysmic technological expansion. The ignition-fuse, figure of the consuming, incendiary power of the bourgeoisie, must be dissevered before its flicker reaches the dynamite. This is a familiar Marxist scenario: that one of socialism or barbarism, voiced by Engels, and echoed by Rosa Luxemburg.[30]

Franz Jung: Revolt

As Benjamin wrote those words on the urgency of revolution in his modernistic pamphlet *One-Way Street*, another revolutionary, Franz Jung, was writing the novel *The Conquest of the Machines* (1923). Both surveyed a desperate arena, yet harboured hopes that all the disintegration might give way to class-conscious action and proletarian revolt. Both reviewed the fragmented scene of Weimar Germany, home of a fissured left and working class and place where the ruins of war still spoilt the landscape. They both translated that fragmentation visibly into their writing through the technique of modernist, montaged vignette. Jung's documentary novel was part of the 'Red Novel' series, published by Malik-Verlag in Berlin. The actions depicted in the novel were, as in Benjamin's *One-Way Street*, explosive and drastic, for the narrative concerned the events of the March Action of 1921 in Germany in which Jung had taken part. Before the March Action, Jung had been one of a group of revolutionary terrorists who, in order to force on revolution, would go out dressed as hikers and set fire to grain stocks and slaughter cattle. At the same time he joined the Dadaists, and together with the mass-media artist John Heartfield, produced and distributed illegal magazines. Jung had been an energetic participant in the 1918 revolution in Berlin and was sent by the Sparticist group to Potsdamer Platz in Berlin's centre on 9 November 1918. There he acted impulsively and with a group of soldiers and bystanders occupied a telegraph office. But the party did not support this action and members of the new provisional government ousted the occupiers. Jung spent the next months holding Sparticist group meetings and agitating for revolution amongst workers but, in his autobiography *On the Way Down*, his reflections on this period are bitter.[31] Intrigue, paranoia and terror within the revolutionary movement disillusioned him. In January 1919 when revolution broke out, Jung was again there but failed to harness the revolutionary fervour. The left parties had no strategic plan and were disunited. Noske put down the rebellion and Luxemburg and Liebknecht were executed. After the KPD's call to work through official political channels, the movement split, and Jung was expelled from the KPD in October 1919. He hitched himself to the Communist Workers' Party of Germany (KAPD) formed in April 1920. A delegation— Jung and Jan Appel—set off immediately to the Soviet Union for a special meeting with the Comintern. They had no money and had to stowaway, in dangerous conditions, on a fishing boat. Once at sea, the stowaways hijacked the boat (with the help of the crew). Diverting the ship's course involved navigation over a mined seabed; beyond Trondheim they had only a small map of the North Pole with an outline of the coasts of Norway, Russia, Siberia and Alaska. The weather was atrocious. In Petrograd they met with Zinoviev, the Chairman of the Communist International, and travelled on to Moscow. Lenin met the delegation and was critical of their impetuousness. At a second reception Lenin read aloud to them extracts from his unpublished pamphlet 'Left Wing Communism—An Infantile Disorder'.

The Third Congress of the Comintern exposed differences between the KAPD and other member parties. The KAPD was told to continue co-operating with the KPD in the old unions and in the democratic assemblies, and to drop the slogan 'All Power to the Workers' Councils!' They refused. Jung distanced himself from the central leadership of the Party, and became involved in illegal paramilitary groups which were often under the cover of hiking or sports clubs. These kept their members ever ready for the final phase of the class struggle. Jung was arrested in September 1920 for the piracy action, and began to write in prison. Once released, Jung became involved in the bloody March Action in the mining district of Mansfeld. In 1919 miners of the region had clashed with the Freikorps and had not relinquished their arms. The Communists were strong there. The security police from Berlin had been drafted in to keep an eye on the workers who were engaging in wildcat strikes and, so the rulers claimed, looting and lawlessness. The workers viewed the presence of the security police as provocation and declared a strike. In nearby Halle the local Communist Party leadership was cautious in calling on workers to strike. However, Max Hölz turned up. He was a revolutionary adventurer who blew up law courts and robbed banks to help fund the KAPD. Famous for leading a 'Red Army' in the Vogtland in the Kapp Putsch days, he raised an armed detachment of 400 men to carry out guerrilla attacks on police posts. The insurrectionary wave spread and the workers in the chemical plant, Leuna, sat in their factory for a week. But there was no general plan. The police crushed the uprising, and the army did not need to be called. It was an episode of ultra-left infantilism. The parties had misjudged the ripeness of the situation. Jung went on the run and in the summer of 1921 he ended up in Petrograd. He worked in the press division of the Comintern, and was then employed, to little avail, by the aid organisation helping the Volga Germans who were suffering famine. He participated in rebuilding the match industry and was then moved to a factory in Petrograd that produced iron drums. Raw material supply difficulties and economic crises made Jung's life so difficult that he once again fled as a stowaway. Wanted by the police in Germany, Jung invented a new identity for himself and went back to his profession as an economic and trade journalist while also dabbling in a number of more-or-less dubious financial speculations. He also wrote a novel, *The Conquest of the Machines*, a reflection on one of the German escapades that marked the closing of the window of opportunity for internationalising the Communist revolution. Perhaps the March Action was foolhardy. Perhaps conditions were not ready. The action never could have been generalised: working-class militancy was localised and sectionalised, the party leaderships were inexperienced. When, in 1923, after the occupation of the Ruhr by the French, insurrections spread across Germany amidst massive economic crisis, the KPD, terrified of a repetition of March 1921, held off. Some tried to promote a policy of united frontism, but the bloody nightmare of March 1921 left a wound on the class memory, and distrust between Social Democrats and Communists held sway. That was the end of hope for revolutionary change. Social Democratic faith in progress had failed. Revolutionary adventurism had failed.

Jung's book *The Conquest of the Machines* was written through this period of class warfare. It is not set in one named place, for Jung insisted that there was a time in Germany when there was hardly a place where similar events were not occurring.[32] He wrote the book on the back of his (and the revolutionary movement's) failure. His conclusion was to reject parties and the trade unions, preferring instead red unions and the *Allgemeine Arbeiter-Union*, a sort of German IWW. In the novel it is the workers and the parties who are to blame for the useless and bloody *débâcle* at Mansfeld. The story of the strike is prefaced by an introduction—three vignettes set the scene. The first, 'Piblokto', describes a disease that affects the Eskimos. Abandoned in their ice-scape, they fall victim to a malady which is brought about by the fear of the future (it is to be assumed that workers too suffer from this malady, and so they fail to act). The second details the horror of imprisonment in the summertime, a deprivation that Jung knew well. And the last outlines Jung's economic analysis. Electricity, 'a dangerous weapon', is pouring into the economic infrastructure, by which he means that governments and state no longer rule. Life is changing—and the pace of life is changing, as the electricity networks web across the world, and dictate the pace and place of activity.

The emotional, the institutional and the economic-technological covered, Jung moves onto the story of class struggle. This too is in three parts. The first details insurrection. It outlines the failures of workers to unite, the inability of parties to act decisively and in unity, and the lack, on workers' and parties' part, of a vision of the future. The second part depicts aspects of capitalist society, with bosses meeting together to plan their class struggle, which involves siphoning off a fraction of the class with enticements and education. The tableau is one of an increasing dependency of government on capitalism and its agents, who are themselves eaten up by capital. Capitalism is concentrated; monopolisation the tendency and rationalisation the trend. Jung shows how the minister of labour, a working-class man, sells out his class of origin, because of his fear of big business. And the union officials care more about their positions than workers' jobs. Disputes develop again, for as a Marxist, Jung knew that the struggle continues despite previous failures—and solidarity develops. It is the 'red union' of the electricians that becomes the core of the movement—like the power they generate, they too are a force.

Political consciousness achieved, the revolutionary workers know that the machines must be taken over, which means social relations must be altered by those who are in a position to alter them and to benefit most clearly from that alteration. This is made evident on the cover of the 1923 edition of Jung's book. Malik-Verlag was owned by Wieland Herzfelde whose dada-revolutionary brother John Heartfield created a photomontage for the book's jacket. The writer Hans Reimann commented on Heartfield's jacket design in 1927:

Heartfield was the first who dared to use scissors to produce dust jackets, cleverly cutting up photos and putting them together again to form a new totality....And his most remarkable achievement is the cover to Jung's *Eroberung der Maschinen*: here the unbearable tension of certain scenes of *Battleship Potemkin* is achieved with a browning pistol, a fist, and a mystical confusion of machines into

which is wedged a red triangle. This is the work of someone who has grasped the meaning of Futurism. And
Expressionism. And accumulation. For Heartfield's work
is truly expressionist—with a practical background.[33]

Heartfield successfully relayed Jung's double-vanguardism—
his *avant-garde* modernist excitement with new modes of
expression—montage, documentary style, aphorism—and
his vanguardist vision of violent revolutionary overthrow,
based on working-class power.

Overcoming their fear of repression, the workers in the
novel begin to act politically and class consciously. The red
electricians lead a strike. They bring the machines to a halt,
in order then to be the ones to say when they may start turning again. They are successful at first, but then they are let
down by the revolutionary parties who lack the confidence to
head a revolutionary government. The leaders are inexperienced and uncertain. Again the movement goes down. The
strike is broken, the leaders arrested and thrown in jail.

The final section of the novel is a utopian fantasy, the
reverie of one of the arrested strike leaders. He dreams that
the red unionists in the copper industry organise a worldwide
strike, the beginning of world revolution. Copper is the
material basis of electricity networks—and is fundamental to
the energy that flows through its wires. The copper web
forms a parallel to the global linking of the workers in net-
worked solidarity. The accumulation of capital will lead to
the combination of workers, making it easier to seize control.
Revolution, when it happens, is presented as spontaneous. A
loose federation of unionists organises it, and its motive is
economistic, produced of the tendency of capitalism towards
collapse. We watch the revolution unfold, not knowing that
this is a dream. But the imprisoned worker awakes.

For the conclusion Jung returns to the vignette form. The
first section is called 'Awakening from the Ice Age'. There
was a paradisiacal period in Europe, where England combined with Scandinavia to form a continent and the North

German plain transformed into a sea. On the strand of this sea, where today Saxony is, there stood wonderful forests of blooms, plants from which today's coal reserves were formed. Then came the ice age; it seems so near, we feel as if we experienced it. For 20,000 years we have been frozen and now, if we are thawing, it is because we sense that we can overcome nature through labour. Although Jung's perspective is long-term, he insists only on the present possibilities of human (that is workers') self-organisation. Work will bring together people in community and co-operation. Workers' self-organisation will allow the knowledge of the workers to come to fruition and put them in the position to distribute the joys of this life amongst themselves.[34]

The second vignette 'The Deposing of God' continues in this vein. God is a product of human alienation from nature, and he is a projection of humanity's own creative powers. God produces loneliness, separation from self and others—in short from real life. God is anti-life. It is good that he is gone, for he was beginning to stink, says Jung. The final section is entitled 'The Meaning of Life'. Life's meaning consists in overcoming fear and solitude, in understanding that essential humanity lies in community. The world has changed. The pace of life has speeded up and will go ever faster. Electricity's agility provides a model for us. Age will be overcome—by the desire to live. The generations will slide into connection, and time will be overcome by human solidarity. All will rush together into a new future.

The Conquest of the Machines is pessimistic in its presentation of abortive action, and in its representation of the failure of workers and parties to act decisively and in concert. It has to turn to the utopian mode to show the possibility of social progress. Perhaps Jung was following the same trail as that other ultra-leftist, putschist August Blanqui. Desperate for the revolution, a participant in repeated uprisings that were precipitant or mismanaged, he too turned pessimist and began to doubt the possibility of progress.

Jung, after writing the novel, distanced himself from

activist politics. He became a playwright and worked with Georg Kaiser, Ernst Piscator, Bertolt Brecht, Kurt Weill and others involved in experimental and political theatre. He produced a magazine called *The Opponent*, that opposed whoever was in power. The Wall Street crash tempted him to concentrate on financial and industrial analysis and journalism. This was a time when economic links between Germany and the Soviet Union were intensifying. Jung manipulated currency deals, credits and investments. He set up a financial agency that invested in theatre, night clubs, Australian gold mines, and massive housing estates planned by Le Corbusier and sympathisers which were to be built in conjunction with trade unions in France and Germany. Cross-border currency controls erected in the early 1930s turned this project into an illegal activity which was condemned vociferously in the Nazi press. The financial agency collapsed, and piles of money— invested by trade unionists—were lost. Jung was denounced and again went underground as the Nazis came to power. These were the darkest years. And they were also the years that submitted the incontrovertible proof of the Marxian slogan—'socialism or barbarism'. Rosa Luxemburg had used the phrase in her campaign against the Social Democratic reformists who were convinced of capitalism's capacity for infinite expansion. She held the view that the system would not expand limitlessly; and that, in due course, it would experience crisis and be compelled to turn to militarism. Rosa Luxemburg was proved right once, when world war broke out in 1914, and barbarism came to the muddy fields of Northern France and elsewhere. There were other chances too, as Benjamin said, to sever the fuse before the point of destruction was reached again. But when, after the war, all the chances to end the cycle and spread world revolution were botched, the punishment was an even greater barbarism, managed through the backlash politics of Nazism. The Nazis' first actions were to smash the workers' movement. In his autobiography, Jung records how he stumbled upon the government decreed 'Celebration Day of National

Labour' on 1 May 1933.[35] The columns of trade unionists were squashed in between the ranks of SA and SS men. Communists and Social Democrats found themselves overrun by uniformed types. The true voices of labour were the least important voices. There were new organisations to celebrate the abstract principle of labour in the Third Reich: Hitler-Youth, *Bund deutscher Mädel, NS-Frauenschaft, NS-Fliegerkorps*, NS-factory organisations, and so on. This elaborate veneration of labour—designed for technological mediation with its spectator tribunes, may poles, loud speakers, lanterns and spotlights and a million banners—was supported by the General Trade Union Alliance (ADG), Jung tells us, for tactically they thought they should show themselves willing to co-operate with their new rulers. Free trade unions were banned on 2 May 1933.

A week later, on 10 May 1933, at a Nazi book burning on Opera House Square in Berlin two of the 'un-German' books to be consumed by the flames were Franz Jung's *The Conquest of the Machines* and Walter Benjamin's *One-Way Street*.

3. Daughters of the Century
The Politics of Women's Liberation 1900–99

Anne Alexander

On the eve of 1900, people in the advanced capitalist countries felt the new century would be one of progress for humanity as a whole. One-hundred years later, many would argue that while nineteenth-century expectations of technological and social change have been surpassed, 'progress' has come at a terrible cost. In the industrialised countries of Europe, North America and Japan, most families can afford a material standard of living which is higher than their great-grandparents in 1900. Yet despite this, the expectations of continued 'progress' have evaporated. The horrors of the twentieth century—the two world wars, the Holocaust, the atomic bomb, the famines—have stained the balance sheet.

This ambivalent evaluation of the twentieth century is conspicuously missing when it comes to the question of women's liberation, however. Discussions of women's role in society in the mainstream press and in the academic world, start from the premise that women have done uniquely well from the social and political changes of the last one-hundred years. Women not only compete on equal terms with men, but have even begun to overtake them. Women managers, doctors, lawyers, politicians, academics, fire-fighters, pilots, athletes, paramedics and engineers may still be relatively rare, but they are no longer remarkable. Women's careers are no longer an interlude between education and marriage. Young women are encouraged to enjoy their sexuality, instead of waiting demurely for their prince to come.

For some equality has gone too far, men are being undermined and boys left without role models. There has been a rash of academic and pseudo-academic books stressing biological and social differences between men and women.[1] Some feminists have also concluded that women's oppression is a thing of the past and those women who fail to make it now have only their own lack of drive and ambition to blame.

The reality for most women is very different. The majority of working-class women work in low-paid, unskilled, insecure jobs and juggle their working lives around child care. Their access to decent health care and education is being steadily eroded. Outside the richest countries, the picture is even bleaker. 'Structural Adjustment Programmes' from the World Bank have forced governments to cut spending on welfare, health and education and thus sweep away the fragile gains of the last thirty years.

The purpose of this chapter is to examine the different ways in which women (and men) have fought to end women's oppression during the twentieth century. My starting point for this discussion is the basic belief that women are treated unequally and unfairly in every contemporary society. This inequality is a social and political fact, not a biological one, whatever proponents of 'evolutionary psychology' or other rehashed versions of social Darwinism may claim. 'Post-feminists' may see 'post-modern irony' in topless pin-ups in *Loaded* and *FHM* magazines, I see old-fashioned sexism.

This conscious recognition of women's oppression, is crucial to the definition of organisations which have fought for women's liberation. I do not accept the argument that only organisations made up of women should be counted as part of the 'women's movement'. There have been many examples of women organising themselves to campaign against women's equality, and in defence of women's 'traditional roles' as mothers and homemakers. In fact, throughout the century, the vast majority of women involved in the struggle for women's rights have not been organised in women-only groups, but have generally been members of trade unions and socialist organisations. It is also rarely been the case that the threads linking any of these organisations have survived unbroken across different generations. The term, the 'women's movement' here is used deliberately loosely. By definition the women and men who have fought women's oppression have pitted themselves against the certainties of the established order. Out of necessity the movements and organisations they formed have been dynamic, but also transient.

The political ideas around which the 'women's movement' has developed during the twentieth century were shaped by two main currents. The first, which may be broadly called 'feminist', argues that the primary cause of women's oppression is men. Sisterhood of all women overrides all ties of class, race or religion. Kate Millet, in her book *Sexual Politics*, puts it like this:

> In the final analysis, it is possible to argue that women tend to transcend the usual class stratifications in patriarchy, for whatever the class of her birth and education, the female has fewer permanent class associations than does the male.[2]

Writers like Millet and her contemporary Shulamith Firestone began to develop the formal theoretical framework for 'patriarchy theory' from the late 1960s, building on the conclusions of earlier generations of feminists.

The second current, which in broad terms can be labelled 'socialist', takes a different starting point. Socialists see women's oppression arising from the structures of class society in general, and capitalist society in particular. Thus, again in the crudest definition, women workers have more in common with working-class men, than they do with their bourgeois sisters. At the turn of the century Elizabeth Gurley Flynn, a leading woman agitator in the American radical trade union, the International Workers of the World, made this call to women workers:

> The 'queen in the parlour' has no interest in common with 'maid in the kitchen'...the sisterhood of women, like the

brotherhood of men is a hollow sham to labour. Behind all its smug hypocrisy and sickly sentimentality loom the sinister outlines of the class war.[3]

The label 'socialist' has described different people at different periods: from doctrinaire Stalinists, to labour-movement bureaucrats to student Maoists. However, at every stage in the development of the women's movement, socialists of one kind or another have played a crucial role in shaping the political debates around the question of women's oppression. Whether they lived up to those promises of liberation should be judged not only on what they said, but how they put it into practice.

These debates point to a history which has been created by millions of ordinary people. The gains which women have made in the last hundred years are a product of this struggle. Women's rights have been won, they have not simply evolved. Social and economic development has not been any guarantee of equality. There have been several periods when, despite technological progress or economic prosperity, women's social and political rights have been restricted (for example the 1950s in the USA or 1930s Germany), or they have come under sustained attack (in Britain in the 1980s). In contrast, the position of women in society has changed for the better at times when the established political and economic order has come under attack from below. This is not something that can be measured by levels of trade-union membership, or even in strike figures: it is when the level of class struggle rises to create an atmosphere where people, downtrodden in everyday life, can challenge the system which exploits and oppresses them.

1900–14

As the celebrations for the new century began in 1900 in Europe and the USA the established political order seemed secure and unshakeable. None of the major industrialised countries had granted women the right to vote. Ideological pressure on women to retreat into the home had grown immensely over the previous two generations. Victorian Britain saw the reinvention of the family, which was supported by legislation against anything which might threaten an idealised picture of domestic bliss. Edward Carpenter looked back on the 'Victorian Age' with revulsion as:

> a period in which not only commercialism in public life, but cant in religion, pure materialism in science, futility in social conventions...the denial of the human body and its needs...the 'impure hush' on matters of sex...and the cruel banning of women from every natural and useful expression of their lives, were carried to an extremity of folly difficult for us now to realise.[4]

Despite the legacy of the previous decades, it was during the years 1900–14 that the question of women's rights first began to shape political debates in Europe and the USA. Women's organisations began to involve more than the privileged and educated few. New organisations were founded, often to lead the campaign for a woman's right to vote. Existing groups, particularly trade unions and socialist parties also began to recruit large numbers of women, and to organise campaigns around 'women's issues'. In Britain, the most significant of the new women's organisations was the Women's Social and Political Union (WSPU) which was founded in 1903. The origins of the WSPU lay in the labour movement, through the Pankhurst family's connections with the Independent Labour Party. As Sheila Rowbotham describes, Emily Pankhurst

> began her political career by standing for the School Board and marching with the unemployed to the Poor Law Office when they demanded the right to work.[5]

The name of the organisation itself—the Women's *Social* and

Political Union reflected a concern for wider issues than simply the campaign for the vote.

However, as the years went by, and as traditional methods of political lobbying seemed to produce few results, the Suffragettes as they had become known, focused on the single issue of the franchise. They also turned to direct action: women took part in vandalism, arson and other forms of individual protest, in contrast to the collective action of the trade unions. At times the suffragettes appeared to be one of the most radical forces in British society, turning to extra-parliamentary action as the political parties made no concessions to their demands. On the surface, they seemed to have more in common with the militant trade unionists of the Great Unrest and the emerging paramilitary armies of Ireland, than they did with respectable politics.

Militant direct action also coincided with a widening fracture within the organisation and the Pankhurst family. After 1912 Christabel Pankhurst prompted a significant shift away from any co-operation with the labour movement, putting her sister Sylvia, who had concentrated her energies on building among the women workers of the East End of London, into an impossible position. Sylvia had been trying to build an organisation which involved genuine mass action by ordinary women, including a possible rent strike for the vote. It was after Sylvia supported a solidarity meeting in the Albert Hall for the release of the Irish trade-union leader and revolutionary James Larkin, that Christabel and Emily Pankhurst told her that if she did not leave the WPSU, she and her East London Federation of Suffragettes would be expelled. Sylvia's description of the discussion gives a sense of the deeper political debates behind this demand:

> They said a deputation to the Labour Party was all very well for us, but one to the king was better for them.[6]

The outbreak of war brought a sudden role reversal. The WSPU, which had been forced to move its headquarters to

Paris during the height of its militant campaigns, suspended all campaigning for women's rights to throw themselves against the national war effort. As George Dangerfield describes in *The Strange Death of Liberal England*:

> So now those hands which had smashed windows, and lighted the stealthy fuse, and poured jam into letter boxes, gave out white feathers to civilian youths and wounded soldiers in mufti. The mouths which had uttered the extreme language of rebellion now made recruiting speeches...So in loyal fervour and jingoistic enterprise, ended the Great Woman's Rebellion.[7]

By contrast, Sylvia and her East London women were now considered dangerous outcasts, as they tried to organise resistance to the war.

The development of the women's movement in Germany followed a similar trajectory. However, the abrupt disintegration of the movement on the outbreak of war did not stem from the capitulation of the mainstream feminist organisations, but rather from the collapse of the SPD (the German Social Democratic Party) into chauvinism. The SPD had from the beginning also played a greater role in shaping the debates over women's rights in Germany. The influence of the SPD was partly a legacy of the repression from the Bismarck era: when women were not only unable to vote, they were forbidden to speak at political meetings. The target of repression, was not women's organisations as such, but the SPD which was banned throughout much of Bismarck's time in power. However, the scale of repression had the effect of ensuring a high profile for the question of women's rights in Germany. The SPD consistently supported female suffrage and made serious attempts to recruit women from the early 1900s. Some of the party's best-known radical activists were women, such as Rosa Luxemburg and Clara Zetkin. After 1890 the SPD grew rapidly, and by 1914, the party counted around one million members; it produced

ninety daily newspapers and won 4.5 million votes in elections.[8] Despite the fact that women were forbidden to join
any political party until 1908, the number of women members of the SPD skyrocketed from 29,468 to 174,474 in just
six years.[9]
The influence of the SPD pulled some feminists and their
organisations to the left. These included radical feminists,
such as Helen Stocker, who founded the progressive *Bund
für Mutterschutz* in 1904. The *Bund* campaigned for access
to abortion, contraception and to end discrimination against
children born to unmarried women. Minna Cauer and Lily
Braun worked to organise women sales clerks and domestic
servants in trade unions.[10] Clara Zetkin attempted to pull
women workers away from their influence into socialist politics. However, as the SPD moved further to the right, her
ideas were watered down to appeal to a broader layer of
women. The emphasis in the SPD's women's paper
Gleichheit (Equality) moved from women's work within the
unions to producing supplements 'For our Housewives and
Mothers' and 'For our Children' after 1905.[11]
However, as in Britain, the real crisis came with the outbreak of war. The war did not only expose the divisions
between middle-class feminists and socialist, it cruelly
exposed the gap between the SPD's May-Day rhetoric and
reality. The party's leadership voted to back the war, while a
small number of left-wingers (in particular Luxemburg and
Zetkin) organised against it.

Revolution and Reaction

The First World War ripped apart the old certainties of the
nineteenth century. European socialist parties collapsed into
chauvinism. The sense of challenge to the established order,
expressed in so many fine anti-war resolutions and so many
rousing May-Day speeches, evaporated in the August of
1914. It was not just the socialist movement which found
itself in confusion at the outbreak of war: there was an

unspoken assumption that the demands for women's political and social equality would have to wait until the war had been won and the majority of feminists threw themselves behind the war effort.

Yet, although the war began with nationalism and flag-waving crowds, it ended in workers' revolution. One by one the crowned heads of Europe tottered. The Austro-Hungarian and Ottoman Empires collapsed. Even Britain was racked by soldiers' protests and strikes. The impact of this revolutionary wave of struggle on the women's movement was immense. The next fifty years were shaped by first, the successful challenge to the system that the revolutions after the First World War represented, and then by the collapse of the revolutionary hopes and the triumph of reaction across Europe. The position of women in the two countries most marked out by this process, Russia and Germany reflects the pressures of reaction and revolt.

In Tsarist Russia strikes and trade-union organisation were illegal, and activists were punished harshly. It was, however, both legal and accepted for men to beat their wives, and a whip hung over many Russian marital beds as a sign of women's subordination.[12] Despite these obstacles women played a vital role in overturning the Tsarist system. The revolution of February 1917 began as a strike by women textile workers in Petrograd to mark the occasion of International Women's Day. Women workers fraternised with the soldiers, urging them to join the revolution. As Leon Trotsky describes:

> They go up to the cordons more boldly than men, take hold of the rifles, beseech, almost command: 'Put down your bayonets-join us' the soldiers are excited, ashamed, exchange anxious glances, waver; someone makes up his mind first, and the bayonets rise guiltily above the shoulders of the advancing crowd.[13]

The transformation in the position of women gathered pace with the Bolshevik revolution in October 1917. In legal terms, women in Russia gained all that even the most radical sections of the feminist movement in Europe had demanded. Decrees issued by the Bolshevik government in the first few weeks after the revolution established women's political and social rights in law. Russian women had the right to vote on equal terms with men more than a decade before they did in Britain, a year before the USA, and 28 years before they had the right to vote at all in France. Divorce became a simple formality. Civil marriage was established and discrimination between legitimate and illegitimate children became illegal. The legal role of the male head of the family was abolished. Women workers were protected with legislation to enforce equal pay for equal work, restrictions on heavy manual work, and granted paid maternity leave. Adultery, incest and homosexuality were dropped from the criminal code. In 1920 free abortion became available on demand, and in 1923 a commission was set up on birth control which recommended the distribution of contraceptives and advice on sexual health.[14]

The Bolsheviks established the *Zhenotdel*, a government division set up to deal with the problems faced by women, which was headed by Alexandra Kollontai. Kollontai had long argued that paper commitments to equality would do nothing to change the lives of Russian women, if the material roots of women's oppression were not addressed. She wrote in 1909:

> The struggle for political rights, for the right to receive doctorates and other academic degrees, and for equal pay for equal work, is not the full sum of the fight for equality. To become really free a woman has to throw off the heavy chains of the current forms of the family....For women the solution of the family question is no less important than the achievement of political equality and economic independence.[15]

So the Bolsheviks attempted to systematically take the work done by women in the home out of the private domain of the household and into the public sphere. Thus they organised childcare, set up communal restaurants, laundries and mending services to release women from the burden of housework. Kollontai, in a speech to the Congress of Working and Peasant Women in Moscow in 1918, described some of the services which the fledgling workers' state was already trying to provide:

> in the Communist city anyone who likes may come and eat in the central kitchens and restaurants…the working woman will no longer be obliged to sink in an ocean of filth or to ruin her eyes darning her stockings or mending her linen; she will simply carry these things to the central laundries each week.[16]

The revolution in Russia set the whole of Europe alight. In November 1918 the storm burst in Germany: soldiers and sailors mutinied, workers' councils sprang up across the country. The Kaiser was bundled out of the country and, in Berlin, a hastily cobbled together coalition of socialists and liberals became the new government. The political change for women was just as abrupt. Women gained the vote in 1918 and by 1919, 10 per cent of the delegates elected to the National Assembly were female. Between 1919 and 1932, 112 women were elected as deputies to serve in the Reichstag. Many women activists had high hopes that this signalled a permanent change in German politics. Maria Juchacz, a Socialist argued: 'The Woman Question in Germany no longer exists in the old sense of the term. It has been solved.'[17]

Liberation meant more than the chance to vote. Weimar Germany witnessed a cultural flowering which seemed to promise both sexual and artistic fulfilment. This was the Germany of Bertolt Brecht, Walter Benjamin and Thomas Mann. This was the world which Georg Grosz, Paul Klee and Otto Dix sketched and satirized. More than 150,000 Germans subscribed to the journals of sex reformers such as

Magnus Hirschfeld and Helene Stöcker, the leading figure in
the radical *Bund für Mutterschutz*.[18] Music hall songs celebrated women's sexual and political confidence—'Chuck all
the men out of the Reichstag' was one popular chorus.[19]

However, beneath the glittering surface of Weimar
Germany different political currents were gathering
strength. The forerunners of the future Nazi SA battalions
had already appeared in the paramilitary gangs which
emerged to crush the communist uprising in Berlin in 1919
and murder Rosa Luxemburg and Karl Liebknecht.
Although the Nazis themselves remained marginal until the
late 1920s, the failure of the German revolution prompted
a shift to the right among the organisations of respectable
politics. This shift is particularly noticeable in the large
women's organisation, the *Bund Deutsche Frauenvereine*
(BDF), which took a firm stand against abortion, contraception and sexual liberation. Gertrud Bäumer, the leading
figure in the BDF supported women who resigned from
political office in the early 1930s and retreated into the
home, on the grounds that the rough and tumble of politics was 'foreign to women's natures'. Richard Evans
argues: 'by 1932 the BDF was joining in the general attack
launched by the right on the parliamentary system and urging the establishment of a fascist-style corporate state.'[20]
The capitulation of former liberals did nothing to soften
the Nazis' grip. Under Hitler's rule, women had one role
above all others: to breed. Motherhood was honoured but
thousands of women who were not 'racially pure' endured
enforced sterilisation, while millions of others were killed
under the Nazis' extermination programmes.

Russia under Stalin also saw reverses in the position of
women as the revolution was slowly crushed from within.
Many of the paper commitments to women's equality stayed
in place, even as the reality of low-paid work, long hours and
lack of basic facilities made life a misery for millions of
Russian women. The organisations which the Bolsheviks had
set up to encourage women's participation in political life,

such as the Women's Department, the *Zhenotdel*, lost any independent function. Stalin's drive to industrialisation saw the needs of workers in general and women in particular completely subordinated to the demands of the economy. One woman miner described her work conditions in 1937:

> I am in the seventh month of pregnancy. In the mine they refuse me the privileges to which I am entitled...I complained to the division chief Samsonov, that if the winch doesn't work I have to load stones by hand. 'Never mind, you can stand it.' Samsonov said.[21]

The economic attack on the working class was accompanied by an ideological onslaught on the gains of the revolution. Motherhood was idealised, and access to abortion and contraception limited. Sexual freedom came under attack as 'bourgeois debauchery'. The decree of 1936 'In defence of Mother and child' reinstated the cult of the family. Women with six children could receive the Motherhood medal, while those with seven, eight or nine were decorated with the award of Motherhood Glory; First, Second or Third degree. Ten children or more conferred the status of Heroine Mother.[22] The ideals of 1917 had been reversed, with women again shouldering the burdens of childcare and work. As Kate Millett points out: 'Stalin's Russia preferred to bolster the family to perform the functions the state had promised but did not choose to afford.'[23]

The twin poles of revolution and reaction did not simply shape the lives of women in Russia and Germany. They also imposed their logic in the rest of Europe and the USA. In Britain, after women gained the vote in 1918, the women's suffrage movement largely wound itself up. However, women did not retreat from political engagement: large numbers were recruited by the Labour Party, others later joined the Communist Party or fascist organisations. The specific question of women's liberation was subsumed by wider political issues. First, by the crucial debate on whether to support or reject the Russian Revolution, which became a litmus test for individuals and organisations alike and second, by the imperative of stopping fascism and, as the 1930s drew to a close, halting the drive to war.

The 1960s

Looking back on her first steps towards political activity in the early 1960s, Sheila Rowbotham asked: 'Why did it take us so long to make a movement like women's liberation?'[24] The generation of women who played a central role in the events of the 1960s: from the Civil Rights movement, to the protests against the Vietnam war, to the foundation of the 'women's liberation movement itself, rarely had any direct connection with the feminist or socialist organisations which had dominated the women's movement before the Second World War. This political hiatus reflected two main factors: first the resurgence of the right, both during the 1930s, and at the height of the cold war in the 1950s, sapped the strength of socialist parties and feminist groups. Second, it reflected the conscious rejection of the established organisations of the left by a new generation determined to break the constraints of the old order.

The demands of the war-time economy of the 1940s saw large numbers of women enter the workforce: poster heroines, such as 'Rosie the Riveter' in the USA, urged women to take up 'men's jobs' in the service of their country. However, this change was short-lived and the 1950s was a sterile decade for the women's movement throughout most of the developed world. A combination of the post-war boom and the cold war prepared the ground for political conservatism. Apart from gaining the vote in France, the last major developed country to hold out against women's suffrage, there was little further progress towards social equality. However forces were gathering behind the façade of domestic bliss that would give birth to the women's movement once again. It was middle-class women who first gave expression to what

Betty Friedan called 'the problem with no name'. In her book, *The Feminine Mystique*, she described vividly the isolation, boredom and mind-numbing misery of housewives' lives. She asked:

> Just what was this problem that has no name? What were the words that women used when they tried to express it? Sometimes a woman would say 'I feel empty some-how...incomplete.' Or she would say 'I feel as if I don't exist.'[25]

The expansion of higher education had also played an important role in fuelling resentment. A university education gave possibilities for a generation of women which their mothers and grandmothers could have barely imagined, but it also threw into sharp relief the inequalities and obstacles placed in their way. Women found themselves at the bottom of the ladder for promotion, or ended up segregated in dead-end 'women's grades', if they were lucky enough to be appointed at all. These factors created a small layer of discontented middle-class women but the ideas of activists like these did not penetrate much deeper into society as a whole. It was only with the unravelling of the post-war boom and the upswing in class struggle at the end of the 1960s that the demands of the women's movement began to reach a wider audience.

The first challenges did not come from the established left, or the organised working class. A range of social movements began to articulate protests against the *status quo* long before workers took centre stage in the struggle; the reborn women's movement grew out of movements such as the struggle for black civil rights and the student protests against the Vietnam war. From these campaigns other movements developed, and ideas and experiences fertilised and radicalised each other. So the non-violent protests for civil rights gave birth to the radical Black Power movement and the Gay Liberation Front were named in solidarity with the Vietnamese National Liberation Front.

These movements, although diverse shared organisational form and political ideas. They arose in opposition to established political parties, and either explicitly rejected, or implicitly criticised the sterility of the monolithic Stalinist Communist Parties. This often translated into a rejection of working-class organisation itself, partly because of the dead hand of Stalinism on the working-class movement, but was also a response to the passivity of the working class itself. Herbert Marcuse, who became a kind of unofficial spokesman for the new social movements, argued that the concept of workers in the industrialised countries playing a leading role in the revolutionary struggles of the future was:

> totally inapplicable to those countries in which the integration of the working class is the result of structural economic-political processes (sustained high productivity, large markets, neo-colonialism, administered democracy) and where the masses themselves are forces of conservatism and stabilisation.[26]

In less pompous terms—workers in the USA and Europe had been bought off by the delights of the consumer society, they had as big a stake in the system as their bosses.

The relationship between the women's movement and the other social movements was contradictory. The impetus for a separate women's movement was often based on an explicit challenge to the sexism women faced within these movements. Within the radical student groups such as the Student Non-violent Co-ordinating Committee (SNCC) and Students for a Democratic Society (SDS), women played a vital part in the protests, the sit-ins, bus boycotts and marches. Yet when it came to organising, acting as the public voice of the movement, or even putting their own ideas forward, they faced hostility and ridicule. When they tried to raise these issues at the SDS national conventions in 1965 and 1966 they were shouted down. Stokeley Carmichael notoriously summed up the attitude of a large number of male activists when he said: 'the only position for women in SNCC is prone'.[27]

These attitudes reflected the contradictions of a society emerging from a period of inhibition and repression. Free love and free sexual expression became the trademarks of the 'hippie scene', just as much as the flowers, bells and incense. Free love could be liberating for both men and women, however as some of the women activists noted at the time, the phrase could also mask double standards and hypocrisy. Sheila Rowbotham has commented caustically that:

> The passivity of the ideal 'chick'—serene and spiritual although she was completely broke and standing in endless NAB queues with a baby on her breast and her tarot cards on her knee—was transparently a new version of the old mystique.[28]

Enjoying sex and sexuality could represent one in the eye for the po-faced moralists of the establishment, but as Dave Widgery pointed out in exasperation a few years later: 'the Underground can't just go on seeing every nipple and grunt as an attack on capitalism'.[29]

The first separate women's groups in the USA made a sharp ideological break with the politics of the student left. The New York Radical Feminists, including Shulamith Firestone, who later wrote *The Dialectic of Sex*, argued in their founding statement in 1969:

> We do not believe that capitalism, or any other economic system, is the cause of female oppression, nor do we believe that female oppression will disappear as a result of a purely political revolution.[30]

A group of students from the American South produced this analysis of the problem in 1968:

> In the life of each woman, the most immediate oppressor,

however unwilling he may be in theory to play that role, is 'the man'.[31]

From 1969 feminist groups sprang up in most major US cities. In Berkley there was Women's Liberation, in Boston Cell 16, and Bread and Roses. WITCH organised several branches across the USA. The Chicago Women's Liberation Union was founded in 1969. The idea of women's liberation leapt into the headlines of the national newspapers at the same time; the famous 'bra-burning' demonstration outside the Miss World pageant in 1968 put feminists' demands on the front pages.[32] As a publicity stunt the protest was extremely successful, however it did not represent a new trend in women's protest. In reality the bulk of feminists' energy was concentrated on the internal dynamics of the new organisations, particularly through the use of 'consciousness-raising'. The feminist magazine *Ms* produced a guide to consciousness-raising in 1972 which explained some of the practicalities:

> The optimum size is six to ten women; larger groups make individual participation difficult...Adding new members after, say, the second or third session is not a good idea. Coming in without knowledge of what's gone before is hard on the newcomer, and hard on the group.[33]

The intense atmosphere of 'consciousness-raising' groups fostered moralism and brought political differences down to a personal level. One woman described her experiences in a 'non-hierarchical' women's liberation group like this:

> In the name of anti-elitism, they were trying to pull off the most elitist thing possible. The meeting ended with charges and counter-charges, and a distinct lack of a feeling of sisterhood.[34]

Most of the groups were also short-lived, and the women

involved did not generally move on into other organisations or even remain active in the women's movement.

This process of fragmentation was not just a product of the organisational tools that the movement had chosen—the women-only groups, the emphasis on lifestyle choice, 'consciousness-raising'. These tactical choices had their roots deep in the political milieu of the new social movements, from which the separate women's movement had emerged. As Sarah Evans argues:

> Separatism was on the cards logically for the New Left was focused on the need for all oppressed groups to organise themselves.[35]

Within the women's movement this dynamic translated into acrimonious splits between lesbians and straight women, divisions over racism, and accusations of 'class-ism'. As Sharon Smith notes:

> As the radical feminist movement disintegrated over the years, the assumption behind separatism took hold: that only those who suffer a certain type of oppression can fight against it.[36]

The development of the women's movement in Britain followed a fairly similar trajectory to its counterpart in the USA. The most important difference lay in the relationship between the women's movement, the left and the organised working class. Women workers in Britain set the trend with the Ford machinists' strike for equal pay in 1968. Although parliament passed the Equal Pay Act two years later, women workers had to fight many other battles to turn legal theory into practice. During 1974 large numbers of strikes took place over equal pay, union recognition, and for the implementation of national wage agreements. The women's paper of the International Socialists, *Women's Voice* noted that:

In most instances the strikes took place among workers with

no previous experience of trade union militancy...women shed their traditionally 'passive and backward' role and led the way showing men how to fight. Women at the National Switch Factory in Keighley led the fight for the implementation of the national engineering wage rates for skilled men, after their own claim for equal pay had been granted.[37]

Asian women workers tore apart the stereotypes of gender and race by leading a militant strike at Imperial Typewriters in Leicester. Male workers supported many of these battles, such as the miners from Nottinghamshire who came with their union banner to join nurses on the picket line.[38]

The campaign to defend abortion rights highlighted the potential to win large sections of the working-class movement to the cause of women's liberation. Socialist women argued that the attempt to restrict access to abortion in James White's Bill of 1975 was a class issue, as much as a women's issue, since rich women could afford to pay the fees for an abortion at a private clinic. This argument clearly had some resonance in the trade-union movement. The first national demonstration called by the National Abortion Campaign in June 1975 drew 40,000 people. Eighteen trades councils sent their banners along with many union branches including AEUW (engineering workers) UPW (post office workers), NUJ (journalists) COHSE (health workers) NUT (teachers) ASTMS and NAGLO (white-collar workers).[39] Although the campaign went on to defeat James White's Bill, the unity of the first few months quickly disappeared. The NAC's conference in Manchester in October 1975 showed the fault lines clearly. *Women's Voice* argued:

> The NAC conference was dominated by those committed to working through the Labour Party machine and parliament. Any sense of action, mass action was missing. There were no spirited feminists even arguing for mass activity by women for women.[40]

The debates within the NAC conference reflected the situation in the women's movement in general. Following the Ruskin College Conference in 1970 which founded the women's liberation movement in Britain, women's groups sprang up around the country. Women picketed Miss World in 1971, organised celebrations for International Women's Day and started up campaigns for 24-hour nurseries. However, this activity was short lived. The Women's Liberation conference in Skegness voted to disband the Women's National Co-ordinating Committee which had been set up at Ruskin the previous year. The conference in Manchester the following year split over the question of whether men should be allowed to come to the conference social night. By the time of the Women and Socialism conference in Birmingham in 1974, the arguments for separatism were gaining ground.[41] As in the USA the number of women involved in the women's movement dwindled. The feminist magazine *Shrew* ceased production between 1974 and 1976, while other publications barely stayed afloat. The opening lines of Hilary Wainwright's introduction to *Beyond the Fragments*, written with Sheila Rowbotham and Lynne Segal sum up the frustration felt by many: 'After a decade of intense socialist agitation, more working-class people than ever in post-war years voted Tory at the last election.'[42]

Backlash: The 1980s and 1990s

The sense of disorientation in the women's movement expressed by the authors of *Beyond the Fragments* was reflected on the rest of the left. The end of the 1970s saw the political spectrum across the USA and much of Europe shift to the right. The tide had begun to turn in the workplaces as well. Reagan smashed the Air Traffic Controllers' strike, while Thatcher set about picking off the British trade unions, one by one. Susan Faludi, in *Backlash* dates the beginnings of the New Right's attack on women to the same period. In 1980, the television evangelist Jerry Falwell solemnly proclaimed: 'The Equal Rights Amendment strikes at the foundation of our entire social structure.'[43]

The growing confidence of the right seemed to strengthen the arguments of those who argued for separatism. Wainwright, Rowbotham and Segal, in *Beyond the Fragments*, proposed the idea of a federal structure linking oppressed groups, such as women, blacks, gays and lesbians as an organisational tactic to overcome fragmentation on the left.[44] In reality, this kind of co-operation became more and more difficult. Feminist thought during the 1980s was based on opposing ideals of 'male' and 'female' values. Although writers rejected the 'male world', and celebrated the positive achievements and potential of women, the categories they chose to define as 'female', began to recall older ideas about unchanging human nature. Women were nurturing, caring and more in tune with the earth, peaceful, by nature opposed to oppression. Lynne Segal quotes Susan Griffin:

> We [women] can read bodies with our hands, read the earth, find water, trace gravity's path. We know what grows and how to balance one thing against another...and even if over our bodies they [men] have transformed the earth, we say, the truth is, to this day, women still dream.[45]

This idealised vision makes stark contrast to the view of men described by writers such as Andrea Dworkin. According to Dworkin all men oppress all women through terror of rape and violence:

> One can know everything and still be unable to accept the fact that sex and murder are fused in male consciousness, so that one without the immanent possibility of the other is unthinkable and impossible. One can know everything and still at bottom refuse to accept that the annihilation of women is the source of meaning and identity for men.[46]

For Dworkin this need to oppress has biological roots, 'violence is male, and the male is the penis.'[47] Male violence is worked out in rape, pornography and ultimately in war. 'Pornography is the theory. Rape is the practice' was a popular slogan of the time. Some leading feminists in the USA even formed alliances with the right to co-operate on drafting anti-pornography legislation.[48]

The two strands of feminist thought, one stressing the positive values of the female, the other the destructive role of the male, combined in the development of the women's peace movement. The campaign against nuclear weapons in Britain and the USA in the early 1980s attracted mass support from women and from men, and became a focus for large sections of the left. The most famous peace camp at the US Cruise-missile base, Greenham Common, was defined as a 'women's peace camp' (although some of the original marchers were men). Many of the 'Greenham women' wanted to make a stand against the 'male violence' of war:

> Greenham is…a women's space in which we try to live out our ideals of feminism and non-violence, a focus for information and ideas, a meeting place and a vital place for women to express their beliefs and feelings.[49]

At its height the women's peace movement radicalised thousands of women. One of the biggest protests organised 300,000 women to 'embrace the base' by surrounding Greenham Common; many thousands more took part in local activities, protests, leafleting, and fund-raising. However, the structure of the movement itself could also lead to isolation since only a few women could afford to make the full-time commitment that living in the peace camp demanded.

Besides living in a women's peace camp, there were other possible ways to try and escape the effects of Thatcherism. The early 1980s was a period of rapid growth for the left-wing of the Labour Party. Although Labour had been swept out of power at national government level, local councils were often dominated by the left. Consciously working within the existing political system, some feminists were able to create an institutional niche where their demands could become part of the fabric of political life. Thus councils adopted non-sexist language, found funding for women's groups, provided nurseries and devised equal-opportunities policies. In the case of the Greater London Council (GLC), this was the work of the Women's Committee which by the time the GLC was abolished had a staff of 70 and an annual budget of £10 million.[50]

The radicalism of the early 1980s began to evaporate by the end of the decade. As Susan Faludi demonstrates in *Backlash*, from access to abortion and rights at work, to the portrayal of women in the cinema and on television, the right made a conscious effort to turn the clock back to the 1950s.[51] This attempt did not succeed in forcing women out of public life. It did, however, undermine what remained of the women's movement. A new breed of 'power feminists' and 'post-feminists' emerged. As writers, journalists, academics and politicians they were conspicuous symbols of the change in women's public roles. Their heroines were women like Madonna, the Princess of Wales and the Spice Girls: successful, good-looking, media-conscious, rich women. For post-feminists, these select few represented proof that women could make it in a man's world. Some of the leading post-feminists welcomed the onslaught of the right in the debates about sex and violence. Kate Riophe, in her book *The Morning After*, attacked the idea of 'date rape', arguing that 'there is a grey area in which someone's rape may be another person's bad night'.[52] Fay Weldon claimed that 'rape was not the worst thing that could happen to a woman', while Camille Paglia devoted a television programme in early 1994 to the penis, arguing that men should now become sex objects for women.[53]

The public debate on sex and sexuality during the 1990s, illustrates the contradictions of the last twenty years. It is widely accepted that women should not be relegated to a passive role in sexual partnerships. Despite the many moral panics about single mothers the traditional view of the family has rarely seemed weaker. Magazines like *Cosmopolitan* and *19* promote the image of the sexually confident woman, who wants raunchy male pin-ups for the office wall. There has also been a greater tolerance of other sexualities in British and American society. Television has reflected this change: from the lesbian kiss in *Brookside*, to the introduction of a transsexual character into *Coronation Street*, to the Channel 4 series *Queer as Folk*, the image of gay sexuality has certainly developed beyond the single stereotype of the past.

Despite all this progress, the debates on sex of the 1990s— from the furore over the age of consent for gay sex in Britain, to the explosive scandals over sexual harassment and adultery which rocked Bill Clinton in the USA—did not take place in a climate of genuine political openness to new ideas. Rather they have taken place on the open market, where the commodification of men's and women's bodies and desires has been the major influence on the debate. For the post-feminists, articulating a confident, aggressive female sexuality is enough to secure an equality which matches men pint-for-pint and conquest-for-conquest. The fashionable new lads' magazines such as *Loaded*, *FHM*, *Front* and *Later* have taken this to mean that men can behave as they like towards women—who are referred to as 'babes', 'chicks' or 'birds'. Old-fashion sexism has acquired a pseudo-radical gloss with its rhetoric of sexual openness and liberation.

Conclusion

The contradictions of the 1990s sum up the experience of the twentieth century as a whole. Women have made real and tangible strides towards equality, but those gains are still fragile. There is still a long way to travel, even on basic issues such as pay, responsibility for child-care, and control over our own bodies. The women and men who have fought to end women's oppression over the last one-hundred years did not build on the gains of each previous generation in a smooth, upward trajectory. Rather, what progress there has been, has come in fits and starts. Rights have been won, lost and re-won time after time. This, I believe reflects the ambiguity of the century for humanity as a whole. The last century has seen some of the finest triumphs of the human spirit over oppression. It has also counted some of the darkest hours in history. Women cannot fight on their own to end inequality, the experience of separatism within the women's movement shows this clearly. What has made gains for women possible has been the struggle to realise the promise of the twentieth century for everyone: a society free from want, misery and oppression.

4. Reformism at the Polls
Workers in the United States, 1918–24

Andrew Strouthous

As the twenty-first century begins the working class of the USA remains without political alternatives. At the beginning of the twentieth century Werner Sombart asked the question 'Why no Socialism in the United States?'[1] and since then 'absence rather than presence'[2] has been the concern of historians and social scientists. It is claimed that the absence of a reformist party defines the nature of the US working class but what that class achieved is ignored at the expense of explanations of what it did not. Sombart wrote his treatise at a particularly depressing stage of US working-class development; at the beginning of the nineteenth century the US labour movement was dominated by the narrow craft unionism of the American Federation of Labor (AFL) which was opposed to independent working-class political activity. During the late-nineteenth century attempts to build industrial unions were defeated and organised labour advocated voting for either Republicans or Democrats. However by 1920 things looked different, with growing union membership and the formation of labour parties. Of course it can be argued that this was, at least until the 1930s, a temporary phenomenon but by the same reasoning so can the period that preceded the First World War.

There is an additional problem in answering Sombart's question and that is, what did he mean by socialism? Did he mean revolutionary or reformist? However rather than Sombart's definition of socialism, it is the lack of a reformist-type party that has become the concern of contemporary social scientists and historians. Labour or reformist parties, to some extent, exist throughout much of Europe and the absence of such in the USA is cited as evidence of a lack of class-consciousness. From this follows the exceptionalist argument that the USA is not a class society in the way European societies are.[3]

Classes exist in relation to the means of production, and it is clear that the majority of the US population has no ownership or control over those means. Nonetheless the reasons for the different political path taken by US labour is of interest to Marxists. But this chapter is not concerned with absence and instead it is argued that the US working class has been more concerned with political activity than it has been given credit for. Labour party activists, perhaps understandably, have not attracted the same amount of attention as Communists, Socialists, anarchists, and the Industrial Workers of the World (IWW). Yet far more workers were involved with the former, in terms of electoral activity, than the latter. Yet this reformist current inside US labour is often ignored or downplayed.[4]

The absence of a labour party is explained by the alleged working-class rejection of independent political action. An example of this approach is that of Gwendolyn Mink who has claimed that 'In fact American Trade Unionism explicitly rejected the idea of independent labor politics'. Mink focuses on the bureaucracy of the American Federation of Labor (AFL); the activities of its rank and file are ignored. The union's national leadership, it is true, rejected any independent reformist activity, but the membership did not. But by ignoring the membership Mink eliminates other possibilities. Perhaps if those who desired an alternative strategy to the AFL bureaucracy were an insignificant minority then this would not be an unreasonable position.[5]

Richard White has commented on the past: 'We eliminate its strangeness. We eliminate, most of all, its possibilities. History should do more than just validate the inevitability of the present.'[6] There was in the AFL a significant section of workers who wanted 'independent labor politics': a party based on the model of the British Labour Party. The evidence that the reformist political activity of US workers has been underestimated can be illustrated by a brief sketch of workers' political activity in the cities of New York, Chicago and Seattle between 1918–24.[7] This short period was an epoch of intense reformist activity by organised labour, and a period with mass sentiment amongst unionised workers for a labour party, thus this chapter will show:

- That between 1918–24 there was desire amongst organised US workers for a reformist-type party (a party modelled on the British Labour Party).
- That some sections of the US labour movement turned this desire into political organisation.
- That the failure of this movement cannot be explained by an abstract theory of 'exceptionalism' but rather by opposition from the bosses and union leaders.

Workers' Response to War

The effect of the First World War on the American Federation of Labor (AFL) was threefold. First its membership grew dramatically, from 2.7 million in 1914 to 5.1 million by 1920, with many involved in mass strikes. Second, its conservative leadership temporarily abandoned its anti-statist[8] principles and co-operated with the state. The first two effects combined to produce a third: the development of a mass reformist political current amongst the membership. It is the third effect that concerns this chapter, for between 1918 and 1924 the AFL was riven by internecine conflict, between those who believed that organised labour should not involve itself in politics, and those who advocated a labour party on the lines of the British Labour Party. The majority of the AFL executive was opposed to any such party and made this clear in its publications. However a majority of the AFL rank and file, led by city local officials, desired such a party. That there was significant support inside the AFL for the 'Labor Party idea' is sustained by a report in the *Intercollegiate Socialist*, in which Abraham Epstein analysed a survey from an organisation that had the 'confidence of labor in a leading industrial state of the East'.[9] Of 285 unions replying to this survey, 89 per cent favoured the formation of a labour party. If further proof were needed of how substantial support for a labour party was amongst AFL membership, Chicago, the best organised union city in the USA, set about building a labour party.[10] New York City's AFL organisations also set about creating a labour party.

In the past those desiring such a party had hesitated to act, not just out of fear of the AFL executive, but also due to the limited power of the local unions. However, the wartime experience had changed the nature of the AFL. In 1917 and 1918 strikes took place across a wide range of industries. Workers demanded higher wages to keep up with war-driven inflation; others struck for shorter hours or union recognition. The metal trades, heavily involved in munitions production, had more strikes than any other sector. Close on their heels came the building trades, shipbuilding, mining and transportation. These were not the only areas involved, and strikes took place across a wide range of occupations, including women telegraphers. All these industries were central to the war effort and the employers were forced to negotiate with the AFL in the conditions of a wartime boom. By 1919, US workers were involved in the largest wave of strikes the country had ever seen. Some of these strikes were national and industry-wide (such as those in steel) and others city-wide (the Seattle General Strike). The outbreak of militancy and subsequent growth of membership strengthened the hand of the lower level of local officials, in particular the strengthening of 'federated unionism'. Federated unionism was similar to the shop stewards' movement in Britain. Wage claims for workers in different unions were combined under the aegis of the local city trades or crafts council which overcame the problem of craft division in negotiating with the employer. One famous example of this form of organisation was the Seattle Central Labor Council (SCLC) the city-wide body for AFL unions, which led the 1919 Seattle General Strike. This strike was defeated and contributed to the rise of the Red Scare of 1919–20. What is less well known is that the local AFL leadership went on to build a successful labour party. However the Seattle AFL leadership were not the initiators of the labour party movement. It was the Chicago Federation of Labor (CFL) that was amongst the first of the AFL's city-based organisations to form its own labour party in early 1919, and it then went on to challenge the National Executive by launching a national labour party. This move was supported by another important AFL centre, New York City. Seattle labour, heavily influence by syndicalist politics at the time, did not rush to do likewise. It was not until after the city unions had suffered defeat from the employers' offensive against the closed shop (with concomitant loss of union membership) that reformist political activity dominated the agenda there.

Communists and Socialists

Nationally the Socialist Party (SP) was ambivalent about the project, indeed it had major issues of its own to resolve. The party was split between the pro-Bolshevik left, and those who supported the Second International. Though the majority of the party's members supported the Bolsheviks it was the right wing that kept control of the party machine. Logically they should have supported the newly rising labour party advocated by the opposition to the conservative AFL leadership. However they took a sectarian approach to the new body for two reasons. First they needed to demonstrate they were more radical than the Communists who, though the majority of the Socialist Party, were expelled due to their support for the Third International.[11] Thus this was not the time for the remaining, mainly right-wing, Socialists to drop their own electoral intervention. Second, some of the leaders had good relations with the conservative leadership of the AFL who bitterly opposed the forming of a labour party. Nor was the rump Socialist Party capable of developing a non-sectarian approach to the newly formed party and relations between the two organisations, with some individual and local exceptions, were often hostile.

The Communists did not organise until late 1919, a major split from the Socialist Party, they remained divided into two separate parties until 23 December 1921. Both factions refused to relate to the AFL, and hence to the national Farmer Labor Party (FLP) launched by the Chicago Federation of Labor (CFL). James P. Cannon noted that a change of attitude did not come about until after the factions had reunited, and then only when initiated by Moscow sometime in 1922.[12] The high tide of labour party activity was effectively over before the Communists changed their policy and considered working inside the labour party movement. But Communists faced hostility from some of those who supported the labour party movement although they did manage, briefly, to work inside the movement in Chicago but between 1922–24 (apart from Chicago) the Communists were usually excluded from AFL, and independent political activity, and were rarely strong enough to challenge such exclusion.

However the SP was not a monolith; it was in decline, and its members reacted differently according to individual preference, factional sympathy, and the geographical locality. In Seattle leading members joined the labour party, in Chicago and surrounding Illinois they were split, some supporting, some opposing and a few joining the new party. But in New York they were basically antagonistic to the new party. However, although a majority of AFL members at the rank-and-file level supported a labour party, the main opposition they faced was from their own national leadership.

Labour Party Activity 1919–20
Chicago

The majority of Chicago locals supported the new party. The CFL claimed to represent over 300,000 workers, all of whom were formally affiliated to the new party. The CFL changed its union newspaper into a political newspaper,[13] the *New Majority*, to support the new party, and for a short time the well-known syndicalist militant W.Z. Foster was its editor. However, the firmest link between the new party and workers was the fact that many of its leading activists were local union officials. The new party also had the added strength that the Illinois State Federation and the majority of Illinois United Mine Workers (UMW) locals endorsed it. The Women's Trade Union League (WTUL) also supported the new party and used its monthly bulletin to advertise its activities. Additionally the CFL had a far better relationship with unions outside of the AFL than its New York counterparts; Hillman, President of the Amalgamated Clothing Workers (ACW), spoke on Chicago Labor Party platforms and donated money to the party's funds.[14]

Chicago was the first of the three cities detailed here in which the FLP made a major electoral intervention. The Chicago Party entered the mayoral election of 1 April 1919, standing John Fitzpatrick, President of the Chicago Federation of Labor (CFL). It also stood an ethnically mixed slate of candidates including well-known Polish, Scandinavian, Italian and Black trade unionists. Fitzpatrick was the flagship candidate and his 55,990 votes totalled eight per cent of the votes cast. Compared with the Republican victors' vote of 37.6 per cent or the main Democrat vote of 34.5 per cent, it was not impressive and many in the new party were very disappointed.[15] However, a more appropriate comparison of labour's impact is to compare the result with previous working-class interventions in the mayoral election. In Chicago the Socialist Party's highest vote ever had been 25,883 in 1911; in 1919 it was 24,079 but the combined working-class vote, in 1919, of 81,557 was the highest. The intervention of the Chicago labourites had increased the working-class vote three fold. Considering that the Chicago Party was but a few months old it was a creditable result.[16]

Fitzpatrick's vote averaged 8 per cent, but it was higher in working-class wards: 16 per cent in the 29th ward but only 2 per cent in the 2nd. In 16 of the 35 wards he received more than 8 per cent. These included the traditionally Democratic working-class 5th, 29th, and 30th wards; all located in the areas of the stockyards where many new immigrants lived. These were also areas where the party had held large rallies and campaigned enthusiastically.[17] Many workers in these wards did not have the franchise, or didn't bother to vote; thus the polling figures have underestimated labours' support. The most successful aldermanic candidate was Ida Fursman, the only Labor Party woman to remain on the ballot, who polled 5,212 votes, far more than any other labour council candidate. However expectations had been high and the results were considered by some to be a failure. Although the CFL remained committed to its new party, and turned itself into the leadership of the Farmer Labor Party nationally, it suffered increasing apathy. In the national elections of 1920 it was clear that the party, in Chicago, had gone into serious decline, receiving only 0.6 per cent of the presidential vote.[18] Only one year earlier the FLP, in Chicago, had out-polled the Socialists; now the tables had turned with the Socialist vote being the greater. However there was little for the Socialists to celebrate either, for Eugene Debs, their presidential candidate, had won 13.2 per cent of the vote in 1912. In the 1919 mayoral election the joint Labor Party and Socialist vote had been 11.6 per cent: now it only totalled 6.6 per cent of the presidential vote. Though the Chicago Party failed to make any electoral impact in the ensuing years the CFL remained committed to its party until mid 1923. It was not electoral failure that finally persuaded Fitzpatrick and the CFL to drop its strategy, but the loss of support from the Illinois State Federation of Labor combined with virulent opposition from the AFL nationally; this included removing the AFL's financial contribution to Fitzpatrick's wages.

Seattle

Seattle labour did not create an independent labour party until 1920 since the leaders of the Seattle Central Labor Council's wanted the endorsement of the Washington State Federation of Labor (WSFL) before launching a fully fledged party. The leader of the SCLC was the well-known and respected James Duncan who had played a leading role in the local FLP. Although the SCLC delayed launching its party, it did have a tradition of supporting labour nominees in local elections and had support from local Seattle unions, including shipbuilding workers and metalworkers. The new party also had the advantage of the support of a well-established daily progressive newspaper, the *Seattle Union Record*.

The endorsement of the WSFL for its independent electoral strategy was rather by sleight of hand. The WSFL delegated its political intervention for the 1920 National Elections to the Triple Alliance (TA), an amalgam of railwaymen, farmers and AFL delegates. The TA in turn decided to put the question of affiliation to the FLP to a referendum which voted by 6,862 to 174 to end the TA in favour of the FLP. David Coates (Chairman of the TA), claimed that the FLP had 20,000 members statewide which was achieved by transforming TA membership into party membership. Nonetheless the FLP could claim that its electoral strategy was officially endorsed by the WSFL, and had certainly gained support from many union activists. The outcome and speed of events was a shock to William Short (President of the WSFL) who feared losing control, but he could do nothing to stop the party's growing support. Although he feigned support for the FLP during the 1920 presidential election he began, at first from behind the scenes, to organise the downfall of the new Party. Between 1920–3 the SCLC would have to contend with the hostility of AFL State and national officials.

The SCLC went on to prepare the ground for electoral activity in an independent guise. One such campaign was the council's support for James Duncan in the 1920 mayoral elections. Duncan did not stand under the aegis of the FLP, but as an independent endorsed by the King County Triple Alliance. Duncan polled 34,053 votes—the largest ever for a defeated mayoral candidate and Hugh Caldwell received 50,850 votes, the largest for a winning candidate. The result represented the extreme polarisation that took place during the campaign: Duncan was vilified as an anti-war Bolshevik and supporter of the Industrial Workers of the World (IWW); in fact he was none of these things but was a Calvinist pro-temperance progressive, and the only card he carried was that of the AFL. However he did support the FLP, and believed that the AFL should be organised on industrial lines. That was enough to earn him the undying hatred of the AFL leadership who eventually drove him out of the movement.

Though Duncan was defeated in the mayoral campaign, the result, rather than demoralising Seattle labour, spurred it on. By 1920 with 'official' support of the WSFL, the party went on to gain the support of the well-known local progressive Robert Bridges. Labour's alliance with Washington State progressives paid further dividends when it effectively won over whole sections of the Democratic Party to the FLP's cause. Thus Seattle labour entered the 1920 national elections in high spirits. The optimism was not misplaced and in most of the posts contested the FLP came second, and the Democrats third. However, even the highly popular Bridges who gained 39,034 votes for governor, the highest vote for any FLP candidate in Seattle's King County, failed to win. Due to a high poll Bridges' share of the vote represented only 36 per cent. However for the Presidency the FLP polled an average of 25 per cent in King County, considerably below votes garnered for state and local positions.

Nonetheless, for the most part, the FLP temporarily replaced the Democrats as the second party in Washington and Seattle. Since they could not claim they were supporters of the Republicans who were the main beneficiaries of the FLP intervention, labour was left without any political influence. The Republicans introduced Prohibition against the wishes of the AFL, and the Democrats would still have lost without FLP intervention although it did carry sway inside some sections of the Washington labour.

The SCLC and Duncan had been responsible for making the FLP the second party; they soon became subject to a witch-hunt from the conservative officials of the local State Federation. Duncan and his allies would never get the opportunity to build on their success of 1920; a combination of drastic membership losses due to unemployment and an employers' offensive against the closed shop strengthened the hand of the union's conservatives. Deprived of official state support, with the unions weakened and riven by internecine conflict the Seattle FLP went into decline. By 1923 Duncan, the SCLC and its allies were forced to drop their attempts to build a party based on AFL support.

New York City

In early 1919, 886 delegates—of whom 360 were affiliated to the Central Federated Union of New York City (CFU), and 180 to the Central Labor Union of Brooklyn, attended the founding convention of the American Labor Party (ALP), which subsequently joined the FLP. Another 50 delegates were affiliated to the WTUL, while 288 came from local unions. The United Hebrew Trades and the United Board of Business Agents of the Building Trades were each represented by two delegates. The support appears impressive, but the number of union locals and local unions represented amounts to only 146, a fraction of New York labour's organisations. Significantly there is no trace of the Amalgamated Clothing Workers attending the conference and the ACW complained that its locals had not received invitations. Unaffiliated organisations like the ACW were only offered two delegates. The ACW believed there was great enthusiasm and support in labour bodies for a labour party. It stated that 58 of its locals had supported Cook County Labor Party. The treatment of the ACW proved to be a serious mistake for the New York Party, one that strengthened the hands of those Socialists who opposed the project. In New York, the attitude of the Socialists proved to be a substantial barrier for a new organisation trying to establish itself. The Socialists had a traditional support from some sections of the labour movement at the polls, and received financial assistance from many progressive trade unions. As well as the Socialists the New York State Federation of Labor also opposed the Party. Nor was the base of the pro-labour party activists particularly secure in New York City, especially in Brooklyn, and a substantial number of conservative trade unionist officials looked to Gompers and the AFL nationally to put down the insurgents.

Electorally the FLP was least successful in New York but, for the most part, its results were derisory. This was partly due to the fact that here the party existed in the most hostile environment. Its enemies not only included the main party machines, with their ability to manipulate the administration of elections, but also union leaders allied with gangsters, the State and national AFL leadership. This, combined with the barrier of a hostile Socialist Party, proved the party's' undoing. Unlike the parties in Seattle and Chicago, city central labour body support was removed at an early stage, and at no stage did the party gain the support of the New York State Federation of Labor. However there were one or two bright spots amongst the gloom.

The presidential vote in the 1920 election was particularly poor, with Parley P. Christensen, the Farmer Labor national candidate, garnering 18,413 votes, a mere 0.6 per cent of the presidential vote cast in New York. In comparison Debs, the Socialist candidate, received 203,201, 7 per cent. Dudley

Field Malone a well-known progressive standing for the FLP got 69,908 votes (for Governor of New York State) with fewer than 9,000 coming from outside NYC. Rose Schneiderman, a well-known trade union activist and leading member of the Women's Trade Union League (WTUL) polled only 27,934 votes for the Senate. Schneiderman, it was believed, had done well amongst women garment workers and in the East Side.[19] However the best result was in the 18th Congressional district (see table below). Here Jerry O'Leary got 25 per cent of the poll which was the most successful result for the FLP.

Table 1: Election Result 18th Congressional District

Democrat	Republican	FLP	Socialist
12,169 (31.2%)	11,148 (28.6%)	9,998 (25.7%)	5, 668(14.5%)

O'Leary probably did well because he was widely known throughout New York for campaigning for Irish self-determination. O'Leary had the advantage of being both well—known in Irish circles, and well connected with many of the community's organisations.[20]

Dudley Malone, a progressive friendly to labour, had also polled reasonably well because of his consistent campaigning for women's suffrage. But such is the nature of US electoral politics that he believed his result was a fiasco; it had not lived up to his high expectations. Malone deserted the new party as did many other progressives, and WTUL support drifted away. Bereft of trade-union and progressive support the New York FLP (also known as the American Labor Party ALP) was effectively dead though it would limp on in different guises until 1924.

Many of the founders of the new party were demoralised by the electoral results of 1920 (except in Seattle). However, as the progressive Frederick Howe noted people don't always vote as they shout. In other words there is evidence that a lot of AFL members wanted a labour party but either didn't vote for it and sometimes didn't vote at all. It is hardly surprising that a party that was only a couple a years old did not have the confidence of those looking for an alternative at the polls. Indeed in the election of 1920 there was a great desire to have an alternative to Woodrow Wilson and his Democratic Party. Labour, and the Irish in particular, had every reason to resent his government. It was Wilson's government that had organised the Palmer Raids, the Red Scare of 1919, with government-led attacks on the radical left and the deportation of immigrant activists. Wilson had also refused to support self-determination for the Irish. The backlash against the Democrats was enormous, but except in Seattle the beneficiary was not the FLP, but the Republican Party. It is not possible here to analyse the reasons why the new party had made such little headway by the end of 1920, although some reasons are implied above.[21] The central argument here is that there was a substantial reformist current in the AFL as evidenced by organised workers, in the three cities above.

However this impulse did not translate into broad electoral commitment. Only in Seattle, with the unique situation of full local and state AFL backing for the FLP combined with the collapse of the local Democrats, did the backlash against Wilson benefit labour. Chicago had State union backing, but lacked a recent tradition of trade-union independent electoral activity. At the end of 1920 New York Labour had lost all union support. By 1922 a genuinely independent labour party movement based on AFL unions was finished. The defeat had come about for a variety of reasons, including economic downturn, and the employers' offensive against union recognition, but not because the instigators were ideologically convinced of the AFL's non-partisan policy. Indeed many hoped that a return to favourable conditions for labour would allow them to relaunch the party.[22]

Thus it was not ideology but the shift in the balance of class forces in the employers' favour after 1919 that was the key to abandoning of the labour party strategy between 1922–3. A short term slump, the Red Scare, rising unemployment in traditional industries and the employers' offensive against the closed shop led to a rapid decline in union membership. This combination of factors subdued the wave of militancy that had engulfed 1919–20 and weakened local union leaders. Union leaders who had rebelled against the AFL national leadership now needed national union backing to survive. Gompers threatened to remove the AFL charter from insurgent local leaders. Even the powerful Fitzpatrick in Chicago was forced to surrender. The FLP was a spent force with little achievement to its name.[23]

Deflected Reformism

By the beginning of 1924 the AFL leadership had quashed the majority of those who wanted to build an independent party. Even the most powerful and radical advocates of reform, John Fitzpatrick and the Chicago Federation of Labor had, under immense pressure, surrendered and accepted the AFL philosophy of non-partisanship. This meant organised labour voting for either the Republican or Democratic Party, depending on which was considered most responsive to the AFL's list of demands.

Yet in the general election of 1924 the AFL broke with supporting the presidential candidate of either of the two main parties, and advocated voting for Robert La Follette. La Follette, a progressive and a Republican Party member (he remained a Republican Party member even after he had stood against it), and labour sympathiser he made it clear that his was an individual candidacy that invited labour support. La Follette opposed a new party in the short run, but would probably have welcomed a progressive-type party in the long run. In a sense La Follette and the AFL leadership were united since neither saw his election campaign as an endorsement of a labour party.

If the AFL's electoral opportunism and manoeuvrings were the only factor, then its support for the La Follette campaign would be of little interest; however support for La

Follette went beyond the wishes of a few full-time national officials; Indeed support for the campaign went beyond the labour activists who had tried to build the FLP; beyond the Socialist Party and Eugene Debs, and deep into the rank and file of the AFL. Labour and working-class voters proved to be La Follette's most substantial supporters.

The Road to La Follette

Between 1920 and 1924 labour experienced devastating defeats: in particular, the railroad workers, miners, steelworkers, meatpacking workers, and shipyard workers suffered at the hands of anti-union employers and the gains made in union recruitment during the war and 1919 were reversed. First under the Democratic Administration employers began their attacks on the unions. The Democrats, hated as the instigators of the Red Scare (Palmer raids), were removed by an electoral backlash. The Republican Party, who had used troops against striking railworkers and miners, proved to be just as bad, using troops against striking railworkers and miners. Thus hatred of the two main parties by organised labour went beyond the AFL's national leadership's hurt pride over electoral manoeuvring. AFL bureaucrats, some of whom even threatened to launch a new party, reflected the deep bitterness of workers in radical speeches. The railway unions set up a Conference for Progressive Political Action (CPPA). Its aim was to get politicians to become more attentive to the needs of labour by pursuing non-partisan political action in a more aggressive manner than the AFL leadership which was ineffective. The CPPA produced a journal, *Labor*, and in some areas supported Farmer Labor Party candidates.[24] Neither of the two main parties felt any pressing need to pay attention to the AFL's, or the more vigorous CPPA's, efforts to get them to offer policies favourable to unions and workers. To overcome this indifference some sections of the AFL and the CPPA talked up the issue of an independent party which explains why some Socialists and other activists wrongly believed that the CPPA could become the foundation of a labour party.

Thus, as the 1924 National Election approached, talk in labour circles increasingly turned to the need for an independent labour party. Some of it was sincere, as in the case of Socialist Party trade unionists, and some of it just rhetoric. Ironically, at a time of growing sentiment for a labour party the FLP had ceased to exist in any effective organisational form. At the same time, as outlined above, the presidential candidates of the two main parties were unacceptable to the AFL. The CPPA seized its chance; it could deliver a rebuke to the Democrats and Republicans by persuading Senator Robert La Follette to stand for president.

For the old labour party activists, and now also the Socialists the La Follette campaign became a substitute for a labour-party campaign. They were aware he was a non-partisan candidate, independent of all parties including a labour party. Nonetheless, both the labour party supporters and the more recent converts, the Socialists, believed that the gathering momentum behind La Follette would spontaneously create a labour party. However, the AFL made it clear that in no sense could this be interpreted as backing for a labour party. The Socialists and other activists said little about this aspect of AFL policy, making no criticism of the AFL leadership or warning that the AFL would ditch the campaign immediately after the election.

This promised support of organised labour was an important factor in convincing La Follette to stand. It is also clear that without this support he would not have garnered the vote he did (over 4,800,000 votes, almost 17 per cent of the total cast). La Follette's vote can be described as a deflected reformist vote and La Follette's vote was a substantial proof of a labour party impulse.

La Follette's vote is usually acknowledged as a progressive vote; the role of labour is, for the most part, played down or treated as insignificant.[25] The evidence usually given for this is that the AFL provided little finance or resources for the campaign. At a national level this is true; but at the local level the picture is completely changed. In Chicago, New York, Seattle and Minnesota local unions and activists provided substantial financial support. Local union officials and national union newspapers campaigned for La Follette.[26] In New York most of the rank and file supported the independent candidate. Socialist newspapers and progressive labour periodicals also actively campaigned for La Follette. In New York FLP activists and Socialists had united to create a new American Labor Party. Eugene Debs also dropped his own candidacy in favour of La Follette. Thus a massive alliance of Socialists, former FLP activists, and Progressives was temporarily created to win votes for the campaign. Only the Communists remained outside of the campaign; and failed to relate in any meaningful way to those who desired a genuine labour party.[27]

This was one of the most substantial votes for an independent presidential candidate in US history. But, as soon as the result was known, the AFL repudiated its policy of supporting La Follette as a grievous mistake. The CPPA did not go as far as that, but it dropped any strategy of supporting a new party, the logic of non-partisan action applied to AFL and CPPA alike. Thus rather than leading to a labour party, the campaign led only to further marginalisation of the Socialists and the complete demise of the FLP as a national organisation.

Completely abandoned by their new-found political allies, the CPPA and AFL, the Socialists had no other strategy to offer than to go back to standing their own candidates. But their uncritical support of the La Follette campaign and the downplaying of their own electoral intervention in the 1924 national elections left them weaker than ever. Unaligned activists, reformists and progressives in the AFL who had fought for a labour party in the past had no organisation left either, and the Communists, at the time, were marginal. The millions who had voted for La Follette were left without political strategy, organisation or leadership. The possibility of creating a labour party was, in any practical sense, completely negated by the La Follette vote. The 1924 general election was an indicator of deep discontent with the two main parties; it also signalled the end of any effective third party activity based on the unions.

The 1930s saw a massive wave of workers' struggles and the founding of the Congress of Industrial Organizations (CIO). With workers joining unions en masse, many looked for an independent political alternative. This could have been fertile ground for an already existing, but fledgling, labour party to grow in, but the AFL had almost completely extinguished the tradition of labour party activity that had risen between 1918–24. Once again in the 1930s many workers looked for a reformist alternative at the polls once again the trade-union bureaucracy did everything it could to frustrate such an impulse.[28]

None of this is to argue that a labour party could have succeeded, but it does demonstrate that at key moments in the class struggle in the USA there has been a major impulse amongst organised workers to build an independent political alternative based on the unions. There are many reasons why these movements have failed however, it cannot be ignored that as well as hostility from the employers and the established political parties, workers also had to deal with hostility from their own union leaders. If those leaders had supported the attempts to build a labour party it is not unreasonable to surmise that the outcome could have been different. If the unions had maintained a commitment to a labour party throughout the 1920s, and had kept a minority of activists together inside a political party, that organisation would have faced far more favourable circumstances by 1936. As Richard White has argued elsewhere, 'Small changes in one period can yield significant differences in another. Contingency is not the whole story, but it is part of the story.'[29]

5. John Reed and the United States of America

John Newsinger

John Reed is best known as the chronicler of the Bolshevik Revolution of October 1917, the author of *Ten Days That Shook the World*. It is sometimes argued that Reed stands outside the American tradition. Certainly, his experiences in Petrograd won him over to Bolshevism and the account of his experiences was to win over many others, but it is the contention here that his politics were always rooted in the US. This chapter will examine Reed's US experiences, and demonstrate that it was the nature of class conflict there, and the repression of the left that accompanied it, that were determining influences on him. This explains Reed's enthusiastic embrace of Bolshevism, an enthusiasm for which, despite all the difficulties and hardships, the suffering and setbacks of the revolutionary struggle, he remained true to until his death in October 1920.[1]

Enter the Industrial Workers of the World

Reed first encountered the class struggle while working as a journalist on Max Eastman's radical magazine, *The Masses*. He was to be sent to cover the silk weavers' strike in Paterson, New Jersey at the end of January 1913. Workers at the Henry Doherty Silk Company had walked out, precipitating a general revolt. The strikers turned to the revolutionary syndicalists the IWW, the 'Wobblies', for help which soon arrived in the shape of Elizabeth Gurley Flynn, Carlo Tresca, Patrick Quinlan and Big Bill Haywood. By the end of March,

Paterson was in the grip of what amounted to a general strike involving 25,000 workers and the closure of 300 mills. [2]

The IWW tried to publicise the worsening exploitation that had precipitated the revolt. Average wages were just $10 a week, but the IWW also identified some cases of super-exploitation, especially of young women. Some employers held back half the pay of adolescent girl employees for a year and if they left or were fired before the end of that time, these girls lost the deducted pay. Among a number of examples Flynn produced included a sixteen-year old who had worked in a mill for forty-two weeks, for fifty-five hours a week, for which she earned only $1.25 per week.[3] The authorities responded to this revolt against injustice with massive repression. According to one historian:

> Rarely was there a strike in American labour history in which mass arrests of the strikers took place on a scale similar to Paterson. Recorder James F. Carroll was kept busy day after day during the strike, sending strikers to jail for unlawful assemblage; on one occasion he sent 164 to jail. One jury found 41 strikers guilty of unlawful assembly because they were doing picket duty around the Harding Mill. Judge Kleinert sentenced 31 strikers to three months in county jail at hard labour, and then suspended sentence during good behaviour. He admonished the strikers that if they did not like the laws they were at liberty to leave the country. All of the strikers thus addressed went right back to the picket line and most of them ended up in jail. Seventeen-year-old Hannah Silverman, a young striker, was sent to the country jail three times during the strike and was on the picket line the following morning each time she was released. In the course of the strike, the police made 4,800 arrests which resulted in 1,300 prison sentences.[4] The 'Wobbly' leaders were as much the victims of legal repression as the rank and file. Haywood, Flynn, Quinlan and Tresca were all arrested and held in custody for varying periods by the police, although only Quinlan

was to be sentenced to a term of imprisonment, serving twenty-two months in the aftermath of the dispute.[4]

While the 'Wobblies' advocated non-violence and passive resistance, there were inevitably violent clashes. On 17 April pickets jeering at scabs were fired on and a bystander, Modestino Valentino, was shot dead. He was buried by the IWW, with some 20,000 people filing past his coffin. It was at this point that John Reed went to Paterson to report on the strike. He arrived on 28 April, joining the pickets outside the mills and within hours was under arrest for refusing to move on. That same day he appeared in court and was promptly sentence to 20 days in jail (he served only four before Upton Sinclair bailed him out). His article describing his experiences, 'War in Paterson' appeared in the June 1913 issue of *The Masses* and gave the strikers and their cause useful publicity. A Paterson policeman was later to complain that jailing Reed had given the IWW more publicity than jailing hundreds of strikers.[5]

It was in Paterson that Reed's lifelong enthusiasm for and commitment to the IWW began. He was completely won over by the strikers, who filled him with admiration, and by the IWW leaders, in particular Bill Haywood. In 'War in Paterson', Reed described the scene in prison:

Surrounded by a dense crowd of short, dark-faced men, Big Bill Haywood towered in the centre of the room. His big hands made simple gestures as he explained something to them. His massive, rugged face, seamed and scarred like a mountain, and as calm, radiated strength. These slight foreign faced strikers, one of many desperate little armies in the vanguard of the battle line of labour, quickened and strengthened by Bill Haywood's face and voice, looked up at him lovingly, eloquently. Faces deadened and dulled with grinding routine in the sunless mills glowered with hope and understanding. Faces scarred and bruised from policemen's clubs grinned eagerly at the thought of going back on the picket line. And there were other faces too lined and sunken with the slow starvation of nine weeks' poverty, shadowed with the sight of so much suffering, or the hopeless brutality of the police and there were those who had seen Modestino Valentino shot to death by a private detective. But not one showed discouragement; not one a sign of faltering or of fear. As one little Italian said to me, with blazing eyes: 'We all one bigga da union. IWW —dat word is pierced da heart of de people'.[6]

What was the IWW? The Industrial Workers of the World was established in Chicago in 1905, a revolutionary syndicalist union committed to organising the unskilled and downtrodden, the immigrant workers, the blacks, women and migrant workers for the overthrow of capitalism. Its constitution proclaimed that 'the working class and the employing class have nothing in common' and that between 'these two classes a struggle must go on until the workers of the world organise as a class, take possession of the earth and the machinery of production and abolish the wage system'.[7] In the period before the US's entry into the First World War, the IWW was involved in at least 150 strikes, many of them brutal, bloody affairs. The union fought the Goldfield, Nevada miners' strike in 1906–7, the Lawrence, Massachusetts textile workers' strike in 1912, the Louisiana and Arkansas timber worker strikes in 1912–13, the Paterson strike and the Mesabi Range ironworkers strike of 1916. These class battles inspired the left and outraged the right, both seeing the IWW as the harbinger of revolution. The IWW fought for the right to proclaim its message, resisting attempts to deny its agitators and organisers free speech. Up until the Great War, it fought some thirty Free Speech campaigns with members and supporters descending on those towns and cities where rights were denied. Thousands were imprisoned, hundreds badly beaten, and some killed. The First World War, as we shall see, provided employers and government with the excuse for a nationwide campaign to destroy the union, a campaign against which no Free Speech campaign could prevail.[8]

Writing much later in the journal *Communist International*, Reed was to celebrate 'the power of the IWW mass tactics':

> The characteristics of an IWW strike are these: the workers are discontented; they are either unorganised, or their union will not support their demands. A spontaneous strike movement occurs. The IWW is called in to take charge. Union or non-union, it makes no difference to the IWW, whose aim is to completely tie up the industry. Other workers are called out in sympathy. The mass is kept constantly stirred up, with speeches, demonstrations, and mass picketing, leading to collisions with the police. Meanwhile, the leaders educate the strikers in a revolutionary way, preaching the necessity for the overthrow of capitalism, advocating the 'perpetual strike': that is to say, 'This is not a strike for wages. When we have won this strike we shall strike again and again and again, until the capitalists are finally ruined and the workers will take over industry'.

He acknowledged the IWW's failure to build stable organisations, even where it won strikes, but put this down to the fact that it was 'an organisation built to fight'.[9]

Reed's own involvement with the Paterson strike did not end with his arrest and brief imprisonment. He was the key figure in organising a great pageant, a celebration of the Paterson workers' struggle that was intended both to publicise their cause and to raise funds. On 7 June 1913, some 2,000 strikers, carefully rehearsed by Reed, descended on New York and marched up Fifth Avenue to Madison Square Garden which displayed an electronic sign of the letters 'IWW' which was ten feet high. Before an audience of 15,000 the strikers re-enacted the story of their revolt, including the funeral of Modestino Valentino, filing past a coffin which they covered in carnations. Haywood and

Tresco repeated their funeral orations. The pageant ended with the singing of the 'Internationale'. It was a tremendous success, moving and stirring its audience to great effect. But instead of making a profit that would have helped sustain the strike, the pageant made a loss. According to some accounts this seriously demoralised sections of the strikers and heralded a turning of the tide against the IWW. By mid-June the Paterson strike had collapsed in defeat.[10]

There is one last point worth making about the Paterson strike: the intervention of the American Federation of Labor (AFL) and its craft affiliate, the United Textile Workers (UTW) in the dispute in April 1913. The UTW had members in Paterson, skilled workers in the mills, who it had refused to call out in support of the strikers and instead allowed to work alongside scab labour. Now at the insistence of the employers, who announced that they were prepared to negotiate with the UTW, but would never negotiate with the IWW, the UTW offered to accept the strikers into membership and to end the strike. On 21 April a mass meeting was called at which UTW and IWW speakers were to present their respective cases to the strikers. Some 15,000 people attended, listening in silence to the UTW speakers and then walking out when the IWW was denied the right of reply. This, as Philip Foner remarks, 'ended the invasion of Paterson by the AF of L'.[11] The strikers hostility to the AFL for its attempt at strikebreaking was very much reflected in Reed's article, 'War in Paterson'. He was to sustain this hostility to the AFL for the rest of his life.

What was the impact of the Paterson strike on John Reed? Certainly the dispute left him with considerable sympathy for the unskilled and immigrant working class and great admiration for the IWW, its leaders and rank-and-file members. It did not change his life however: there was no transformation from John Reed, aspiring poet and bohemian journalist, into John Reed, the dedicated revolutionary. The decisive experience that effected this transformation was to take place not in Petrograd in 1917, but at Ludlow in Colorado in 1914.

The Ludlow Massacre

The Colorado miners' strike began in September 1913 when members of the United Mine Workers of America (UMW) went on strike against the mine owners who were completely dominated by John D. Rockefeller Jnr's Colorado Fuel and Iron Company. The mine owners had deliberately recruited a mix of immigrant workers in an attempt to undermine solidarity and had imposed one of the harshest labour regimes in the US. Colorado had the worst mine safety record in the US, which in turn, had the worst in the world. In 1910, 319 miners were killed in accidents, more than one in 50 of those employed. The mine owners routinely rigged the pithead scales so that they underweighed, and thus lowered the miners' wages. One state official, who weighed 155lbs found that when he stood on the scales at the Eagleville mine, he added only 92lbs to the coal truck load, at the Sopris mine he added only 70lbs and at Rockefeller's Starkville mine he added only 35lbs. The mine owners also exercised almost feudal control over their workers, control that was maintained by armed guards and company spies. In 1912 over one-thousand miners throughout the coalfield were sacked on suspicion of union membership.[12]

An earlier attempt at organising the Colorado coal field had been defeated after a protracted strike in 1903–4. The deportation of strikers and importation of scabs, intimidation, beatings and murder had defeated the union on that occasion. By 1913 the UMW was strong enough for another attempt.

The miners demands were: union recognition, an eight-hour day and 10 per cent pay increase, the right to elect their own checkweighman to end company fraud, the withdrawal of company guards, and the enforcement of Colorado's mine safety regulations. Over 90 per cent of the Colorado miners (more than 11,000 men) walked out on 23 September 1913 and, with their families, were promptly evicted from company housing and escorted out of the company towns at gunpoint.

The UMW established eight tent colonies outside of company property, the largest at Ludlow. Philip Foner describes what the strikers had to endure that winter:

> The miners' wives and children tried to keep warm that winter, in temperatures as low as forty to fifty degrees below zero, by shovelling out from under four to six foot snowfalls, while their men fought a bloody war against strikebreakers, company guards, and Baldwin-Felts detectives sworn in as deputy sheriffs...Day after day, mine guards wearing deputy badges, fired at the strikers. On 5 October, the operators shipped four machine guns into the strike zone. The machine guns were not just for show.[13]

The strike held through the winter in the face of intimidation and murder, occupation by the National Guard, and the hardship of living under canvas in appalling weather. The mine owners were losing patience by the spring of 1914 and the tent colonies were fearful of an all-out assault. It came on 20 April when National Guardsmen under the command of a former company guard, Lieutenant Karl Linderfelt attacked the Ludlow colony. They raked it with machine-gun fire before setting alight to the tents. They continued firing as the miners and their families fled. A number of strikers were killed, among them the union organiser, Louis Tikas, who tried to intercede. He was severely beaten and then summarily executed on Linderfelt's orders. Even more horrifying, women and children were killed while sheltering in the tents. The exact number of strikers and family members killed at Ludlow is not known. It was at least sixteen (including two women and eleven children) but was believed to be much higher. According to Foner, over thirty people were killed with the National Guard disposing of a large number of bodies in secret.[14]

The Ludlow massacre provoked what amounted to an armed insurrection in the coal field with the local UMW openly arming its members and supporters for war. Mines were attacked, company property destroyed, and scabs and company guards killed in a series of ferocious revenge attacks. At Aguilar, the company men retreated underground when the strikers attacked: they dynamited the shaft, trapping 35 people inside. At Forbes, after a fierce gun battle, the strikers overran the mine, killing nine guards and burning buildings and equipment. In the face of this labour rebellion, President Woodrow Wilson decided to intervene. He sent federal troops into the coal field to restore order. They were ordered in on 28 April, a week after the massacre, not to protect the strikers and their families, but to protect company property. By the time the army arrived, more than 70 people had been killed in the 'Colorado War'.

Reed travelled to Ludlow with Max Eastman and both men produced savage accounts of the massacre, the events leading up to it, and its aftermath. Reed's long article, 'The Colorado War' that appeared in the July issue of *The Metropolitan* magazine is one of his most powerful pieces.[15] As Eric Homberger has argued, Ludlow in 1914 had much the same effect on Reed as Barcelona in 1937 had on George Orwell.[16] What Reed saw and heard in Colorado defined his political commitment, placing him unreservedly on the side of the radical labour movement inspiring a fierce hatred for US capitalism. His experience in Russia was to build on this foundation, but it had been laid down at Ludlow.

Violence and the Left

Soon after Ludlow, Rockefeller gave testimony before the House Committee on Mine and Mining and made clear that he was determined that his mining camps 'shall be open camps', that is non-union. It was an absolute principle as far as he was concerned. He was asked by Congressman Foster if he would stick to that principle even 'if that lost all your property and kills all your employees'. Rockefeller replied that 'It is a great principle.'[17] He was, of course, not alone in this particular determination. Many other US employers were similarly committed to the 'open shop', determined to resist unionisation at any costs, even the use of violence.

In his article celebrating the 'Wobbly', 'The Fighting IWW in America', published in 1920, Reed made his understanding of the realities of the class war in the US clear:

> Industry in the United States is civil war. Almost every strike is a battle, in which the workers are opposed by the whole machinery of the state, and also by private armies equipped with rifles and machine guns. The worker in the United States who goes on strike takes his life and the lives of his family in his hands. Workers are murdered by gunmen with impunity and the strike leaders are charged with murder....All over the United States today hundreds of men once active in strikes, languish in jail, convicted of murders they never committed. The list is endless. Savage imprisonments, lynchings, deportations are the lot of workers in America who try to organise their class.

Reed provides a brief list of some of 'the countless martyrs of the American Labour movement': The McNamaras, Schmidt and Kaplan, Tom Mooney, Ford and Suhr, Joe Hill, Frank Little and the 'Wobbly' leaders jailed in the great Chicago show trial.[18]

The catalogue of repression is impressive. Not only did it impel Reed along the revolutionary road, it also played a crucial, but neglected role, in weakening the American labour and socialist movements. This is not to say that anti-labour violence was the only factor, but rather that its importance has not been generally recognised. It was a systemic phenomenon rather than an occasional aberration.

Patricia Cayo Sexton in her *The War on Labor and the Left* makes the point that the working class everywhere has 'war stories' to tell of great strikes and confrontations, 'but nowhere has the record been as violent as in the United States'. There are no reliable figures available for the numbers of people killed and injured in industrial disputes (which she finds suspicious in itself!), but she cites one estimate that between 1877 and 1968 there were 700 people killed and many thousands more injured during strikes in USA. These figures might well 'grossly understate the total casualties', she notes, an observation with which this writer concurs. Sexton gives more concrete figures for specific periods to demonstrate her central point: from 1890–7, 92 people were killed in strikes, while from January 1902 to September 1904, 198 people were killed. These figures contrast dramatically with the level of anti-labour violence in other countries with representative forms of government. The Paris Commune and the German Revolution of 1918–23 are, of course, periods of greater violence than that experienced in the US, but these were revolutionary situations. In the US, the violence was more often than not generated by employer resistance to union organisation.[19]

One point worth emphasising is that this violence does not indicate the violent proclivities of the US working class, whether 'native' or immigrant. It cannot be legitimately described as 'labour violence', and is more accurately characterised as 'anti-labour violence', involving attacks on union organisers, strikers, and working-class communities by the police, company guards, private detectives, state militia, and federal troops. What we are confronted by here is an unremarked proclivity towards domestic violence on the part of the US capitalist class. Indeed, as a contribution to the debate on 'US exceptionalism', a case can be made that the US capitalist class is more deserving of attention than the US working class.

Sexton provides useful studies of the steel industry and the railroads; her account of the Homestead strike of 1892 is an example of industrial warfare US style. Andrew Carnegie and Henry Frick were determined to smash the steelworkers' union and took extraordinary measures to accomplish their objective:

Frick's first act was to build a ten-foot-high, three-mile-long wooden fence around the entire mill, running down to the river approaches. The fence was pierced with holes every twenty-five feet for gun emplacements and topped with barbed wire. Behind the fence were guard towers with searchlights beamed in all directions.

Once the strike was underway, Frick attempted to ship 300 armed Pinkerton detectives into the plant. This precipitated a thirteen-hour gun battle that left three Pinkertons and seven strikers dead. The gunfight provided an excuse for the intervention of the National Guard under whose protection scab labour was imported into the plant which formed part of Frick's plan. While most of the strike leaders were arrested for 'treason' for their part in the Homestead battle, none of the company's agents were charged and the union was smashed. In Frick's words: 'We have taught our employees a lesson that they will never forget'.[20] This was a remarkable way to conduct an industrial dispute. It indicated a determination to win, to maintain the 'open shop' at any cost, and the necessary political influence to make these methods legitimate. From this point of view, anti-labour violence clearly demonstrates the ruthlessness of the US capitalist class. It also indicates how powerful it was within US society.

Reed had, of course, seen the consequences of the American capitalist's commitment to the 'open shop' at first hand in Ludlow. The First World War and its aftermath were not only to provide him with the inspirational example of the Russian Revolution, but also with the repression of the IWW and the socialists during the war, the postwar 'open shop' drive and the 'Red Scare' that almost overwhelmed communism in the USA. The repression of the left occasioned by the war was certainly more severe than anything experienced in Britain, but also arguably more severe than in any other of the major combatants. Thousands of IWW members were thrown into prison (Reed estimated between 20,000 and 30,000) with the dreadful procedure culminating in the

Chicago show trial, 'US vs. W.D. Haywood et al.', a trial of 166 defendants eventually reduced to 101 which began, appropriately, on 1 April 1918 and lasted five months. For Reed this crucial event revealed the class nature of American society in the raw. The men on trial were 'out-door men, hard-rock blasters, tree fellers, wheatbinders, longshoremen, the boys who do the strong work of the world'. He went on:

> To me, fresh from Russia, the scene was strangely familiar. For a long time, I was puzzled at the feeling of having witnessed it all before: suddenly it flashed upon me. The IWW trial in the federal courtroom of Chicago looked like a meeting of the Central Executive Committee of the All-Russian Soviets of Workers' Deputies in Petrograd.[21]

They were all found guilty, even those no longer involved with the IWW. Thirty-five received sentences of five years; 33 of 10 years; and 15 of 20 years; others received nominal sentences. There were also fines totalling over $2 million, a crippling blow for the IWW.

In many ways more symptomatic was the fate of the Socialist Party leader, Eugene Debs. He was prosecuted under the Espionage Act for opposing the war in September 1918 and was sentenced to ten years' imprisonment. Debs was not alone, as other members of the Socialist Party, both leaders and rank and file, fell victim to wartime repression and the war was made use of as a convenient opportunity to smash the American left.[22]

The American Revolution

Reed wrote *Ten Days That Shook The World* both to rally international support for the embattled Bolsheviks and to carry the lessons of the Bolshevik Revolution to the international working class, especially to the US. Reed felt that what had taken place in Russia was pregnant with significance for the US working class. Nevertheless, he was always clear that the lessons of the Bolshevik Revolution had to be adapted to the experiences of the US working class, rather than, as some early Communists seemed to believe, the other way round. This was to be one of the causes of a split in the Socialist left which left the two rival Communist parties busy squabbling with each other while the postwar 'Red Scare' engulfed them both. The two CPs began with a joint membership of some 40,000, but within a short time this had fallen to 10,000. While the ferocity of the repression they faced accounted for much of this collapse, internal divisions certainly exacerbated the problems that American Communism faced.

What was Reed's own contribution to the split from the Socialist Party and the foundation of the Communist Labour Party in September 1919? Biographical studies have neglected the efforts he made to develop a revolutionary understanding of the development of American politics and society. His biographers generally prefer to view him as a romantic figure who fell in love with an idealistic image of Bolshevism and the Bolshevik Revolution and they have shied away from the evidence that shows a strong commitment to the revolutionary overthrow of US capitalism. Revolution in Russia can be (or could be) excused because of the nature of Tsarism, but revolution in the USA was a different matter. This aspect of the last eighteen months of Reed's life has been passed over and Reed edited a revolutionary weekly newspaper, the *New York Communist* from mid-April 1919 until the end of June that same year. This was at a time of what one author has characterised as a 'crusade against radicalism' in the city.[23]

The newspaper's first editorial proclaimed:

Comrades! Across the sea the workers are rising, wave on wave. The surf of Social Revolution beats on the crumbling dikes of the old order.

The nations of the world are bankrupt. The Capitalist system is bankrupt. The headlong competition of the two imperialist groups of nations, resulting in the great war, has wrecked the international credit system upon which Capitalist Imperialism is based, and taught the industrial proletariat that there is no hope for the world but in the Socialist Commonwealth.

It went on to repudiate the 'Moderate' Socialist leaders' whose adherence to the parliamentary road had ended with them upholding 'capitalism in its grand climactic crime'. In Russia and Germany, the moderate socialists had 'found themselves on the capitalist side of the barricades, shooting down workers to preserve their *petit bourgeois* theories'. Instead, the *New York Communist* proclaimed:

> We take our stand with the Russian Communist Party (Bolshevik), with the Spartacists of Germany, and the Communists of Hungary and Bavaria, believing that only through the Dictatorship of the Proletariat can the Socialist order be brought about.[24]

The *New York Communist* vigorously supported the efforts of the leftwing of the Socialist Party to capture control of the organisation and had a limited coverage of revolutionary developments abroad. It carried articles from Russia (Lenin's 'Proletarian Dictatorship' occupied the front page on 21 June 1919), reported the purging of the left from the Socialist Party ('Forty Thousand Expelled by Seven' on the front page on 7 June and 'Scuttling the Ship' the following week) and debated the meaning of the Russian Revolution with the IWW (John Reed's 'The IWW and Bolshevism' that appeared on 31 May 1919). What it did not cover at all was the industrial struggle that gripped the United States at this time.

According to Philip Foner, 1919 was 'the year of strikes'.[25] In March there were 175 strikes, in April 248, in May 388, in June 303, in July 360 and in August 373.[26] New York was certainly not exempt from this explosion of working-class unrest. Conditions in the city:

were similar to those existing throughout the country. There seemed to be no end to the succession of strikes in 1919, estimated at more than five-hundred in New York City alone. Labor disturbances reached a peak in October when sixty thousand men were idled. A strike in the clothing industry just four days after the Armistice was the first of many industrial disputes in the city. Two strikes on the waterfront brought all shipping in the port of New York to a standstill. A pressman's strike tied up the printing industry while an actors' strike darkened the Broadway theaters.[27]

The *New York Communist*'s failure to relate to this explosion of unrest is a serious political weakness (one factor in this was certainly Reed's hostility towards the AFL, a hostility he had maintained since the Paterson strike). Instead the newspaper focussed on the struggle inside the Socialist Party.

While the *New York Communist* failed to recognise the importance of the industrial conflict that raged in New York and across the country, it did carry a series of articles by Reed, 'Why Political Democracy Must Go' that argued the revolutionary cause in an American context. The series appeared between 8 May and 21 June and in it Reed examined 'the character of American political democracy' and 'the question of whether or not we shall try to win socialism by means of political democracy, making use of capitalist state machinery'. Alongside a discussion of US historical development, he lamented 'the disastrous effect of political democratic ideology upon the growth of class consciousness' in America. American workers remained believers in political democracy, in legislative reformism long after the capitalist class 'had learned that government is not carried on in legislatures, but in banks and chambers of commerce'. It would be the action of the capitalist class that disillusioned them.

Reed discussed the performance of American Moderate Socialism, chronicling the compromises, betrayals and treachery, but made the point that it was not this that was crucial to his argument. What was crucial was the fate of those Moderate Socialists who did not betray. He argued that:

in cases where the Socialists in office actually tried to follow socialist principles, capitalist action was swift and merciless. In Minneapolis, for instance, Mayor van Lear having manifested a mild hospitality towards free speech, the state government promptly took away his police power and governed the city through the State Council of National Defense, which was composed of the representatives of big business. Mayor Hoan, Socialist mayor of Milwaukee, was completely divested of his powers as a city executive by the business interests of Wisconsin acting through the governor and Council of National Defense. In Cleveland, two Socialists were elected to the City Council; one was disbarred, because a woman reported that 12 months before he had been heard to say that he did not believe in the Red Cross and the other councilman was expelled because he belonged to the same political party as his colleague. Victor Berger ran for United States Senate in Wisconsin in the spring of 1918. In order to prevent him from taking his seat, the business interests of his state and of the country at large secured his indictment in the federal courts, Berger then ran for the House of Representatives. This was the signal for still further indictments. He was elected by an overwhelming vote and another indictment was clapped on him: and after the armistice had been signed, Berger was tried and convicted, and sentenced to 20 years in jail.

This was the fate of Moderate Socialism in the United States.

Why? Reed argued his own account of US exceptionalism: 'nowhere in the world is the capitalist class so strongly organised and so firmly entrenched as in America'. The absence of a feudal class meant that the capitalist class never had to make concessions to the working class to win their support and was not weakened by confronting two rivals at once. 'In America', he insisted, 'there was no feudal class to divert the capitalists from their war upon the working class'. Seventy years later, this seems a useful starting point for understanding the history of the US working class in the twentieth century.[28]

Conclusion

Reed died from typhus on 17 October 1920 in Russia, just days before this thirty-third birthday. His premature end in the land of Bolshevism helped fix his identification with the Russian Revolution to the detriment of his identity as an American revolutionary. Moreover, it gave a spurious credence to those who have argued that Reed died disillusioned with the failure of the Revolution. If Reed had survived what we know with certainty is that on his return to America he would have joined the other leaders of American Communism in prison. This would have substantiated his belief that revolutionary politics was the way forward in the United States, despite the repression that descended on the left in the postwar years. Would he have remained an American Communist? It is hard to imagine Reed endorsing Stalin's massacre of the men and women who had led the Bolshevik Revolution, many of whom he knew and admired. Similarly, it is hard to imagine that Stalin would have tolerated the man who neglected to mention him in the classic account of that Revolution, *Ten Days That Shook The World*.

6. The Success and Failure of the Comintern

Ian Birchall

In assessing the achievements of the century, socialists have a particular responsibility to examine the successes and failures of their own movement. It is sadly true that in 2000 a smaller proportion of the working class aspires to the achieving of socialism within the coming century than did so in 1900. Obviously a number of reasons for this can be cited, but important among them must be the two great historic failures of the socialist movement.

The first came in 1914, when the Socialist International, despite its mass base in many European countries, capitulated at the outbreak of the First World War. It was that betrayal, combined with the impact of the Russian Revolution, that led to the foundation in 1919 of a new organisation, the Third (Communist) International. In its initial manifesto it set out explicitly to avoid the mistakes of its predecessor, whose leaders had been 'bogged down in reformism and in adaptation to the bourgeois state'.[1] Yet within two decades, it was guilty of betrayals as horrendous as that of 1914. The Comintern's lunatic sectarianism in refusing a united front against fascism made possible Hitler's accession to power in 1933, and hence the Holocaust, the Second World War and the development of nuclear weapons. (The German Communist Party's children paper even demanded that the 'little Zörgiebels' [social-democrats] be driven out of 'schools and playgrounds'.[2]) Four years later, in Spain, its opportunistic class collaboration strangled the possibility of a socialist revolution that could have reversed the defeat of

1933. A substantial contribution to the negative balance-sheet of the century.

The reasons for the collapse of the Second International remain a matter of debate, but at least the fact of defeat is generally acknowledged. In the case of the Comintern, the combined pressures of Stalinism and anti-Communism have meant that serious analysis has been relatively rare. It is important then, to welcome Pierre Broué's recent history of the Comintern,[3] the culmination of a career devoted to a study of the Bolshevik Party, the German and Spanish revolutions and the life of Trotsky,[4] it draws together standard histories of various Communist Parties with newly available material from the Moscow archives. Broué combines a commitment to the ideals of the original Comintern with a recognition that this was not some smooth-running conspiracy or ideal manifestation of perfect Marxist principles. During its heroic years the Comintern was very much a ramshackle improvisation, which made enormous mistakes. As he puts it, history sometimes progresses 'by stammering'.[5]

Broué's account raises the study of the early Comintern to a new level. What follows will be an attempt to discuss a few aspects of the success and failure of the Comintern, based on Broué's history and on the writings of Victor Serge[6] and Alfred Rosmer.[7] Both men worked in the Comintern apparatus in its early years; both became left critics of Stalinism, and though neither stayed long in the ranks of orthodox Trotskyism; both died intransigent revolutionaries. We can draw on the testimony not only of their memoirs, written decades later, but on their writings from the 1920s. Within the confines of a short chapter the account will necessarily be sketchy and focused on a few major areas; there will be no mention of minor irrelevancies like the corrupt and impotent Communist Party of Great Britain.

There is a huge literature on the history of the Comintern. Unfortunately much of it suffered from the monstrous distortions of the cold-war epoch. Within the Stalinist camp historiography was dominated by cowardly lickspittles who justified every twist and turn of the Russian bureaucracy. A sad example is Palme Dutt's history of the Internationals—which makes no reference to Zinoviev's role in the Comintern, and which sees the theory of 'social fascism' in terms of 'errors of excess of zeal...easier to judge today in the light of fuller subsequent knowledge'.[8]

On the other side of the fence, the distortions were equally great. For the anti-Communist historians of the cold war, the Comintern could be dismissed merely as a 'technique of civil war, of manipulating and disciplining the masses, of totalitarian tyranny'.[9] Such histories generally fail to distinguish between the Leninist and Stalinist phases, although a glance at Broué or Rosmer reveals the total contrast between the lively and open debate of the early congresses and the later authoritarian period.

Even within the dissident Marxist tradition severe problems persisted. Trotskyist historians were able to criticise the crimes and betrayals of Stalinism, but because of the smallness and isolation of the left opposition, the treatment was overwhelmingly defensive of an orthodoxy. Hence the myth of the 'first four congresses' (those dominated by Lenin and Trotsky) which were seen as free of fault, a model school of tactics and strategy. As Pierre Broué has pointed out, Trotsky's defeat and isolation left him in a position in which he had to defend orthodoxy at the price of developing original thought.[10] The limitation was often communicated to his followers. The best Trotskyist histories—James's *World Revolution 1917–36*[11] or more recently Duncan Hallas' s *The Comintern*[12]—are valuable in that they defend what was best in the early years of the Comintern (and there was much worth defending) while clearly distinguishing that early period from the later Stalinist horrors. Yet they remain essentially defensive.

A different emphasis emerges in volume four of Tony Cliff's *Lenin*[13] which is markedly irreverent towards the period of the 'first four congresses'. Though I suspect neither author would be happy with the comparison, it can in some ways be seen as a forerunner of the approach developed in Broué's history.

Over the last thirty years or so, with the decline of Stalinism, a more pessimistic account of the Comintern has emerged among left historians. In 1970, Fernando Claudin, a veteran member of the Spanish Communist Party expelled in 1965 after thirty years as a Communist, broke new ground with his serious and well researched account of the history of the Comintern.[14] While in full sympathy with the aims and aspirations of the Comintern, he offered a sharp critique of the actual practice of the organisation even in its early years. Unlike the self-serving cold-war critics, he thus presented a challenge to which defenders of the Comintern had to respond. His criticism focused on two themes: first that the 'Comintern was shipwrecked on the fact of nationality';[15] second that the Leninist Comintern was premature because the majority of Western workers had not broken with reformism, so that 'the break with reformism...resulted in a break with the mass of the workers'.[16] Only when the continuing grip of reformism was broken could a new international be formed.

Many critics of the Comintern argue that the basic problem was excessive domination from Moscow. In a sense they are right; the point was made very effectively in Lenin's last speech to the Comintern, in October 1922, when he scorned those who were satisfied with 'hanging (Russian experience) in a corner like an icon and praying to it.' He concluded that the most important task at present was 'to study'.[17] Obviously a Communist Party could only hope to make any effective intervention if it was thoroughly rooted in the life and institutions of its native country. All too often the young Communist Parties imitated Russian language to the extent of making themselves incomprehensible to their own working classes, as when the Italian Communist Party referred to Mussolini's 'blackshirts' as 'white gangs'.[18]

Lenin's speech was a prophetic warning of the damage to be wreaked by the Zinovievite 'Bolshevisation' imposed on the parties of the Comintern in the years immediately following his death.[19] The famous 'Twenty-One Conditions', so often denounced as blanket Moscow interference in the life of constituent parties, merely laid down a number of requirements for party activity. In particular, they required that any party claiming to be communist should commit itself to anti-imperialist and anti-militarist activity.[20] The imposition of leadership friendly to Zinoviev—such as Treint in France and Ruth Fischer in Germany—was quite a different matter.

Those accounts, whether from left or right, which stress the manipulative aspects of the early years of the Comintern are not so much wrong as one-sided. Certainly Comintern functionaries cut the occasional corner; money crossed frontiers in considerable sums and Comintern officials—some of them plainly not suited to the job—threw their weight around.[21] The German Party (KPD) received money from Moscow enabling it to run twenty-seven daily papers; unfortunately, as Brandler pointed out, Moscow could not supply editors, and a party short of cadre was forced to rely on 'workers who could not write or "drop-out' students".[22] But to abstract these phenomena from their context is to deprive them of all meaning. As Georg Lukács remarked to Victor Serge: 'Marxists know that dirty little tricks can be performed with impunity when great deeds are being achieved; the error of some comrades is to suppose that one can produce great results simply through the performance of dirty little tricks'.[23]

Europe was seething with revolutionary discontent. The Russian Revolution had aroused enormous enthusiasm among millions of working people. Hence the rapid growth of Communist Parties. Leading militants from a wide range of positions made the journey to Russia to see for themselves. Victor Serge, who crossed Europe at the risk of his life, testifies to this powerful attraction, as does his account of meeting a group of British soldiers in a café in post-war France and experiencing the powerful solidarity they felt with their Russian comrades.[24]

The essence of the Comintern was internationalism. Its much reviled centralism was devised precisely in order to ensure no repetition of 1914, when the national leaderships of the Second International had preferred their own bourgeoisie to the international working class. It is nowadays fashionable on the left to stress the power of nationalism and to deride the very idea of proletarian internationalism. Thus Eric Hobsbawm, projecting post-Falklands depression back on the entire history of the twentieth-century working class,[25] claims that workers in 1914 joined the armed forces with 'spontaneous zeal'[26]—neglecting the fact that the British ruling class, for example, found it necessary to wage a substantial campaign of intimidation and ideological persuasion to get the 'volunteers' they required.[27]

The fundamental point that must be made in rejecting Claudin's criticism is that there is no such thing as the 'fact of nationality'. Modern nationalisms are generally of relatively recent origin (somewhere in the last two-hundred years), and arose not spontaneously but by dint of hard effort—for example the measures taken during the French Revolution to ensure that the French people should speak French. As the recent history of Yugoslavia has shown, nationalism can decline—and revive with startling rapidity— under the impulse of economic and political circumstances.

The period at the end of the First World War—after millions of workers had experienced the futility of defending the national flag—was precisely a moment when national identity was being called into question. The Comintern was quite right not to accept the 'fact of nationality', but on the contrary, to fight vigorously to develop the potential for internationalism that existed in this period.

Perhaps the finest manifestation of internationalism was shown at the time of the French occupation of the Ruhr in 1923, in pursuit of unpaid reparations. Despite the recent hostilities between France and Germany, it proved possible to mobilise substantial opposition in the French working-class movement to the occupation. Young Communists from

France went into the Ruhr area and carried out an intensive campaign of propaganda and agitation amongst the French troops, despite the severe repression exercised by the French military authorities. As the report by Voya Vuyovich (the Yugoslav secretary-general of the Young Communist International) makes clear, the most lively and imaginative methods of propaganda were employed in order to get the internationalist message across to French soldiers.[28] Likewise, the Communists succeeded in avoiding the racism towards Senegalese troops which was all too common among some sections of the left. Propaganda was distributed to the Senegalese, showing that the struggle of German workers was linked to that of the Senegalese people for national independence As illiteracy was widespread among the Senegalese troops, innovative methods of propaganda such as pictures were used.[29] (As Morgan Philips Price noted in the Rhineland, racist hostility to the African troops came mainly from the middle classes, while there was frequent fraternisation between black soldiers and working-class Germans.[30])

This vigorously waged internationalist campaign awakened real echoes in the French working class. Even the most opportunistically nationalist leaders of the PCF, such as Cachin (who was actually jailed), found themselves obliged to participate in the campaign.[31] And Internationalism remained alive in the French working class. A leader of the French Young Communists, Jacques Doriot, sent a telegram to the Moroccan nationalist leader Abd-el-Krim in 1924, urging him to continue 'the struggle against all imperialisms, including French, until the complete liberation of Moroccan soil'.[32] Despite this 'treachery' to his own nation, Doriot remained a highly popular working-class leader, elected as deputy and mayor of the proletarian suburb of Saint-Denis, and re-elected in 1935 and 1936 despite opposition from the Communist Party with which he had by then broken.[33]

The crucial task facing the Comintern was to win over that section of the working class that still remained loyal to the reformist parties. Those, like Claudin, who argue that the formation of Communist Parties was 'premature' are aware of this problem, but the answer they give is untenable. If revolutionaries had remained inside the mass social democratic parties, they would have proved unable to offer a focus to the newly radicalised militants who were disgusted with the opportunism and betrayals of the old leaderships. Moreover, unless they had been prepared to temper their criticisms to such an extent that they would have been unable to communicate their politics, they would have faced expulsion, and been forced to adopt independent organisation on the basis of their opponents' timetable and not their own. The grip of reformism, like that of nationalism, was seriously shaken in the immediate post-war period. It re-established itself because the new Communist Parties were not quick and efficient enough at filling the vacuum.

The strategy of the 'united front' posed serious problems for Comintern parties. Often within a few months of having made the decisive break with the reformists, with all the polemical denunciations that such breaks involve, they had to address the reformists in order to seek united action. Many of the members of the new Communist Parties were genuinely confused; moreover opportunist elements in the new parties often used that confusion to pursue their own ends. Rosmer's account shows the difficulties of the fight for the united front line in the French Communist party, and the deliberate attempts to sabotage the policy on the behalf of such ex-social democrats as Frossard.[34] Only a clear-sighted cadre with significant tactical experience, able to explain the new tactics patiently to the rank and file, could have succeeded in carrying through the new line—and such a cadre simply did not exist. Rosmer and others did their best through articles in *L'Humanité*, but they were too few.[35]

Far from being a manual of 'correct' tactics and strategy, the Comintern was a constant improvisation, in which the pressures of ultra-leftism and reformism repeatedly threatened to drag the organisation off course. That the centre held firm to a reasonably sound line and avoided disastrous deviations to left or right is largely a tribute to the tactical sense of Lenin and Trotsky and a handful of their colleagues.

Ultra-leftism is an endemic phenomenon in any revolutionary situation. Workers and young people newly radicalised by a rising wave of struggle, who have not seen the defeats and difficulties faced by the movement in the past, tend to underestimate the scale of the task, and to believe that everyone can be won over as rapidly as they themselves were. When ultra-leftism is based on enthusiasm for struggle, rather than on purist passivity, it has positive qualities that must be mobilised by the revolutionary movement rather than lamented over. However, such mobilisation can only be effective if the movement already has a reliable experienced cadre—something missing in all too many of the Comintern's sections, even the strongest.[36]

Lenin wrote *Left Wing Communism: An Infantile Disorder* to make a sharp criticism of the ultra-lefts; but it is also true that he devoted great efforts, despite competing demands on his time, to trying to win over anarchists, syndicalist and associated antiparliamentarians,[37] for example finding time to debate with Nestor Makhno.[38] Lenin fought ultra-leftism politically, not administratively; he vigorously opposed the expulsion of the anti-parliamentary and anti-trade-union left from the German Communist Party.[39] Lenin was one of the relatively few who understood, as the German Crispien put it at the Second Congress, that 'it is easier to divide workers than it is to win them over and unite them'.[40]

The Comintern (despite opposition from Radek and Levi[41]) consciously set out to win over anarchists and syndicalists. Rosmer recalls Bukharin reprimanding a Spanish comrade who spoke of waging 'a pitiless struggle against the anarchists', telling him: 'It's not a question of 'fighting' them, but of discussing frankly and cordially, seeing if we can work together, and only abandoning the attempt if there is an irremovable obstacle.'[42] Serge and Rosmer, given their backgrounds in anarchism and syndicalism, had a particular role to play in this process. The establishment of the Red

International of Labour Unions (RILU), with its specific aim of drawing in revolutionary syndicalists, was one manifestation of this strategy.

But Germany was the key to the fate of the Comintern. A German revolution between 1918 and 1923 would have enabled encircled Russia to break out of its isolation and enabled the building of socialism in an industrially developed country. The errors of leadership in the KPD had colossal impact on the entire course of the world revolutionary movement.

That such errors were made is indisputable. The March Action of 1921—when the KPD made a premature insurrectionary bid for power, allowed massive repression and victimisation of KPD members. This was a mistake of catastrophic proportions. It led to the loss of half the KPD's membership only a few months after it had achieved a major advance by winning over the majority of the Independent Social Democrats.[43] Indeed, it is arguable that the failure of revolution in 1923, when objective circumstances were much more favourable, can be attributed in part to the 1921 débâcle. If the March Action had not happened, the KPD would have been considerably bigger in 1923 and better placed for a bid for power. Social democratic workers were more distrustful of the KPD's united front proposals than if the 1921 madness had not occurred.

Yet it is difficult to follow Broué in his admiration of Paul Levi.[44] Levi, joint KPD president, resigned office shortly before the March Action. After it he published a pamphlet sharply denouncing the position of the KPD leadership. He was expelled by the KPD, a decision endorsed by the Comintern without proper debate. Levi gave up the struggle, and soon became a member of the SPD, despite an offer from Lenin that he should keep his head down for a few months while writing educational pamphlets under a pseudonym, after which he was promised reinstatement into the KPD leadership.[45] (Lenin was so keen to hang on to him precisely because of the shortage of experienced cadre in the

Comintern.) Levi was undoubtedly correct in his criticisms of the March Action. His crime was not the formal breach of discipline of quoting internal polemics in a publicly distributed pamphlet. Lenin had done something very similar in 1917.[46] His real dereliction was failing to carry through his fight once embarked on it. It would be hard to imagine Lenin taking such dramatic action against the party leadership and then simply walking away. But the absence of competent and experienced leaders, after the murders of Luxemburg, Liebknecht and Jogisches, meant the KPD had had to turn to people like Levi, talented but temperamentally unsuited to a top leadership role. Rosmer summed him up as 'an educated, well-informed man, capable of making brilliant analyses, but not of coming to conclusions, nor even of formulating the logical conclusions of his analyses. His origins and way of life seemed incompatible with being the leader of a revolutionary workers' party'.[47]

The failure of the KPD to carry through a revolutionary bid for power in 1923 has been much discussed. Often the whole thing is attributed to the failure of the Russian leadership to give the right instructions to the KPD. Certainly there were serious disagreements among the Russian leadership, and Broué's book contains the results of recent research in the Comintern archives which draws out the sharp differences between Russian leaders.[48]

But ultimately what mattered was the situation on the ground. On this question Victor Serge's reports from Germany provide invaluable evidence. Germany in 1923 was in a state of profound crisis. Hyperinflation destabilised every aspect of everyday life, from the collapse of book publishing to the closure of public baths.[49] The state machine was stretched to its limits: Serge observed a policeman looking miserable as he supervised a bread queue, and commented: 'Perhaps his wife is there, with the others'.[50]

Hitler—financed by Henry Ford[51]—was on the rampage. There were anti-Jewish pogroms on the streets,[52] yet the KPD made a serious challenge to the Nazis' base, not only in the notorious formal debates that took place,[53] but more significantly in the thousands of informal street arguments between the competing ways of thought. As Serge reported: 'All day, until midnight, at busy cross-roads, groups of men are discussing. The unemployed. I've often listened to their discussions: the communist, the social democrat and the national socialist are usually all there; and the communist has the best of the argument.'[54] On another occasion he described working-class women mocking uniformed Nazi students and asking ironically 'Will you bring me some bread?'[55]

The sense of impending revolution was not merely a question of Moscow fixing dates; there was a profound will for revolution running through the KPD at every level. Serge described a group of comrades discussing the situation. After various intellectuals had voiced doubts, a young man spoke up saying: 'I believe in the revolution, because I want it; because I live among people who want it.' Serge noted that he was a district organiser.[56] Revolutionary voluntarism did not just affect a few leaders; it permeated the party cadre at all levels.

But Serge also showed the sheer desperation of the German working class. Five years of revolutionary upheaval and economic crisis left a profoundly weary working class. Serge quoted a doctor from a working-class area: 'Have you noticed the complexion of faces you see (in east Berlin). This greyish, yellowish, discoloured hue puts the brand of hunger on people's foreheads....Are you surprised that these people are slow to awaken to revolutionary consciousness?'[57] Moreover, workers were shy of a second attempt at insurrection after having been so badly bitten in March 1921.

Serge described vividly the sheer pace of events in 1923; militants moved from demonstration to strike to confrontation with the police to bread queue, struggling to maintain a revolutionary press amidst hyperinflation and state bans. He told of a worker who travelled fifty miles by night to attend a meeting,[58] and of 'comrades who for weeks on end did not have a full night's sleep'.[59] Amid such hyperactivity it is perhaps not surprising that the KPD's theoretical journal had a print-run of just 3000—for a membership of over 200,000.[60] There was not much time for studying the falling rate of profit. And the Party had no stable and trusted leadership. Its senior figures had changed several times since the deaths of Luxemburg and Liebknecht, and the failure of October 1923 led to yet another purge. Germany 1923 suggests all too clearly that there is not time to build a revolutionary party amidst the frantic haste of a pre-revolutionary situation.

The German defeat had a catastrophic effect in Russia, where a Bolshevik Party, already partly bureaucratised, was substituting itself for a virtually non-existent working class.[61] The argument for 'socialism in one country' was enormously strengthened. As Zinoviev paved the way for Stalin, defeat inside Russia and defeat in Western Europe reinforced each other.

The crisis of leadership was not just a problem in Germany. Throughout the International there was a shortage of experienced leaders who could implement the difficult strategic and tactical shifts necessary in a fluid situation. As Rosmer summed it up: 'the young communist parties...had many devoted members and the rank and file were impelled by deep and sincere revolutionary feelings. However, the inadequate number of cadres and their inexperience prevented them from making the best use of the forces at their disposal.'[62]

The case of Zinoviev is crucial here. Before 1917 Zinoviev had a bad reputation in the party and had not yet discovered a large enough audience to display his talent for oratory.[63] His role in October 1917, when he opposed the insurrection in the non-party press, might have been expected to lead to his removal from any position of responsibility; yet precisely because of the shortage of personnel he not only remained in the party leadership, but occupied key positions of responsibility in the Comintern. As Borkenau comments, 'this man, who was not deemed suitable for a major office in the Soviet state, was made head of the Communist International'.[64]

Serge, who worked closely with Zinoviev and knew him

well, recounts that it was widely considered that Zinoviev was 'Lenin's biggest mistake'.[65] Rosmer publicly differentiated himself from Zinoviev at the founding congress of the RILU on the question of the nature of syndicalism, suggesting that he had not understood the French labour movement.[66] While Lenin was still there to exercise a countervailing influence; Zinoviev's role was not too pernicious; but once Lenin was out of activity, Zinoviev used his position in the International to begin to build his own faction under the guise of 'Bolshevisation'. At the end of 1924 Rosmer was expelled from the PCF by the new Zinovievite leadership. It is interesting to note that in 1926 Rosmer, an astute observer little given to hysterical or overpersonalised reactions, wrote an article in *La Révolution prolétarienne* in which he argued that Zinoviev would be seen by history 'as mainly responsible for the lamentable functioning' of the Comintern, whereas Stalin was 'a revolutionary by temperament and by will' who had spoken 'the language of a man aware of the necessities of the present moment and concerned to create a collective leadership'![67] Certainly a naïve misjudgment of Stalin, but a clear recognition of Zinoviev's role in preparing the way for something worse.

Ultimately, in fact, everything comes down to the question of personnel. As Marx wrote: 'Human beings make their own history'.[68] The Comintern was made—and unmade— by human beings. Hence the ramshackle and improvised quality of so much of the early Comintern—the Bolsheviks were not superhuman, but very fallible human beings. Rosmer notes that one of the debates at the Third Congress took place 'amid the apathy normal at the end of congresses'[69] (the congress in question had lasted twenty-one days). Indeed, Broué shows that some of the early Congresses descended into chaos; very different from the later Stalinist events.[70] Such descriptions are a vital corrective for those who would like to take the 'first four congresses' as having some scriptural quality.

Tony Cliff has pointed that when the Bolsheviks took

power, they faced a severe shortage of personnel. A man who had once studied finance at London University was seized on to become director of the state bank.[71] Hence the emergence of 'radish bureaucrats'—thin red skins and white inside.[72] The same was true of the apparatus of the International. Certainly it was correct, as Rosmer points out, that the 'Revolution... had made all the militants greater', the experience of revolution giving added stature to individuals who would not have had it in more peaceful circumstances. He gives the example of Lozovsky, whom he had known in Paris before the war, a man 'not of the greatest stature or of a steady character', but who in Moscow in 1920 acquired 'an air of assurance, of self-confidence, decisiveness and certainty'.[73]

But the Comintern, too, did not have the personnel it needed. A man like Rosmer was kept in Moscow to work in the Comintern apparatus, thus depriving the French Communist Party of someone who could have become one of its key leaders. In 1923 he did take effective responsibility for *L'Humanité*, but he could not be in two places at once.[74]

Serge writes contemptuously of the 'outstanding mediocrity' of his comrades in Berlin on the Comintern press, describing one as 'the Communist NCO type, neither a blockhead nor a thinker: obedient only'.[75] More serious was the case of Bela Kun, whose intelligence Lenin despised so much that Congress minutes had to be amended because Lenin had called him an imbecile so frequently. Yet Kun was sent to Germany and played a key role in the March Action. Even after that débâcle he was re-elected to the Comintern Executive.[76] The Bolsheviks had a civil war to fight and an economy to plan; the number of people able to take on roles of major responsibility in the Comintern was therefore of necessity limited.

Because of the bankruptcy of the old working-class leadership, a new leadership had to be built effectively from scratch, from those who had courageously opposed the war and participated in the great class battles that followed it, but who had never developed a homogeneous strategic and tactical approach and style of leadership. Yet the high tide of revolutionary struggle came as early as 1919–20, and by 1923 the whole post-war upheaval had subsided. Rosmer later quoted the Italian anarchist Malatesta's warning that the revolution must be made as quickly as possible, 'for if we let the favourable moment slip, we shall later have to pay in tears of blood for the fright we are now giving the bourgeoisie'.[77] It was not true, as Jacques Sadoul told the First Congress in 1919, that Russia produced revolutionary leaders unparalleled elsewhere because of its climate and geographical features;[78] the cause lay in the Bolshevik Party's development.

The Comintern faced enormous problems in a volatile and unprecedented situation. That it remained, more or less, on course for as long as it did can largely be attributed to the political skill and experience of Lenin, but the task was too much for any individual. In the parties of Western Europe and further afield there were individuals of talent and integrity, but without experience of working together as a team. The Comintern was just beginning to forge a new revolutionary leadership when the revolutionary crisis reached, and passed, its peak. As Tony Cliff has put it, 'no administrative measures could free the Comintern from its dependence on the actual level of leadership, consciousness and training in the different sections of the organisation'.[79] A striking example is the Hungarian Communist party. In November 1918 it had only 4–5000 members. In March 1919 it was in power.[80]

It is clear that revolutionary parties and a revolutionary international cannot be built amid the frantic tempo of a revolutionary situation. But the amorphous nature of the left in the Second International, and the deep divisions between syndicalists and social democrats, meant that when the leaders of the European working class betrayed it in 1914, there was no alternative leadership available.

7. 'Revolutionary Gymnastics' and the Unemployed
The Limits of the Spanish Anarchist Utopia, 1931–37

Chris Ealham

The Spanish revolution of 1936–37 was accompanied by one of the most extensive experiments in workers' self-management in the twentieth century and constituted the last great stand of European libertarianism. Although in its early stages this revolution was far more profound than the 1917 Russian Revolution,[1] a complex series of factors—ranging from the hostile international and domestic contexts to the political shortcomings of the main revolutionary forces—converged to isolate, and ultimately destroy, the sources of popular power. This was an historic defeat, a decisive turning point in twentieth-century European history, paving the way for the barbarism of the Second World War and the political tyranny of the Franco dictatorship. Because the history of the revolution and its demise is already well covered,[2] my aim here is to explore some of the contradictions within the libertarian revolutionary utopia; these contradictions underline, in a highly concentrated form, the insurrectionary and tactical limitations of European anarchism as it had evolved since the 1860s.[3] This will be achieved through an analysis of the libertarian response to mass unemployment, a new challenge to the inter-war labour movement, and one that demanded a revision of existing modalities of struggle, politics and organisation. This emphasis on anarchist mobilising strategies among the jobless is also justified because both the 'pure' libertarians of the *Federación Anarquista Ibérica* (FAI—Iberian Anarchist Federation) and, to a lesser extent, the anarcho-syndicalist leaders of the *Confederación Nacional del Trabajo*

(CNT—National Confederation of Labour), regarded the unemployed as a vanguard force within the ranks of the dispossessed. Furthermore, the attraction of this focus on the struggles of the out-of-work is that it facilitates a discussion of the anti-statist, anti-political utopia of the anarchist movement and enables us to explore one of the central contradictions of the Spanish revolution: the hostility of the CNT and the FAI to any stable revolutionary organisation and their dogged opposition to revolutionary politics.

The focus of this chapter on the contradictions of the CNT and the FAI should not be taken as confirmation of Eric Hobsbawm's deterministic and teleological characterisation of Spanish libertarianism as 'primitive rebellion'.[4] For Hobsbawm, anarchism was a chiliastic or millenarian form of pre-industrial revolt that was destined to collapse under the twin pressures of economic development and its own internal contradictions, whereupon it would be replaced by a more modern, urban-based, Marxist-led social movement. The Spanish case reveals the shortcomings of this 'stages theory of history'[5] and the impossibility of establishing a cut-off point at which economic development provokes a definitive rupture with past modes of social struggle.[6] Rather, protest strategies in Spain and elsewhere were always far more varied and complex, particularly at times of deep social and political crisis when, to use Charles Tilly's much-quoted words, 'repertoires of contention' might be drawn from the vast historical and cultural frames of reference at the disposal of resisters.[7] The variable nature of 'repertoires of contention' was most discernible in Spain, where it was magnified by diverse factors, such as the socio-economic impact of combined and uneven development, the eclectic tactical repertoire of the CNT, which constituted a bridge between more 'modern' forms of protest like the strike and 'pre-modern' tactics of riot, and the ideological readiness of the anarchists to mobilise beyond the traditional factory proletariat. That anarchism was not an atavistic, exclusively pre-industrial movement, waiting to be superseded by capitalist modernisation, is shown by the success of anarchism in Cádiz, one of the most economically developed areas of Andalucía, where southern anarchism enjoyed its strongest base, and by the ability of the industrial unions of the CNT, the most enduring revolutionary syndicalist union in twentieth-century Europe, to establish a firm foothold in the industrially advanced plants of Barcelona.[8] Spanish anarchism therefore adapted itself to urban struggles in the explosive circumstances provided by largely unmediated industrial relations, popular alienation from the state and a mass struggle against an intransigent and obdurate economic oligarchy that resisted even the most gradual change.[9]

Had anarchist strategies been inappropriate for the social setting in which they developed, or had they failed to express the experiential concerns of local workers, then they certainly would not have proved as popular as they did, an argument that has been convincingly advanced by Temma Kaplan, Clara Lida and Jerome Mintz, who maintain that anarchism represented a logical response to capitalist exploitation.[10] Yet this view must be nuanced by several caveats, for while the CNT and the FAI were, as we will see, firmly rooted in local social and community structures, this did not always make for rational practices, particularly when the anarchists moved beyond the local and attempted to articulate a strategy for transforming national politics: witness the manner in which the increasingly urban-based libertarian movement of the 1930s espoused an essentially ruralist vision of the revolution.[11] There is also a possibility that, in different circumstances or contexts, the direct action mobilising role of the anarchists could have been fulfilled by a radical socialist or a communist party, with entirely different results.[12]

It is first necessary to gauge the scale of unemployment in 1930s Spain. While the unreliable nature of official statistics renders this task difficult, we can safely conclude that the Spanish unemployment rate was relatively low, particularly when compared with Britain and Germany.[13] Yet Spanish wages were also very low: according to International Labour

Office figures for Europe, only Portuguese workers earned less than their Spanish counterparts, who were also cheated of a large part of their wages by rampant inflation, resulting in profound material distress among the urban and rural working classes.[14]

This material context gave rise to a powerful cycle of social protest in the 1930s which corroded another great utopia of the Spanish left: the liberal-reformist Second Republic (1931–9).[15] Before 1931, middle-class republicans and their social-democratic allies channelled this protest cycle against the monarchy, promising structural reforms of agriculture and the economy, unemployment benefits and public works, while mobilising around the nineteenth-century idea of the Republic as the embodiment of political equality and social progress.[16] Consequently, in 1931, broad sections of middle- and working-class opinion welcomed the Second Republic as a panacea for all social ills.[17] But once in power the popular expectations were unfulfilled, as successive governments, both with and without socialist representation, pursued traditional liberal economic policies based on an obsessive desire to balance the budget and appease domestic and international financiers. Clearly then, there was no room for a reformist 'new deal' for the unemployed and welfare benefit and public works schemes were deemed unaffordable luxuries, during a time when the spread of unemployment overwhelmed local charitable initiatives and municipal socialist projects.[18] Indeed the traditional economic policies pursued during the Second Republic were accompanied by state repression: there was a sharp closure of the republican polity in the summer of 1931 as the liberal-democratic state stockpiled repressive legislation that effectively castrated the freedoms offered by the new constitution.[19] Even if the Second Republic signified a limited increase in civil and political freedoms, in material terms the position of the working class remained unchanged

Despite the manifest boundaries of the new democracy and its repressive, anti-working-class nature, the Second

Republic is frequently depicted as a noble democratic experiment, a golden era of liberalism in twentieth-century Spain. This vision reflects the high profile of a number of liberal-left historians, who tend to view the history of the Second Republic through the prism of the long winter of Francoist repression;[20] accordingly, these historians look back at the ephemeral democratic experiment of the 1930s with nostalgia because it contrasts with decades of right-wing domination of Spanish politics and the authoritarian drift of the rest of Europe during a decade that ended in world war.

In 1931 the CNT leadership also had enormous illusions in the new democratic régime. Formed in 1910, as a revolutionary syndicalist organisation, the *raison d'être* of the CNT was to transcend the limitations of traditional trade unionism and its narrow, economistic concern with wages and conditions by struggling in the workplace and in the streets for grassroots proletarian democracy. Unsurprisingly, then, *cenetismo* was subjected to fierce and unrelenting state repression by the monarchist authorities, an experience which inclined much of the Confederation's moderate anarcho-syndicalist leadership towards the view that a democratic republic would defend trade-union freedoms and favour organised labour, or at least adopt a neutral stance in industrial affairs. To expect a bourgeois-democratic state to allow a mass, revolutionary syndicalist union like the CNT to consolidate its organisation is a clear measure of the political naïvety of the moderate anarcho-syndicalists, who resembled the leaders of the Second International in that their revolutionary discourse, masked an essentially reformist practice: they were captivated by the practicalities of everyday union struggles and syndical organisation, whereas the anarchist goal of a classless, stateless society was a distant dream.

Notwithstanding the incipient reformism of its moderate leadership, the CNT's impeccable credentials of militant class struggle guaranteed that it was perceived by revolutionary and militant workers as the best vehicle for proletarian self-defence. In fact, while the Confederation is generally viewed as an anarcho-syndicalist union, it normally encompassed all those workers who most acutely felt the need to fight capitalism and its base was always ideologically pluralistic, consisting of anarchists, anarcho-syndicalists and communists.[21] By the middle of 1932 therefore CNT membership stood at around 1.2 million members nationally (about one-third of whom hailed from Catalonia), making the Confederation the largest radical current within the Spanish labour movement, while its unions were a central reference point in working-class life.[22]

Besides misinterpreting the nature of the Second Republic, the moderate CNT leadership also misjudged the combativity of the grassroots *cenetistas*; it was these rank-and-file supporters who impelled the all-important middle-level trade-union activists and community organisers forward in an attempt to reshape material realities from below during the 'hot' summer of 1931, when a wave of labour conflicts swept across Spain: in August 1931 alone 41 strikes took place in Barcelona city, some of which paralysed entire industries. Due to the decentralised, flexible nature of the CNT, which gave considerable autonomy to the base militants, many of these conflicts were beyond the control of the union leadership. Strikes frequently began as spontaneous protests by grassroots workers and only later did they gain support from the CNT.[23] The question of unemployment was placed at the centre of the strikers' petitions, as the employed took up the gauntlet in defence of the out-of-work, raising demands for worksharing arrangements, employer-funded unemployment subsidies, a reduced working day without a cut in wages, an end to redundancies and the abolition of intensive forms of labour such as piece-work. As working-class radicalism became an acid that dissolved many of the hopes invested in the Second Republic, some revolutionaries—including many communists—felt that a revolutionary situation was developing in 1931: on occasions isolated local conflicts over redundancies culminated in factory occupations; from the Basque Country in the north to Andalusia in the south, a succession of armed clashes between hungry workers and the security forces occurred; and there were general strikes in CNT strongholds such as Barcelona, Zaragoza and Sevilla.[24]

In the opinion of the anarcho-syndicalists, the unemployed were best organised in CNT *bolsas de trabajo* (labour exchanges). These had a variety of attractions. First, from a syndicalist-corporatist perspective, they allowed for an important extension of union control over the supply of labour and promised an increase in syndical power over the economy and society; second, the *bolsas* maintained a vital connection between the unemployed and the labour movement, ensuring that the jobless remained under the influence of class culture. This was particularly true for the young, male, unemployed for whom the *bolsas* represented schools for industrial activism in which they were educated in fly-posting and picketing; the *bolsas* were also a conveyor-belt for recruits to the para-military CNT *comités de defensa* (defence squads) that were entrusted with a variety of self-defence functions at meetings and demonstrations.[25] Last, and perhaps most importantly, the *bolsas* enhanced the militancy of those still in work, who could launch strike actions without fearing that the jobless might become a weapon in the hands of the employers.

The second major collective action linked to the unemployed in 1931 was the Barcelona rent strike, a mobilisation that began spontaneously in some of the poorest neighbourhoods of the Catalan capital immediately before the birth of the Second Republic.[26] But the rent strike did not occur in a vacuum: it was inextricably bound up with the radical mobilising culture propounded by the CNT over the previous twenty years[27] and proletarian traditions of direct action that extended back into the nineteenth century. Moreover, although none of the CNT unions had initiated the rent boycott, *cenetistas* were highly active in the street committees and neighbourhood groups which organised the strike. When, in the summer of 1931, the rent strike was 'appropriated' and channelled by the CNT unions, it spread like wild-fire across Barcelona and extended into surrounding towns; at its pinnacle, over 100,000 people in the Barcelona area withheld rent payments from their landlords.[28]

Given the profound level of solidarity and mass participation underpinning these collective struggles, it is striking that they were replaced by new modes of conflict characterised by small group resistance. There are several reasons for this. First, the growth of unemployment in 1931 and the collapse of industrial structures threatened the authority of the unions, thereby stimulating a shift in the arena of struggle from the factory to the streets, and propelling the unemployed towards irregular and non-institutionalised mobilisations which were based on loose social networks and direct action at community level. This exposed the limits of the anarcho-syndicalists' attempts to organise the unemployed through the trade unions. Along with the fact that the jobless possessed markedly fewer bargaining resources than the employed, only a fraction of the unemployed was willing to throw itself headlong into a militant life of activism in the CNT *bolsas*; most jobless workers—especially those with families—simply wanted work and were therefore reluctant to pay the potential costs of this agitation.

Second, state repression closed many of the legal, political and urban spaces in which mass mobilisations had previously occurred, thereby favouring the emergence of new forms of street politics. The 1931 Law for the Defence of the Republic, which labelled pickets and strikers as 'enemies' of the state and allowed them to be interned without trial, rendered much mass mobilisation ineffective. The repressive apparatus of the republican state was also directed at the rent strikers, although a combination of resilient social networks, intense community hostility towards the police and acute material need ensured that rents continued to go unpaid in a few 'liberated zones' in the housing projects and ghetto districts.[29]

Last, and most crucially, the switch to small group resistance owed to the rise of the radical anarchists of the FAI within the CNT. Modelled on the Bakuninist secret society, the FAI was an exclusively libertarian organisation of so-called 'pure' anarchists, whose fundamentalism resembled that of the nineteenth-century followers of Errico Malatesta.[30] The FAI has been described as a 'guerrilla organisation',[31] and this is most apt, for it was based on *grupos de afinidad* (affinity groups), consisting of anything from 4 to 12 members/comrades/friends, who were united in the pursuit of a set of common goals. The *faístas* employed a discourse and practice of immediate revolutionary violence which, they believed, should be spontaneous and audacious; accordingly, the maximalists of the FAI excoriated the inherent 'reformism' of the short-term palliatives advanced by anarcho-syndicalists and trade unionists.[32]

The FAI exploited the discontent of the CNT rank-and-file at the economic crisis and republican repression to replace the moderate anarcho-syndicalists at the top of the Confederation. Essentially, the FAI accused its enemies in the CNT of betraying the interests of the unemployed. The irony here was that resolute action on behalf of the unemployed presupposed a powerful, united and massified CNT, something that was inimical to the FAI goal of an anarchist trade union, a project that led to the expulsion of many anarcho-syndicalists and dissident communists from the Confederation, and which produced a massive haemorrhage in union membership during 1932–3.[33] The attendant decline in syndical muscle eroded the combative power of the CNT; it became more difficult now for the unions to win strikes, and the *bolsas* lost much of their effectiveness and attractiveness for the unemployed.

From the end of 1931 until the outbreak of the civil war, the FAI applied insurrectionary-maximalist tactics to the question of unemployment. The FAI perceived the issue of unemployment as a matter that could only be resolved 'after the revolution'. Not only were demands for welfare benefits and public works denounced by the anarchists as an immoral request for state charity which humiliated the proletariat before the authorities, but the anarchists also feared that the implementation of such measures would weaken the insurrectionary appetite of the masses and stabilise capitalism. Instead, it was necessary to make the unemployed ready for revolution and convert them into insurgent shock-troops by 'launching the jobless into the streets' in what the FAI described as 'revolutionary gymnastics',[34] insurrectionary essays which would leave capitalism ungovernable and encourage the masses to surmount their fear of the security forces through streetfighting. The *faistas* also calculated that their 'revolutionary gymnastics' would compel the state to implement increasingly repressive measures, thereby eroding the veneer of bourgeois legalism and forcing the masses to shed any remaining popular illusions in the Second Republic.[35]

The 'revolutionary gymnastics' resulted in a proliferation of street guerrilla warfare by the unemployed, or what we might term the anti-politics of the unemployed. Despite the extensive nature of these guerrilla actions, we encounter a number of problems when assessing this phenomenon. For instance, at times guerrilla actions by the unemployed were underreported in the daily press, whereas on other occasions, and for reasons of political expediency, they were overstated.[36] It is also difficult to distinguish between the 'spontaneous', and often illegal, direct action of the unemployed in the streets, and protests that were organised by activists. This situation is further complicated by the tendency of the CNT to adopt popular practices and by the efforts of the anarchists to intensify the street practices of the unemployed as part of their own insurrectionary agenda.[37]

The guerrilla struggle of the unemployed was waged on diverse fronts. One element was the practice of jobless workers to tour factories looking for work. These excursions were also organised by *cenetistas* and there were reports of up to 300 workers paying visits to employers. On occasions, the jobless also put themselves to work in factories and then demanded to be paid by management at the end of the day.[38]

Second, we have the 'appropriation' of meals in restaurants. It was common for hungry jobless workers—either alone or in small groups—to eat in restaurants and then refuse to pay. CNT activists organised this practice and sometimes groups of up to 150 workers entered restaurants, hotels and bars to demand food. There was a strong normative or 'counter-cultural' element of resistance here, with those who participated in this type of action regularly asserting their 'social right' to life.

Another form of 'appropriation' was known euphemistically as 'proletarian shopping trips'; these ranged from the small-scale requisition of foodstuffs from local shops, bakeries, lorries and warehouses, to well-planned, mass raids on markets. Groups of unemployed were also known to enter farms and seize produce. Again there was evidence of a pronounced normative element in this 'appropriation', perhaps most vividly demonstrated in the so-called 'sacrilegious robberies' of gold icons and collection boxes from churches in working-class neighbourhoods.

At the top of the hierarchy of unemployed direct action was armed robbery.[39] Because armed robbery—like all forms of illegal 'self-help'—was deeply embedded in the property relations of 1930s Spain, it is possible to emphasise its class character. Indeed, the social geography and the targets of armed robbery underscored the degree to which it was directed at the upper and middle classes. For example, attacks on the commercial establishments of the urban middle class (tobacconists, bars and jewellers) and banks were widespread, as were armed raids at the weekend residences and apartments of the rich. During an era when car ownership was the exclusive preserve of the economic oligarchy, highway robbery on the isolated roads where town met country was also common. Meanwhile, taxi-drivers, many of whom supported the fascist Falange, were regularly targeted in city centres. There is considerable evidence that unemployed CNT members and *faístas* were involved in all of these forms of armed robbery.[40]

One common denominator uniting all of these forms of direct action was that they were based on conflictive relations with the police. This was the everyday norm for the unemployed, who spent much their time in public spaces. Moreover, because the streets constituted the only sphere in which the out-of-work could register their protest, the jobless were repeatedly persecuted by the police, who viewed the unemployed as a visible and persistent threat to public order. Yet anti-police sentiments also ran deep in working-class communities. In part, this reflected the fact that a considerable faction of the urban and rural labouring population found it difficult to guarantee its physical survival without stepping outside the law. Popular illegality also dovetailed with a collective working-class memory of police brutality which can be traced to the beginnings of organised labour in Spain, when the police and para-military bodies such as the *Guardia civil* (Civil Guard) were deployed as instruments of state repression and class rule. These anti-police traditions became even more generalised after the emergence of a mass trade-union movement in the post-First World War era, when labour insurgency was quelled through a combination of saturation policing and the selective assassination of CNT activists. The extent of anti-police sentiments was frequently reflected in popular resistance to policing, particularly when the security forces attempted to make arrests in working-class districts.

These popular anti-police traditions and practices commingled with anarchist mobilisations and protests to a quite significant extent during the 1930s.[41] One of the strengths of the *comités de defensa* was that they—like most CNT and anarchist activists—formed an integral part of the working-class neighbourhoods in which they operated: most activists were genuinely proletarian, and were often important and respected figures in local communities.[42] This osmosis between movement and community was a central objective of anarchist revolutionary strategy and it was this reliance upon powerful neighbourhood support networks that enabled the CNT and the FAI to survive even during periods of intense repression.[43] Similarly, the level of social loyalty upon which the CNT was based explains how it became the connecting point for a world of protest on the streets that was outside formal institutional channels.[44] Indeed, the direct action of the CNT and the FAI was inspired by the resilient street culture of the neighbourhoods and, as we saw with the rent strike, direct action protests often belonged more to the streets than to the union organisation. These neighbourhood struggles for space and local self-determination were united with the para-military struggle of the anarchists against the state: at certain times this amalgamation of community resistance and anti-state mobilisation gave the CNT tremendous mobilising power; it also holds the key to the CNT's incessant and unremitting confrontations with the state.

Yet the anarchists miscalculated the degree to which they could build upon popular anti-police violence. In part, this was the outcome of their exaggerated faith in spontaneity and the accompanying conviction that radically dispossessed constituencies could be transformed into a conscious revolutionary actor without any active or organised political intervention. Also, the anarchists misinterpreted many of the street conflicts with the police which, rather than an indication of the simmering revolutionary aspirations of the dispossessed, were, more often than not, *defensive* in nature, reflecting either the everyday battle of the unemployed, the unskilled and the low-paid for survival, or community resistance to policing. In short, it was difficult to give these essentially defensive mobilisations a more *offensive* complexion and to channel them into anti-state insurrections.[45] Indeed, if street conflicts became intense, the withdrawal of the police from the neighbourhood often calmed the mood of protesters; if, however, the insurgency continued, the full repressive arsenal of the state could be mobilised, including the army and the courts, and at this stage the resisters had little chance of victory. Last, the anarchists were unable to appreciate the inherent limitations of unemployed protests. The fundamental problem here was that while certain sections of the jobless were easily mobilised and, more often than not, ready to engage the police in streetfighting, the 'revolutionary gymnastics' could only ever be the insurrectionary politics of a specific segment of the unemployed: generally-speaking, the young, unskilled, male workers, who had little to lose during a confrontation with the repressive forces of the state. Most unemployed workers, however, were unprepared to face the risks demanded by the direct action mobilisations of the anarchists, and this was especially true of those with dependents, who could ill afford a spell in hospital or jail. Accordingly, the neighbourhood-based *comités de defensa* always constituted a vanguard armed force within the working class, something that is reflected in the mute popular response to the various anarchist insurrections (January 1932, January 1933 and December 1933) which were little more than uncoordinated putsches and the cause of only minor irritation to the state.[46] Much anarchist action was therefore substitutionist, small group, élitist violence. But because this violence was usually directed at individuals who were unpopular with workers, such as local policeman and other agents of the state, the *comités de defensa* were at least tolerated, if not celebrated in working-class districts as a symbol of neighbourhood strength. Thus, the para-military activists of the *comités de defensa* were able to swim in a sea of community support, safe in the knowledge that they would not be betrayed to the authorities.

The reliance of the CNT and the FAI on its community strongholds produced a largely containable, defensive politics in the 1930s. This situation was further compounded by a succession of factors—the absence of any strategy capable of allowing the CNT and the FAI to progress onto an offensive plane, the split in the unions between anarchists and moderate anarcho-syndicalists, the enforced experience of clandestinity, and the intense state repression that the 'revolutionary gymnastics' invited upon their movement—all of which guaranteed that the anarchist movement spent long periods of time in a political ghetto during the early 1930s, from where it was thoroughly unprepared for the challenges presented by the 1936 revolution.

Let us now examine the most important trends within the anarchist movement that constrained the development of the Spanish revolution. The first area we need to consider is the movement's rejection of institutionalisation. For the most part, anarchists regarded revolutionary organisation as a contradiction in terms: they execrated organisation and institutionalisation as a dangerous compromise which could result only in reformism and the betrayal of the revolution. This unalloyed celebration of revolutionary spontaneity sealed the hostility of the anarchists to all organisational projects, even those of anarcho-syndicalist inspiration, designed to improve the effectiveness and coordination of anti-capitalist mobilisations at national level.[47] Consequently, there was no leap forward in organisational modes that might have produced new ties between the jobless by transcending the frontiers produced by everyday community interactions. Wider organisational bonds might also have generated ties with the rest of the organised working class, allowing for the maximisation of the scarce protest resources of the jobless and providing a form of linkage between the defensive, direct action of the unemployed and a more sustained, mass movement capable of forcing the authorities to act on behalf of the unemployed.

Instead, the anti-organising impulses of the anarchists undermined their long-term revolutionary goals and they remained trapped in a defensive mode of struggle in their community enclaves,[48] unable to address what Frederic Jameson has described as 'the enormous strategic and tactical difficulties of coordinating local and grassroots neighbourhood political actions with national or international ones'.[49] An understanding of these dilemmas is central to any appreciation of one of the most distinctive features of the 1936 revolution: the proliferation of independent, community-based local revolutionary committees. As in the case of the jobless mobilisations, the local revolutionary committees enjoyed tremendous power at community level, where they were anchored in informal contacts, but they could not initiate an offensive, 'high-risk' strategy—this had to be rooted on the firmer social relations which can only be produced when neighbourhood solidarity is refined and bolstered by a stable revolutionary organisation. Quite simply, the anarchist movement possessed neither the means nor the strategy to channel the insurgent energies of its grassroots towards the revolutionary transformation of the state structure at national political level. In the absence of a political nerve centre, the profound revolutionary impulses emanating from the working class in the 1930s failed to find any genuine institutional expression, whereupon they were doomed to remain localised and, eventually, to dissipate.[50]

The second area concerns the sectarianism of the radical anarchists. During the 1930s the FAI launched a war against all rival factions in the labour movement: it appropriated the discourse of the so-called 'Third Period' of the Comintern to denounce the 'social-fascism' of the social-democrats, while its attacks on the 'anarcho-reformism' of the moderate anarcho-syndicalists and communist 'red dictators' culminated in a debilitating split within the CNT. Besides engendering bitter divisions within the organised working class, anarchist fundamentalism undermined the struggles of the unemployed which, if they were to succeed, had to rest on unity. For instance, during the rent strike, public meetings were sometimes hijacked by the FAI in order to extol the virtues of anarchist communism; at one meeting, violence broke out when communists in the audience demanded the right to reply.[51] Unemployed workers' meetings organised by rival leftist groups were also targeted for aggression, such as in the libertarian stronghold of l'Hospitalet de Llobregat, where anarchists attacked communist meetings with fists and pistols.[52]

While anarchist hostility towards the PCE might be explained in terms of the notoriously divisive policies of the Stalinists towards the CNT,[53] this does not account for the

unrelenting antipathy that the *faístas* felt towards the dissident communist BOC, which emerged as the most disinter-
ested advocate of revolutionary unity. The first step on the
road to unity for the *bloquistas* was the creation of an
Alianza Obrera en contra de l'Atur Forçós (Workers' Alliance
Against Unemployment) in Catalonia, through which it was
hoped to build a united, mass movement from below around
the struggles of the unemployed. The anti-Stalinist BOC
hoped to attract the anarchists to the Alianza Obrera and,
given that it shared the anarchists' revolutionary conviction
that unemployment could only be eradicated through socialist transformation, one might assume that this was not an
unreasonable expectation. However, the BOC's insistence
upon the desirability of uniting the jobless and the organised
labour movement in a struggle for a series of short-term
goals such as rent cuts, free travel and unemployment benefit did not meet with the approval of the maximalist FAI,
which embarked on a sectarian, anti-organisational campaign
against the Alianza Obrera, which it portrayed as numbing
the insurgent spirit of the jobless by 'begging' from the state.
Although the boycott of the anarchists effectively killed off
the *Alianza Obrera en contra de l'Atur Forçós* in Catalonia,
the BOC had nevertheless succeeded in popularising the
need for unity. Indeed, the BOC initiative for the unemployed was a precursor to the *Alianza Obrera contra el fascismo* (Workers' Alliance against fascism), which was formed
throughout Spain in response to the increasing fascist danger, both nationally and internationally.[54] In some places,
such as Asturias, this new proletarian anti-fascist alliance
attracted the support of anarchist groups, including some
from the FAI. This groundswell of worker unity paved the
way for the united proletarian front which laid the basis for
the Asturian Revolution of October 1934, a revolutionary
uprising of the entire Spanish left (the anarchists, the anarcho-syndicalists, the socialists and the communists, both dissident and orthodox alike), a mobilisation which became a
beacon of what the united left could achieve.[55] Yet any hopes

that the Alianza Obrera might provide the basis for revolutionary unity in action were stymied by the ultra-sectarian Catalan anarchists—then hegemonic within the CNT and the FAI—who feared any initiative that seemed to confirm the wisdom of the policies of their dissident communist rivals. Nevertheless, in the context of fascist aggression, both nationally and internationally, the need for unity remained. This point was not lost on the leaders of the CNT and the FAI who, for all their revolutionary rhetoric, finally endorsed the reformist, inter-class unity inherent to the Popular Front. Anarchist sectarians triumphed over revolutionary politics. The failure of the Workers' Alliance project during 1934–5 can be regarded as a missed opportunity to arrive at a revolutionary pact during the last few months of relative peace before the violent convulsions that were about to engulf Spain, and all attempts to establish a similar degree of left-wing unity in the fray of civil war and revolution after July 1936 were to prove elusive.

Finally, it is necessary to explore the anti-politics of the libertarians. This trait flowed from the theoretical confusion that lay at the centre of anarchist ideology, especially its absence of a clear analysis of the nature of capitalist exploitation. In the final analysis, the libertarians understood the oppression of the working class to be a function of politics more than economics.[56] As we have seen, anti-politicism inclined the anarchists to repudiate the struggle for unemployment benefit, thereby absolving the state and the bourgeoisie of all responsibility for the welfare of the jobless. In essence, the anarchists looked upon politics in the same way as Christians view original sin: there were no 'good' or 'bad' politics, there were simply politics which, whether 'bourgeois' or 'proletarian', would distract the masses from their ultimately revolutionary vocation, and allow a new oppressive (political) leadership to enslave the workers (the example of Stalin's Russia furnished the anarchists with a powerful example of the process whereby the pursuit of politics led to 'the dictatorship of the party' over the proletariat).[57]

This anti-politicism—the veritable Achilles Heel of the movement—highlights the utopian essence of libertarianism which, even when coupled with revolutionary trade unionism (in the guise of anarcho-syndicalism), baulked at initiating struggles on the political plane. Such a renunciation of politics was both counter-productive and utopian, because all mass movements, including those that are formally anti-political, nevertheless form part of a national political framework, particularly when the movement concerned is devoted to militant class struggle.[58] In practice, given that all class struggles, including those spearheaded by revolutionary syndicalists, have profound political consequences, the CNT could not always ignore politics; thus, the pressure of political events and dynamics periodically impelled the anarchist movement to break with its anti-political shibboleths, such as in the elections of April 1931 and in February 1936, when the CNT and the FAI leaders discretely invited their supporters to vote for the republicans as a 'lesser evil', calculating that a government of the liberal-left would bring a diminution in state repression. Meanwhile, in the November 1933 elections, anarchist disenchantment with liberal-left politics inspired a policy of abstention (the 'electoral strike') which, while more consistent with libertarian anti-political philosophy, nevertheless favoured the election of a right-wing clerical alliance.

The consequences of this anti-politicism were twofold. First, by diverting working-class votes towards petty bourgeois parties, it inflated the presence of the middle classes in national politics. Second, anti-politicism militated against the creation of a revolutionary proletarian political leadership; instead, the working class, particularly its most radical wing, was unrepresented, politically emasculated and reduced to impotency. The CNT epitomised this process: while it aspired towards class consciousness by surpassing sectional or corporate consciousness, its guiding anti-politicism led it to focus exclusively on ideological and economic struggles, thereby reducing the movement to the living equivalent to economism.

The extent to which the anarchist rejection of political struggle, including the struggle for state power, tended towards a compromise with bourgeois political forces became most evident after the July 1936 revolution. Satisfied that it could make *its* revolution simply by seizing the means of production, and confident in its power in the workplaces, fields and proletarian communities of Spain, the CNT and the FAI saw no danger in allowing the fragments of the bourgeois state to survive. However, once it became apparent that the multiple demands of revolution and civil war presupposed some form of political organisation, the anarchist leadership faced a sharp dilemma: it could not allow its enemies in the republican camp to dominate the political sphere and was therefore forced to choose between forging a new revolutionary power and collaborating with the parties of the Popular Front who had rallied to the defence of the collapsed liberal-capitalist state. Given the anarchists' record of hostility to proletarian politics during 1931–6, its tendency to express itself politically though middle-class political formations, and its doctrinal opposition to any centralised revolutionary-political authority, it was no surprise when the libertarians opted to support the liberal-democratic state, first joining the Catalan regional government in September 1936 and, just a few weeks later, in early November, entering the central government. The bizarre logic and consequences of anti-politicism is therefore central to any explanation of why the profound upsurge of the masses in the summer of 1936 remained unarticulated and why the revolution failed to destroy the capitalist state.

Although during the civil war the erstwhile anti-political leaders of the CNT and the FAI were forced to face the very political dynamics that they had always denied, the anarchist ministers were untrained in the 'art' of politics and they were easily outmanoeuvred by their bourgeois republican and Stalinist opponents, who exploited the collective responsibility of the Popular Front governmental alliance to erode the sources of popular power established by the July revolution.[59]

Thus, between September 1936 and the end of the civil war, the anarchist ministers—along with the leaders of the CNT and the FAI—connived in the reconstruction and stabilisation of the bourgeois republican state. The legacy of their anti-political culture left the libertarians bereft of political sense and, while most political commentators, including the enemies of the revolution in the Popular Front, appreciated that it was only a matter of time before the reconstructed bourgeois state clashed with the revolution, the anarchist leadership remained tied to the inter-classist Popular Front strategy. Because the CNT-FAI leaders could see no revolutionary strategy, they remained tied to Popular Front tactics and trapped in its view of its governmental colleagues as 'friends', even at a time when the latter had effectively broken their civil war alliance and were openly attacking the power of the revolution.[60] Finally, when the much-expected trial of strength between a resurgent bourgeois-democratic state and the last vestiges of popular revolutionary power occurred in May 1937, the anarchist hierarchy preferred to shore up its damaged governmental alliance with its republican-Stalinist enemies rather than pursue its own independent political line. The 'May Days' signified a huge political defeat for the CNT and the FAI, and the power of the anarchist movement underwent a sharp and irrevocable decline.[61]

There were attempts from within the anarchist movement to renew the tactical and strategic perspectives of the CNT and the FAI. Perhaps the most significant project for the ideological renewal of the anarchist movement emanated from the *Amigos de Durruti* (Friends of Durruti), a dissentient libertarian affinity group which emerged in the spring of 1937 and which became the most outspoken critic of the leaders of the CNT and the FAI. Composed largely of radical anarchists, a number of whom had previously figured among the most sectarian, isolationist and anti-political currents of the CNT and the FAI, the *Amigos de Durruti* recoiled against the 'collaborationist' Popular Frontism of the anarchist hierarchy and proposed a new revolutionary offensive based on an Asturian-style proletarian alliance with other anti-capitalist groups.[62] In spite of its origins within the 'purist' wing of the anarchist movement, the *Amigos de Durruti* included a slogan in its programme that had never figured in any previous libertarian manifesto: the formation of a revolutionary junta elected by workers', peasants' and soldiers' assemblies. In short, a section of the anarchist movement had finally grasped the importance of the struggle for state and therefore political power. By advocating an exclusively proletarian power that would repress the enemies of the revolution, the *Amigos de Durruti* proposed a new revolutionary praxis and simultaneously underscored the limits of the anarchist anti-political utopia.[63]

Yet the *Amigos de Durruti* were swimming against the current. First, the timing of the irruption of the *Amigos de Durruti* on the political stage—its critique of the Spanish anarchist tradition was issued in the spring of 1937, when the exigencies of the civil war had already eroded many of the revolutionary positions conquered in July 1936—meant that its impact was muted. Indeed, the chances of fashioning a vanguard revolutionary political leadership in the heat of civil war battles against domestic and international counter-revolutionary forces were remote. The second problem facing the *Amigos de Durruti* was the hostility of the anarchist leadership, who used bureaucratic methods and threats of expulsion to isolate the dissidents within their ranks. Last, the journey of theoretical and political discovery embarked upon by the *Amigos de Durruti* was detained by their inability to break entirely with their anarchist past (take, for instance, the way that their personalised attacks on the anarchist 'ministers' ignored the underlying doctrinal confusion that had led libertarians to sit in a bourgeois government in the first place).

In conclusion, the balance of the 1930s is that the leading sections of the anarchist movement remained trapped in their anti-political dogma as they fought a defensive struggle to retain hegemony over the most revolutionary sections of the labour movement. In these circumstances, there could be no great advance in the realm of ideas nor could there be any significant re-appraisal of past revolutionary experiences.[64] Had the anti-political, anti-institutional utopia of the anarchists been discarded and replaced by a more coherent transforming project, then the outcome of the Spanish revolution, and the history of twentieth-century Spain and Europe, would have been different.[65]

8. Recent Trends in the Historiography of Italian Fascism

Tobias Abse

Fascism is crucial to any general account of the twentieth century, particularly of the short twentieth century (1914–91) or 'Age of Extremes', to adopt Hobsbawm's label. Fascism is clearly one of these extremes, whatever definition is offered of the other, where controversy obtains as to whether Communism and Stalinism are one and the same, an issue with which Ian Birchall deals elsewhere in this book. Ernst Nolte originally defined the 1919–45 period as the epoch of fascism.[1] Whilst the notion of fascism being reduced to a marginal force after 1945 has been called into question by political developments over the last decade, especially in Italy, Austria, Turkey and Croatia where politicians from forces in the fascist tradition have participated in government, it is not unreasonable to see the period between 1919 and 1945 as dominated by fascism. Fascism is a twentieth-century ideology that arose in the aftermath of the First World War.[2] Therefore, the ways in which historians appraise fascism is crucial to the judgement they pass on the century as a whole. The widespread consensus, once the full story of the Nazi death camps became common knowledge, that fascism was the greatest evil of the twentieth century, although surviving in some texts by younger left liberals like Mark Mazower's *Dark Continent: Europe's Twentieth Century*,[3] has started to break down as an historical revisionism associated with the political right that seeks to relativise fascism in order to brand communism as the greatest evil of the twentieth century has become increasingly popular over the last fifteen years. This relativisation of fascism is the essence of Ernst Nolte's project in Germany[4] and was at the core of the last book written by François Furet in France.[5] However, the continuing popular association of Nazism with the Holocaust has limited the extent to which Nolte and his allies have been able to change German opinion, whilst in France the trials of Barbie and Touvier have tended to give a more, rather than less, negative image to the Vichy régime whose complicity in the deportation of the Jews had been minimised by French historians. Only in Italy is it possible to argue that the politically motivated revisionists may be winning the argument since, by the time of his death in 1996, Renzo De Felice was undoubtedly the best-known historian of Italian fascism and was treated with respect in the Anglophone world, although his reputation was higher in the US than in the UK. De Felice and other Italian revisionists have sought to differentiate Italian Fascism from German Nazism, especially in relation to anti-semitism, going so far as to repudiate the very notion of a generic fascism. This intellectual trend cannot be separated from political developments in Italy where, in the context of the collapse of the governing parties as a result of the corruption scandals of 1992–94, the neo-fascist *Movimento Sociale Italiano* was able to transform itself into the allegedly post-fascist *Alleanza Nazionale* and become a major force in Italian mainstream politics, even participating in government for seven months in 1994.

It is also worth noting that Italian fascism has proved singularly attractive to American culturalist historians, partly because the Italian regime's attitude towards the arts was much less rigid than that of its German counterpart. (Hitler's hatred of all forms of modern art set the tone of cultural policy, whilst some symbiosis between fascism and modernism undeniably took place in Italian painting, architecture and, to a lesser extent, theatre.) Therefore, the dangers from an anti-fascist point of view of the apparently apolitical culturalist approach to history are much more clearly demonstrated from a discussion of recent historiography on Italy than they

would be from a discussion of recent literature on Nazism.
I want to examine two recent trends in the historiography
of Italian Fascism: the emergence of a cultural history
approach and the growing respectability of a revisionist
approach that rehabilitates the *Duce* or pours scorn on the
Italian Resistance.[6] The trends are not unconnected but it
would be crass reductionism to conflate them because many
American proponents of the culturalist approach would dis-
associate themselves from the politics of revisionism and
identify themselves in a generic way with the left, even if, as
we shall see, Emilio Gentile, the leading Italian proponent of
the cultural approach, is a pupil of the Italian revisionist
Renzo De Felice.[7]

The turn away from social history towards cultural history
is a general movement in no way specific to, or originating
in, the study of Italian Fascism. Whilst the Department of
Historical and Cultural Studies where I teach is probably
exceptional in a British context in having committed itself to
a 'cultural history' approach in public statements linked to
the Research Assessment Exercise, such a decision is indica-
tive of a more general atmosphere in British and American
historiography in the wider context of the 'linguistic turn'
and the rise of post-modernism, in which genuine social history of the kind associated with Edward Thompson has been
marginalised by a combination of a resurgent political history
on the one hand and the new cultural history on the other.
The cultural history approach to the study of Italian Fascism
has become widespread during the 1990s. My detailed comments in this chapter will be confined to works by Emilio
Gentile, Mabel Berezin, Simonetta Falasca-Zamponi, Marla
Stone and Jeffrey Schnapp, but this quintet is by no means
isolated. The 30th anniversary issue of the *Journal of
Contemporary History* in 1996 contained nine papers on
Fascist art, architecture and spectacles, and the last few years
have seen the publication of a number of articles by the
British historian and theorist of comparative fascism Roger
Griffin, which adopt similar perspectives.[8]

However, whilst a case can be argued that the general climate in American historiography in particular was favourable to the growth of a cultural history approach to the study of Italian Fascism, the specific trigger was Italian. Emilio Gentile's *The Sacralization of Politics in Fascist Italy*, first published in 1993 and translated into English in 1996,[9] has precipitated both research into, and vigorous theoretical debate about, the myths, rituals, symbols, monuments and other spectacles of Fascist Italy. The two most direct responses to Gentile have come from two American female sociologists, Mabel Berezin at UCLA and Simonetta Falasca-Zamponi at Santa Barbara.[10] The two authors, whose viewpoints—both broadly defined as post-modernist—are in some respects as far apart from each other as from Gentile, might find the direct comparison invidious but one must assume that no sociologist would ascribe such synchronicities in intellectual production to coincidence.

It was always likely that the kind of cultural history centred on rituals, spectacles and symbols influenced by Foucault and other post-modernist theorists and originally more focused on Early Modern Europe, which has gained particular prominence in certain American universities, might have seen Mussolini's regime, whose theatrical character was commented upon by contemporaries, as a suitable area for investigation. However, Gentile's precipitant role should not be under-rated and that Gentile's open acknowledgment of an enormous intellectual debt to George Mosse should not detract from this. No American scholar spontaneously considered applying Mosse's German-centred theories to the Italian instance, despite the decades of renown enjoyed by the author of the *Nationalization of the Masses*.[11] The 30th anniversary issue of the *Journal of Contemporary History* (Mosse was a co-founder) is dominated by articles adopting a Mossean culturalist approach to Italian Fascism and appeared three years after Gentile's book which suggests the American Mosseans were following in the wake of his Italian disciple[12] and Jeffrey Schnapp's book,[13] whilst preceding the monographs by Berezin, Falasca-Zamponi and Stone,[14] was not published until 1996, even if sections of it had appeared in an article in 1993.[15]

There is a considerable degree of overlap in the subject matter of the three books by Gentile, Berezin and Falasca-Zamponi. All deal in various ways with Fascist spectacle, a side of Mussolini's regime that both traditional Anglo-Saxon empiricists and most European Marxists—although not Falasca-Zamponi's key influence, Walter Benjamin—have tended to neglect, ridicule or dismiss as instrumental propaganda because of their own rationalism. However Gentile's analysis is conducted in terms of 'political religion', whilst Berezin's conceptual armoury employs 'ritual' and 'identity' and Falasca-Zamponi is primarily preoccupied with 'the aestheticisation of politics'. Gentile is an empirical historian who has adopted the emphasis on the use of archival material and contemporary sources preached, although not always practised, by his teacher Renzo De Felice. Given the controversies unleashed by De Felice himself, it ought to be underlined that Gentile is best characterised as a left De Felicean: left is a relative term here, given the rightward drift of De Felice in his last years. Whilst Gentile shares his mentor's anti-Marxism and distance from the Catholic tradition (a distance that some might argue has had a negative effect on Gentile's understanding of what constitutes a religion), he is committed to the Anglo-Saxon ideal of liberal democracy and is not an intellectual fellow traveller of Gianfranco Fini, as De Felice had become by the end. Inspired by Mosse's work and encouraged by his direct personal incitements, Gentile has sought to adopt the interpretation propounded in *The Nationalization of the Masses* to any Italian primary sources that seemed relevant to such a project.

Gentile's book is the most accessible of the three works of cultural history I am considering at this stage and the one whose merit is least dependent on agreement with its general theory, even if it is less empirical and more widely focused than the book by Marla Stone.[16] The body of Gentile's text is largely made up of a mixture of narrative and description of the type associated with traditional historiography. Admirably lucid, it is easily comprehensible to any historian with a basic knowledge of modern Italy. Gentile's account is the best brief introduction to the Italian Fascists' use of public spectacle, ranging from annual commemorations of the March on Rome to the construction of monumental architecture. Although at times his allocation of space to particular themes may be over influenced by the ready availability of vivid primary sources, there are few glaring omissions, even if the regime's use of film, as opposed to theatre or still photography, has been neglected. Furthermore, 'the question of reception' as Berezin calls it, is acknowledged to pose an historical problem. Despite his consistent, and mistaken, use of the label 'totalitarian' to describe the Italian Fascist Regime, Gentile does not seek to present consensus for Mussolini— which he acknowledges to be more widespread than consensus for the regime—as universal. However, he dodges the issue of the degree, motives and intensity of such consensus by stating that it is 'not a task within the scope of this book' (p.149).

Despite the fascination of his material, the clarity of his exposition and the persuasiveness of some of his comparisons with French revolutionary spectacles, Gentile's central theory that Italian Fascism can be explained as a political religion is unconvincing. Gentile distinguishes 'political religions' from 'civic religions' both of which he presents as variants of 'secular religion', a phenomenon he maintains was prevalent in the increasingly secularised societies of the nineteenth and twentieth centuries—by arguing that the former are characteristic of closed totalitarian societies whilst the latter are to be found in open democratic ones. Thus, his theoretical framework is dependent on reviving the bankrupt notion of Italian Fascism constituting a totalitarian regime to be ranked alongside Nazism and what Gentile calls 'Bolshevism'. It is revealing that Gentile writes as if the concept of totalitarianism was unproblematic in the Russian and

German instances, but this apparent ignorance of debates about Nazism and Stalinism is not crucial to an argument about Fascist Italy. Nobody would seek to dispute the aggressively totalitarian aspirations of Mussolini and many leading Fascist ideologues, and few would challenge Mussolini's claim to have copyrighted the word 'totalitarian'. However, it seems ridiculous to write as if the massive amount of detailed empirical research into the workings of the Fascist mass organisations such as the *Dopolavoro* (leisure organisation) or the *Balilla* (youth organisation), the practical embodiments of the Regime's totalitarian ambitions, had never been undertaken and the gap between rhetoric and reality remained unexplored. Despite his pretensions to theoretical sophistication in anthropology and sociology, Gentile seems to have regressed to the political science clichés of Germino's *The Italian Fascist Party in Power*[17] as if scholars such as Tannenbaum, De Grazia and Koon had never investigated Italian society under Fascism.[18]

Berezin rejects Gentile's view of Italian Fascism as a political religion. But she seems reluctant to enter into a debate that would clarify her differences with him for those readers whose prime interest is Italian Fascism rather than sociological or anthropological theory. Berezin's analysis centres on the notion of political rituals, although the following statement: 'public political spectacles or rituals (I use the words interchangeably)' (p.5) suggest that for practical purposes she is writing about very similar phenomena to Falasca-Zamponi and Gentile himself. Berezin's attempt to retheorise fascism, which ultimately concludes that it is a form of anti-liberal but non-Marxist communitarianism, fails to advance our understanding.

Falasca-Zamponi agrees with Gentile that 'The 'sacralisation of politics' doubtless accounts for the regime's recourse to liturgical practices as a means to transform politics and induce the populace to share a panoply of myths and cults' (p.187). However, she believes there are many aspects of fascism, particularly its apparent contradictions, that cannot be explained within Gentile's framework. Falasca-Zamponi accords a centrality to Mussolini that is absent from the work of Gentile and Berezin. This emphasis is in part a product of the nature of her empirical research, for her primary source has been Mussolini's own writings and speeches. Mussolini's interest in Le Bon and other crowd theorists is not a startling discovery and those characteristics on which Falasca-Zamponi focuses, such as Mussolini's ability as an actor and his growing self-delusion in later years, have long been remarked upon by Mack Smith and other biographers. Where Falasca-Zamponi displays originality is in situating Mussolini's self-conscious efforts to create a myth about himself in the context of a general cultural shift in early twentieth-century Europe and North America, in which the notion of 'personality' replaced that of 'character' and the rise of the charismatic leader can be correlated with the rise of the Hollywood film star. It should be stressed to any unwary reader who assumes Falasca-Zamponi is a Situationist that, despite her chosen title and the reference to 'the society of the spectacle' in the blurb, there is no sustained engagement with the work of Guy Debord who is mentioned only in one of her 843 footnotes. Finally, in contrast to Berezin, who seems to suggest that the role of violence in Italian fascism has been exaggerated and that 1938 saw a shift in foreign policy, and to Gentile, who lays his emphasis on the attempt to create 'collective harmony' within Italy, Falasca-Zamponi believes 'The spectacle of fascism exuded war and narratively prefigured the imperialistic outcome of the totalitarian state's aims' (p.148), a viewpoint that even if it employs the mystifying description 'totalitarian' is nonetheless clearly anti-fascist and in a generic sense left-wing.

Marla Stone's *The Patron State* is a more traditional empirically based study of the policies adopted by the Italian Fascist state towards the visual arts in general, and exhibitions, both artistic and thematic, in particular. It is based in large part on diligent excavations in the archives, and also makes deft use of contemporary printed sources and the relevant secondary literature. Whilst there is acknowledgment of Mosse and De Felice in the introduction, the body of the text is not weighed down with the considerable theoretical baggage that dominates the works of the sociologists Berezin and Falasca-Zamponi. Stone argues that until 1937, Italian Fascism was characterised by 'aesthetic pluralism' and the state was keen to patronise and integrate all artists within a structure of state-run corporations and state-sponsored exhibitions so long as they showed no signs of overt anti-fascism. She claims that 'consent on the part of the artists involved a dialectic of legitimation in which the dictatorship offered artists official commissions and a livelihood, often with few aesthetic constraints, in exchange for artists lending their prestige and work to the state's projects' (p.15). Her other principal thesis concerns the relationship between Italian Fascism and modernism as an artistic trend. Stone underlines that 'Modernism and its offshoots, from abstraction to neo-realism, their post-war designations notwithstanding, were not genetically anti-fascist' (p.7). Whilst the increasingly close relationship between Fascist Italy and Nazi Germany coupled with the drive towards war in the late 1930s 'elevated alternative, more regimented, cultural politics, and strengthened the power and position of the Fascist intransigents' (p.177), Stone shows that even in this last phase the faction around Farinacci, who shared Hitler's views on art, were never able to obtain the complete victory achieved by their German equivalents. However, occasionally one has an uneasy feeling that her vivid descriptions of 'the dynamic, modernist, and successful exhibition formula' (p.223) exemplified by the *Mostra della Rivoluzione Fascista* sometimes slip into an apologia, seeming to imply that artistic merit can be completely divorced from overtly propagandist content.

In his work on 18BL, Schnapp is aware of possible objections and, argues 'I do not view the effort to dissect a work like 18BL, and to reconstruct and interpret the complex social choreography and myth-making that accompanied its staging, as an attempt somehow to rehabilitate a fatally flawed experiment, an experiment that, measured by any purely qualitative yardstick, might well be found wanting. Rather I view it as a challenge to some of the modes of writing cultural history that have prevailed in the study of Italian fascism' (p.10). Despite Schnapp's rationalisation of his own procedures, such a detailed description and analysis of a theatrical work that only ever had one performance and was regarded as a disaster by both its audience and most of those involved in writing and producing it, is likely to leave any reader who does not have a deep knowledge of the period with the erroneous impression that 18BL, an allegory about the First World War, *squadrismo* and the draining of the Pontine Marshes, whose central character was a Fiat truck, that involved a cast of around 2,000 and was presented to an audience of 20,000 at the 1934 *Littoriali della Cultura e dell'Arte* (Fascist youth games) in Florence, was significant. Arguably, a more focused history of Italian Fascist theatre that concentrated on the 'Thespian Cars' (travelling theatres) and open-air festivals in places such as the Roman Arena in Verona, phenomena that Schnapp discusses in passing, might have served a better historical purpose since millions of Italians attended such performances during the course of the Ventennio. However, such a history would have demonstrated that the kind of modernism in which Schnapp is interested and finds attractive was a minority current within Fascist theatre and that the Regime's approach to theatre was more traditionalist than its approach to painting and architecture, since the less *avant-garde* theatrical spectacles were more effective in generating enthusiasm for the dictatorship. Schnapp's discussion of the parallels between Fascist theatre represented by 18BL and contemporary theatrical developments in the Soviet Union and Weimar Germany gives the impression that the theatre of the Regime was in the vanguard of European culture and that there was something revolutionary about Fascism itself. As Bosworth has sagaciously remarked: 'Schnapp's work is an extreme example of how, in their determination to be apolitical and to treat Fascism on its own terms, the cultural historians often credulously report what Fascism said rather than critically exploring what it meant.'[19]

My brief discussion of the cultural history approach has been incomplete and in some ways harsh and one-sided. I have focused on its theoretical weaknesses that flow from its abandonment of any class-based or materialist perspective, such as confusing the Regime's totalitarian aspirations with the degree of consensus it had in practice or generating definitions of fascism which do not clearly differentiate it from other non-Marxist and non-Liberal ideologies, rather than expounding its genuine empirical merits in pioneering a serious examination of Fascist ceremonies, architecture, films, theatre and photography. Nonetheless, it is essential to address the question of the revisionist interpretation of Italian Fascism whose political agenda is more sinister than the posturings of some post-modernist culturalists.

The most prominent figure in Italian revisionism is the late Renzo De Felice, the author of an eight-volume biography of Mussolini: the first volume appeared in 1965 and remained unfinished at the time of De Felice's death in 1996. The posthumous final volume published in 1997 broke off in January 1944 but the 6,425 pages already published by that stage form a basis on which to judge the whole enterprise— even if the anonymous author of the preface to the final volume had to point out that 'it is not possible to say how many and what chapters the author foresaw himself composing to end the volume' (p.ix). The biography is turgid and rambling—frequently turning into a history of Italy during the Fascist period rather than remaining within the framework of an historical biography as the genre is usually conceived either in Italy or abroad—and I suspect that very few people have read it in its entirety.[20] De Felice, born in 1929, had been a Communist in his youth but left the PCI in response to the events of 1956; it was some years before this ex-Communist became notorious for his anti-Communism. The first three volumes of the biography did not arouse much controversy, although Stuart Woolf was critical of the first volume in the first issue of the *Journal of Contemporary History* in 1966, a journal with which De Felice was later to become closely associated. Even the fourth volume, *Mussolini il Duce: Gli anni del consenso, 1929–1936*[21] which described the Italian victory over Ethiopia as 'Mussolini's political masterpiece and greatest success'[22] did not initially stir up as much of a storm as might be imagined in retrospect, given the subsequent heated controversy over the degree of consensus for the regime which De Felice argued was 'more extensive and...more totalitarian'[23] than the enthusiastic but shallower and more ephemeral consent of 1935–6 at the time of the invasion and conquest of Ethiopia which historians have conventionally seen as the peak of the Regime's popularity. Indeed, a debate between De Felice and the veteran Communist leader Giorgio Amendola in the pages of the weekly *L'Espresso* a few days after the volume's publication was both mild and courteous.[24] De Felice's notoriety as a public figure was founded not on the prolix biography but on his more concise and accessible *Intervista sul fascismo*[25] with the American academic Michael Ledeen in July 1975 that went into six editions before the landmark election of June 1976 when the Italian Communist Party appeared to be on the threshold of power. Those who believe I am exaggerating the political relevance of an interview with an historian would do well to remember that the Italian industrialists' association equivalent to the CBI (the *Confindustria*), bought up copies of the *Intervista* to distribute free in the belief that it was cost-effective anti-Communist propaganda.[26] Unlike the biography which has never been translated into any language, De Felice's interview was translated into English and published in the USA in 1977 under the title *Fascism: An Informal Introduction to Its Theory and Practice*.[27] This controversy's ramifications spread well beyond Italy provoking Denis Mack Smith, hitherto primarily an historian of the *Risorgimento*, albeit with a longstanding interest in Fascism,[28] into writing not just a critical review of De Felice's biography and the *Intervista*[29] but two books on Mussolini—*Mussolini's Roman Empire*[30] and *Mussolini*,[31] putting forward an alternative and more hostile view of the *Duce*. The *Intervista* advanced De Felice's thesis about Fascism as a movement of the 'emerging middle classes' and made a distinction between 'Fascism movement' to which he appeared sympathetic and the more reactionary and conservative 'Fascism regime' of which he was more critical. De Felice also contrasted the allegedly forward-looking Italian Fascism with backward-looking German Nazism and tried to undermine any notion of a generic fascism that encompassed both phenomena.

Subsequent volumes of the biography contained what amounted to an apology for Italian Fascist foreign policy in the 1930s, broadly endorsing the more overtly nationalist viewpoint of his pupil Rosaria Quartararo in her book *Roma tra Londra e Berlino*[32] which blamed the British for pushing Fascist Italy towards Nazi Germany by refusing to concede what the De Feliceans regard as her legitimate demand to be a major Mediterranean power. De Felice's volumes on Mussolini between 1940 and 1943[33] put forward a strange Italocentric vision of the Second World War in which Mussolini had done his best to direct Hitler's wandering attention to the Mediterranean which Mussolini, according to De Felice, rightly perceived to be the central theatre of the war.

The final controversy unleashed by De Felice was the result of another short interview book, *Rosso e Nero*.[34] As should be obvious even from the compressed account of De Felice's work in this chapter, *Rosso e Nero* is the latest in a series of attempts on De Felice's part to denigrate the Italian Resistance and dismiss the significance of anti-fascism in order to partially rehabilitate the Fascist Regime—not overtly of course but by implication. *Rosso e Nero* is all the more dangerous for De Felice's apparent distancing of himself from Fini and the AN.[35] De Felice always masqueraded as anti-Communist, anti-Catholic, cold-war liberal democrat of a surprisingly Anglo-American and thoroughly un-Italian type. This political posture was connected to his claim to be an empiricist who followed the documents wherever they led, without any preconceived ideas or ideological bias. Occasional journalistic pronouncements made long before Fini's much-vaunted transformation of the unashamedly neo-fascist MSI into the allegedly post-fascist AN cast some doubt on the credibility of De Felice's overt politics; he announced in the leading Italian daily newspaper *Corriere della Sera* as early as 27 December 1987 that 'It is plain that the great alternative of Fascism and anti-Fascism now falls. It does not make sense any more either in public consciousness or in the reality of the daily political struggle'. However, in *Rosso e Nero*, De Felice equated AN's changed attitude towards anti-fascism with the changed attitude to anti-communism on the part of the PDS, only to mock at both transformations. He affected to criticise AN for using the discussion of 1943–5 solely as a means of rehabilitating the RSI,[36] and distanced himself from Fini's thesis that Mussolini was the greatest statesman of the twentieth century, believing, according to his interviewer, that Churchill should bear this palm instead.[37] Moreover, in contrast to both the French revisionist François Furet and Britain's foremost rightwing historian, Norman Stone, not to mention Jeffrey Schnapp, De Felice was at pains to keep his distance from Ernst Nolte. De Felice's defence of revisionism stressed that it could not be equated with Holocaust denial, relativism and justificationism; the notorious German was never named, but his lurking presence would have been evident to any informed Italian reader, because Nolte's most controversial text, *The European Civil War*, was rapidly translated into Italian, doubtless finding a ready market amongst AN's more hardline members.

Nevertheless, there was plenty in *Rosso e Nero* with which to take issue. Perhaps the most outrageous assertion— namely that Mussolini's assassination was ordered by an

English secret agent because Mussolini had in his possession compromising letters from Churchill—was surreptitiously slipped into the text and is unsupported by any evidence.[38] Whilst the exact details of who shot Mussolini, and precisely where and when it was done, may remain blurred, the essence is that the partisans shot him out of a desire for vengeance upon a tyrant and from a longing to redeem Italian national honour from twenty years of submissiveness and not on the instructions of a foreign power. De Felice has helped to create for future generations of fascists a legend of a national hero murdered by foreign spies.

Another absurd contention of *Rosso e Nero* was that Mussolini returned to Italy from Germany to head the Salò Republic out of pure patriotism, to prevent Hitler turning Italy into another Poland. Whilst the motivation adduced by De Felice may have played some role, to deny that Mussolini had any desire for revenge against those responsible for his overthrow on 25 July 1943, or that he had any remaining belief in fascist ideology, is grotesque, especially in view of the very last interview he gave, on 20 April 1945.[39] Whilst the restored Mussolini was intermittently deeply depressed and arguably in some senses a rather tragic figure, to present the ageing dictator as a selfless Italian patriot would be risible, were it not so politically dangerous in an era in which Fini's party has participated in one government (in 1994) and poses a real challenge to *Forza Italia*'s precarious hegemony over the Italian Right. De Felice adopted a typically shifty and ambiguous position in answer to the question he posed, of whether Mussolini's alleged choice—returning home to help the Italian people—was the right one for him to have made, stressing that Mussolini obtained some of his objectives but paid too high a price.

Overall, De Felice argued that Salò had its good side, attacking the 'historiographical myopia' of those who contested this. Two conspicuous examples of this side were the philosopher Giovanni Gentile and the 'black prince' Junio Valerio Borghese. Gentile allegedly believed in national reconciliation and only gave his allegiance to the RSI because of his longstanding personal links with the *Duce*. In De Felice's hagiographical version, Gentile was supposedly killed to thwart his noble efforts at conciliation, and not because of his status as the official philosopher of the Regime. Like Mussolini, he was apparently the victim of a plot organised by British intelligence.

Whilst some of us have long since grown weary of contemporary Italian intellectuals being far more preoccupied with the killing of a Fascist ideologue like Gentile than with the mass murder of innocent civilians by Germans and RSI forces, De Felice's enthusiasm for Prince Borghese struck a more original note. Borghese, we were informed, was a patriotic soldier, first and foremost. A concern for national honour, not Fascist ideology, led him to choose the RSI rather than the monarchy. De Felice predictably stressed Borghese's role in fighting Tito on the Yugoslav border and tried, unconvincingly, to argue that he was in serious conflict with both the Germans and the ideological Fascists. Needless to say, his decades of continuing participation in conspiratorial anti-democratic politics, culminating in his leadership of a failed *coup d'état* in 1970, were omitted from the record.[40]

Whilst a good deal more could be said about *Rosso e Nero*, about De Felice's other work and about other Italian revisionists like Galli della Loggia,[41] the examples given here explain the general thrust of this intellectual and political offensive by the Italian nationalist right which some have argued has been more successful than its German equivalent.[42]

9. Woodrow Wilson is Amongst Us

The Consequences of the Principle of Nationality in South Asia

Barry Pavier

The nineteenth century was characterised by the creation of colonial empires of a new type. They were markedly different from of the tribute and revenue-producing empires of the pre-capitalist epochs, some of which survived into the twentieth century (Iran, the Ottomans, China, Portugal, Spain and Austria-Hungary among them). They were even fundamentally different from the commercial 'mercantilist' empires of early capitalism: British, French and Dutch. These empires of global capitalism arose out of the expansion of a number of branches of capitalist production beyond the boundaries of their national economies and consequently coming into ever-intensifying competition. By the 1880s this competition had already reached such a point that a new coherent concept of empire was being developed in the major capitalist states. Put briefly, it argued for three roles for empire:

- A captive source of raw materials for the home country's economy
- A captive market for the home country's manufactured goods
- A location of settler colonies for the home country's 'surplus population'

Out of these grew various strategic demands for military and naval bases. Once this idea was in general circulation, it became easy for a combination of industrial and commercial interests (notably shipbuilding, shipping, and mining) and various shady adventurers (e.g. Cecil Rhodes, Karl Peters, and Leopold II) to bounce their respective governments into diplomatic and military offensives to grab as much as they could before their competitors beat them to it. Between 1880 and 1905 most of the available globe was partitioned between the Great Powers. Of the potential targets only the Ottoman Empire remained.

If the last century was that of empire, then in contrast the twentieth was that of national liberation and decolonisation. Far from 'solving' the national question, however, the ending of the colonial empires has led the former colonies into a series of disorders involving conflicts between various of the successor states and inside the states themselves. One type of conflict has arisen between states formed from a partition of the original imperial entity. These have been carried out on the basis that various elements of the population cannot live peaceably and democratically with each other inside the same state. Why it should be thought that states formed on this basis could then live peaceably side-by-side with each other is a mystery and it could only be upheld by invoking the liberal principle of nationality. In its bare essential this states that nationality is the foundation of all human existence and identity, and that any international order has to be organised around national states. Partition, therefore, should resolve all conflict by creating these essential units. A brief look at the partitions carried out on this basis: Ireland, India, Palestine and Cyprus, immediately puts this proposition into question. This chapter will look at the largest and most extensive of these partitions, that of the British Indian Empire in August 1947, and attempt to draw from it some conclusions capable of more general application.

It has to be said that the British empire in India straddled the periods of mercantilism and of finance capital. One of the problems in dealing with its history has been that there has been a tendency to treat it as one seamless process, which has led to the backwards projection of the imperialism of the late nineteenth century onto the conquests after 1757, and indeed to the entire period of the operations of the East India Company after 1602. It is clear that the British appeared to significant sections of the Indian population to be playing a much more ambivalent role until at least the 1820s, making collaboration an action in concert with (supposed) partners rather than with an alien ruler.[1]

The Indian state system prior to British rule was based on various systems of dynastic rule. The epitome was the Mughal state, and the British attempted to model their relationship with the rest of Indian society upon their conception of that state.[2] However, distinct regional entities existed within the dynastic framework. Bengal, Maharashtra, and the 'Tamil Country' (Tamilnadu) existed as such entities for many centuries prior to the establishment of the Mughal state in 1525 and significant elements of society in those regions embraced them as an element of their identity.

What was missing was the notion that such identities should be embodied in a state. In this they were not unique: although the concept of 'England' existed for many centuries, Hobbes and Bolingbroke articulated the dominant pre–1640s but always challenged view that 'political England' was embodied in the monarch. 1688 transferred that to an oligarchic parliament, but it was the French revolution, following the American, which decisively broke with the old tradition by counterposing *La Nation* and *Le Peuple* against the dynasty. The notion of a nation, as a homogenous entity, being the legitimate embodiment of the state became generalised throughout Europe during the next century. 1848 represented a general attempt to establish such states, only to reveal the fatal flaw in the conception: the absence of homogenous nations. The Czech revolt against first the Frankfurt Assembly and then the Habsburgs was a window into the future of national identity and the nation state. Competition for both territory and people became the constant feature of state formation.

The establishment of the Italian state in the 1860s, the

Liberal High Noon, was the model for the first wave of Indian nationalists, notably Surendranath Banerjee of Bengal. Although he did not see it this way, the manner in which standard Italian was created out of a particular regional language was another window to the future for state building in South Asia. Once it became clear that membership of a nationality was not something that was simply taken for granted, then some kind of 'objective' criteria had to be brought into use. Language seemed to be an obvious choice, except for the problems caused by the use of different languages for public and cultural purposes on the one hand, and personal and family use on the other. A nation has to have a national language.[3]

The reason why disparate groups—liberal westernised petit-bourgeois and anti-western dispossessed Brahmins from widely dispersed regions—came together to form the Indian National Congress in 1885 was the impossibility of doing anything else. After 1857 there was no chance of restoring any state system on the old model. The British had destroyed any dynasty that attempted to keep even a vestige of independence, and replaced them with 'royalty' of their own creation. On the other hand, they had also denied the opportunity for desperate would-be collaborators such as Banerjee to collaborate on even the most modest terms. The INC therefore took on the form of a kind of pressure group within which were contained lobbying and direct action wings, which eventually split in 1907, when for the first time they found themselves in the position to lead a large-scale movement on an All-India scale.

The truth was that before the First World War none of the Indian nationalists had a clear idea of what they would replace the Imperial state with. A practical model then occurred to them in the shape of the Irish Home Rule movement. Thus from 1915 to 1918 a mass campaigning organisation, the Home Rule Movement became the focus of Indian politics. It eventually drew in all shades of Congress opinion, which was made more easy because it was fronted by the unlikely figure of Annie Besant, who after joining up with the Theosophical Movement had been resident in India for over twenty years. The campaign assumed the existence of an Indian people, whose specific nature in terms of religion, region and language were subsumed inside a general national identity as the inhabitants of Hindustan.

This campaign became subsumed within a wider movement against the British in 1919–22, which saw the arrival of M.K. Gandhi in the leadership of the Indian National Congress. The Congress-led Non-Co-operation Movement existed in parallel with another began by Muslim political figures, the Khilafat Movement, against a perceived British intent to depose the Ottoman Sultan, the present claimant to be Khalifa of the Muslim community. In fact, the Ottoman Sultan was deposed by Mustapha Kemal rather than the British, and the movement faded out. The point is that these were openly complementary rather than exclusive campaigns, and there was no concept of the Muslims being a separate nationality embodied in the Khilafat Movement.

What happened with all Gandhi's mass movements—the Non-Co-operation Movement, the Civil Disobedience Movement of 1930–2, and the Quit India Movement of 1942—was that after they had eventually been contained by the British they faded away, and on each occasion, in the aftermath of failure communalism re-emerged. However, communalism, political mobilisation on lines of religion, ethnicity, language, caste, region, etc., does not by itself lead to a claim for partition of the state on the lines of nationality. Rather, it is a campaign for a privileged position within the state for the particular communal group. The jump from communalism into a demand for a separate state required the proposition that the Indian Muslims were a distinct nationality, and that could only take place in a context where nationality was the primary criteria for the formation of a state.

In this context the timing of the first demand for the creation of a Muslim state out of the British Indian Empire is no great surprise, nor is the venue. This was the University of Cambridge, and a group of Indian Muslim students led by Choudry Rehmat Ali, who published two pamphlets calling for Pakistan (Punjab, the Afghan provinces, Kashmir, Sind and Baluchistan) in 1935 and 1937. The Muslim League had not even begun to consider such as possibility at that time, and only established a study group on the issue in 1939. This then lays the League leadership in general, and M. A. Jinnah in particular, open to the charge of rank opportunism. While this may indeed be well founded, it does rather beg the question of how that alternative was available to them in the first place.

Here the impact of the 'peace' settlements at the end of the Great War seem to be to be decisive. It is not simply the case that a series of dynastic states (Germany, Russia, Austria-Hungary, the Ottoman Empire) containing a number of subject nationalities collapsed and were replaced by states which were mainly established on the principle of nationality. Rather it is that this process was theorised at the Peace Conference as the desirable and legitimate process for state formation, largely but not solely as a result of the intervention of Woodrow Wilson. That Wilson's performance at the Peace Conference fell lamentably short of his proclaimed objectives and aspirations is too well documented to require further elaboration at this juncture. What is crucial, however, is the level of ideological consensus among significant sections of the British ruling class and the bureaucratic apparatus of the British state.[4] By the time he became Prime Minister in 1937 one of the reasons Neville Chamberlain adopted his version of appeasement was a conviction that Germany could legitimately claim border revision on the grounds of nationality. Nothing else explains his overlooked statement on returning to Croydon in 1938, where he proclaimed that he hoped that the Munich agreement would lead to a general settlement of all outstanding European problems.

It is one thing to establish that the principle of nationality is a central part of the theory of liberal democracy. It is another to find that dominant politicians in bourgeois parliamentary democracies (for that is what Chamberlain was in 1937) enthusiastically embrace it. What this reflects is the extent to which the concept of nationality as the basis for state formation had been generalised by the late 1930s. Cynical realpolitik simply shifted its ground, from dealing with dynastic states to the partitioning of others against the will of the majority of their inhabitants, as happened to Czechoslovakia in 1938. It had been preceded by another, Ireland in 1921 which was not legitimised on that basis (although it is being done so now). It was followed by others—most notably Palestine and Cyprus.

This generalisation of the principle of nationality makes the behaviour of the Muslim League after 1939 quite explicable. While they had not done as badly in the provincial elections in 1937 as has sometimes been made out, they still required a general principle to serve as the focus for their party. Otherwise the League could collapse as it has done before, after 1906 and in the 1920s. Embracing the principle of nationality and the demand for a state— although they were not very clear as to the extent of the nationality on whose behalf they were claiming a state— would appear to be an escape from marginalisation, especially when they would be aware that it was one to which the British would be receptive, even apart from the desire to use the League as a counter-weight to the Congress, which was not evident in 1939.

Once this demand had been released into an environment where the principle of nationality was the accepted criteria for state formation, however, even an opportunist manoeuvre could not simply be packed back into the box. It is not easy to retreat from a claim for a state without appearing to have capitulated, which is the position that the Muslim League got themselves into after 1945. Having made the running in the lengthy negotiations with the British and the Congress, and having paralysed the Interim Government set up in 1946 which was supposed to prepare the way for independence, they were left helpless when the Congress agreed to a partition, but one that left Pakistan with only Muslim majority areas: that is, without the non-Muslim parts of the provinces of Punjab and Bengal that they had calculated on becoming part of Pakistan. Jinnah was left with his famous 'moth-eaten Pakistan', which he clearly recognised would have great difficulty in becoming a viable state.

The disaster of Partition, which is often described as a communal holocaust, or ethnic cleansing on a mass scale, created states which could not escape from the condition of their creation. Both states of Partition had communalism embedded in their existence, and the embracing of the principle of nationality came back to visit Pakistan with a vengeance in 1971 with the separation of Bangladesh. This was carried out on exactly the same grounds that had been employed in the 1940s—in this case, on behalf of a Bengali Muslim nation. Both the Indian and Pakistani states have had to face down other challenges based on the principle of nationality: Pakistan in Baluchistan, India in the Punjab.

The principle of nationality that established Pakistan and Bangladesh, and which influenced the nature of the Indian state, was not simply one of benign co-existence. The existence of the 'Muslim' nationality meant that there had to be a 'Hindu' nationality as well, which was in an antagonistic relationship with the Muslim one. The states, therefore, had to exist in a state of antagonism, since otherwise the entire concept of the Muslim nationality and the rationale for Partition would fall. Thus, far from being a 'solution' to existing problems, partition locked conflict in place for any conceivable future, since the very existence of Pakistan was dependent upon the existence of a threatening India. It was precisely this prospect that led the 'nationalist' Muslims to oppose partition:

Eleven-hundred years of common history have enriched India with our common achievements. Our languages, our poetry, our literature, our culture, our art our dress, our manner and our customs, the innumerable happenings of our daily life, everything bears the stamp of our joint endeavour. There is indeed no aspect of our life that has escaped this stamp...if there are any Muslims who wish to revive their past civilisation and culture, which they brought a thousand years ago from Iran and Central Asia, they dream...and the sooner they wake up the better...I am one of those who believe that revival may be a necessity in a religion but in social matters it is a denial of progress.[5]

In their eyes it would mean disaster for the Muslim community in South Asia, for partition would rip it apart. The Muslim League always avoided the unpleasant issue that tens of millions of Muslims would have to be left in India. In the partitionist world view, they would be abandoning them to perpetual slavery in a Hindu-dominated state. Given this, it is not surprising that contemporary Pakistani history largely edits the remaining Muslims out of the picture.

Partition produced the circumstances in which communal and ultra-chauvinist forces could grow. Despite its 'secular' and pluralist professions, the Indian state has never been able to escape its creation by a communal partition. Although the long boom provided the conditions in which these forces could be contained, the early onset of economic crisis in the mid–1960s set in motion an extended process of political decomposition which in the end has aided the network of organisations known as the *Sangh Parivar* (The Brotherhood of Organisations) in promoting their political strategy of *Hindutva* (Hinduness). The *Sangh Parivar* is a peculiar mix of ultra-conservative and frankly fascist forces, drawing its support from the usual social layers. The unusual aspect from those used to European fascism, is that the mass paramilitary organisation that is the fountainhead of the Parivar (the RSS) has always been antagonistic to taking power itself, wishing to influence the state from outside. In

practice, this has led the political party, the BJP, being drawn
into Indian parliamentary politics. However, the overall
effect in the last decade has been clear: the Sangh Parivar has
been making the pace not only in politics but in society itself,
making its agenda the centre of debate and not only have liberal bourgeois politics become marginalised but so have
those of the left. The Indian election of 1999 was a dramatic
illustration of this. The BJP became the largest single party
with 189 out of 543 seats, the Congress suffered its worst
performance ever with 112, the Communist parties and
other openly socialist organisations hardly passed 40 between
them, and the other seats were captured by a galaxy of over
thirty parties, all of which were communal in one sense or
the other: religious, caste, or ethnic.

One reason for this has been that the left itself has
become colonised by the concept of nationality. Stalinism
embraced the concept of nationality as a means of legit-
imising the strategy of Socialism in One Country.[6] The failure of most of the left to break from this, even when they
have broken from the more obvious features of Stalinism,
means that in India they have been marginalised in every
crisis which has involved nationality—from the Tamil
nationalist agitation in the early 1960s, through to the serious crises over Assamese chauvinism and Sikh separatism in
the 1980s. More importantly still, they have been ineffec-
tual in combating the growth of the Sangh Parivar and have
missed more than one golden opportunity to build an
effective revolutionary force in the country. Today, they
face their most marginalised position since 1919, at a time
when the Indian ruling class appears to be girding itself up
for a major assault on the public sector.

The confusion that the principle of nationality has sown
shows no sign of abating, as the recent Balkan war shows.
It has allowed a series of opportunists and charlatans, from
Lloyd George to Tony Blair, to parade as defenders of small
peoples while promoting their own schemes of expansion
and partition. Fifty years on, we can see clearly the outcome

of those politics in the situation in South Asia: their 'solution' has produced conflict and a carnival of reaction. Our latter-day Woodrow Wilsons are attempting to make this the pattern for the next century but, looking at the performance so far, I would say that one century of such efforts is enough.

10. The Long Boom and the Advanced World 1945–73

Michael Haynes

In 1945 the wife of John Maynard Keynes wrote in her diary, 'World in a disheveled condition.' Leading economists of the time worried not only about the difficulties of overcoming the chaos of war, but the longer term capacity of capitalism to grow. The USA was producing half the world's manufacturing output by 1945, but at the start of 1939 it had still had an unemployment rate of 19 per cent. It was the war economy that had solved this problem. The question now was whether an expansion of productive output and full employment could be sustained in peacetime. And if this posed problems for the USA how could it act as an engine of growth for the world economy? As late as the summer of 1949, Joan Robinson was still recalling that in the inter-war years, 'slumps appeared to have grown deeper and more prolonged, and there was heavy unemployment even in times of boom....There is every reason to expect this situation to repeat itself as soon as the period of post-war readjustment has come to an end.'[1]

Such fears were unfounded. The period of capitalism's greatest crisis in the 1920s and 1930s gave way to its golden age in the three decades after 1945—a period of growth that looks outstanding not only in relation to the past but also in relation to the more uncertain pattern of the last quarter of the twentieth century. The aim of this chapter is to clarify some of the elements of the boom and to relate them to the key issue of the long-run dynamism of capitalism.

Capitalism as a World Economy

There are problems with the measuring the changing dimensions of capitalism. Global capitalism has spread from an Atlantic core to the rest of the world; more primitive modes of production have been subverted and integrated into capitalism. As early as 1945 this process was more or less complete—what would soon be called the Third World was internal to the system. But what of the Soviet bloc? The official ideology of these countries claimed they were part of the socialist sixth of the world, a parallel but separate global economy, and this was accepted even by many of Stalinism's critics on the left. If, however, we concede the argument that the system in the Soviet bloc was some kind of state capitalism, then these economies do appear as an integral part of the recent global capitalism and their development has therefore to be integrated into any analysis of the capitalist system and the dynamics of capital accumulation and profitability.

But measurement then becomes a major problem. Conventional western measures of economic output often conflict with basic Marxist concepts; and although heroic efforts have been made to extend conventional national income accounts backwards and across countries, the coverage of the data remains uneven and the foundations of the estimates often disturbingly slight. Nevertheless, this is all we have to work with.[2]

Maddison's long-run data suggests three distinctive features of the boom.[3] First, in the period from 1945 to 1973 the world economy grew faster than ever before. After 1973 growth slowed considerably compared to the 'golden age' or 'the thirty glorious years.' Growth rates since 1973 have been higher than in the inter-war years but in many cases only slightly higher than those of before 1914 and, in some cases, not significantly different from that era.[4]

Second, world capitalism in the boom was much more stable. For many ordinary people, whose family experience had been marked by the difficulties of the 1930s, the most

Table 1 Growth Rates of Real GDP per Capita[5]

	1870–1913	1913–1950	1950–1973	1973–1989
Australia	0.9	0.7	2.4	1.7
Austria	1.5	0.2	4.9	2.4
Belgium	1.0	0.7	3.5	2.0
Canada	2.3	1.5	2.9	2.5
Denmark	1.6	1.5	3.1	1.6
Finland	1.4	1.9	4.3	2.7
France	1.3	1.1	4.0	1.8
Germany	1.6	0.7	4.9	2.1
Italy	1.3	0.8	5.0	2.6
Japan	1.4	0.9	8.0	3.1
Netherlands	1.0	1.1	3.4	1.4
Norway	1.3	2.1	3.2	3.6
Sweden	1.5	2.1	3.3	1.8
Switzerland	1.2	2.1	3.1	1.0
UK	1.0	0.8	2.5	1.8
USA	1.8	1.6	3.2	1.6
Arithmetic Average	1.4	1.2	3.8	2.1

important aspect of this stability was the existence of full employment apparent in Table 2. In Britain the lowest peace-time level of unemployment was recorded on 11 July 1955 when a mere 184,929 were registered unemployed, 0.9 per cent of the labour force (compared to the January 1933 British peak of 22.8 per cent of the insured population). Switzerland (population 6.6 million) entered the record books at the very end of the boom with a mere 81 registered unemployed in December 1973. Indeed so strong was the demand for labour that the long boom was also an era of mass migration to the heartland of the world economy. The strength and continuity of the boom led many to believe that problems of the economic cycle had been overcome. But they were rudely awakened after 1973.

Table 2 Standardised Unemployment Rates %[6]			
	1920–38	1950–73	1973–98
Western Europe	5.6	2.9	7.1
France	2.6	2.0	8.6
Germany	6.2	2.5	5.7
Italy	4.4	5.7	8.3
United Kingdom	9.4	2.5	8.2
USA	11.2	4.6	6.6
Japan	na	1.6	2.5

Third, there was a clear process of convergence between the advanced economies. This convergence can be identified at the level of the advanced national economies within groups such as the OECD economies or the economies of Eastern Europe. Data for the OECD group is set out in Table 3. There is also convergence between regional groupings with Eastern Europe converging on the OECD and there is some convergence between regions within and between economies.[7]

Table 3 Levels of GDP Per Person at 1990 International $ Prices as % of US Level[8]						
	1870	1900	1913	1950	1979	1992
USA	100.0	100.0	100.0	100.0	100.0	100.0
Australia	154.7	104.9	103.7	75.4	75.1	75.3
Austria	76.3	70.8	65.7	38.9	68.1	79.6
Belgium	107.4	89.2	77.8	56.1	71.7	79.6
Canada	65.9	67.3	79.4	73.6	82.2	84.2
Denmark	78.4	70.8	70.9	69.8	80.8	84.9
Finland	45.1	39.6	38.6	43.2	64.9	67.9
France	75.6	69.6	65.0	54.5	77.9	83.3
Germany	77.9	76.5	76.2	44.7	79.1	89.8
Italy	59.7	42.6	47.2	35.8	62.7	75.3
Japan	30.2	27.7	25.1	19.6	66.3	90.1
Netherlands	107.4	86.2	74.4	61.1	76.9	78.4
Norway	53.0	43.0	42.9	52.1	61.6	81.4
Sweden	67.7	62.5	58.3	70.4	81.3	78.5
Switzerland	88.4	86.2	79.3	93.4	108.1	97.6
UK	132.8	112.1	94.8	71.5	72.7	73.0

Consideration of this data suggests the hypothesis that the more strongly the frontier of capitalist development advances and the more stable its advance, the better the conditions for convergence. The less strongly it advances and the more unstable its development the more difficult the process of convergence, and the more chance that positions will be fixed or there might even be fall back. In this perspective three questions obviously arise. First, what is it that determines the pace of advance of the frontier? Second, what determines the general pattern of convergence-divergence behind the frontier? And finally, what explains outstanding examples of convergence—such as, Japan and outstanding cases of fallback—for example, the 'relative decline of the British economy'.

The Advance of the Frontier in the Long Boom

If we take the performance of the most advanced economies as a proxy for the advancing frontier, then it quickly emerges that long-term growth rates were only marginally higher for the US and the UK in the long boom than their historical average. Long run OECD income growth appears to average around 2 per cent and the long-run rate of growth of whichever economy is leading tends towards to this average. The key feature of the long boom for the two most advanced major economies in 1945 was therefore not its speed so much as its stability. This also points more clearly to the link between stability in the most advanced economies and the catch up effect. The long boom, by producing conditions of relative stability, enabled catch up to occur behind a frontier that was moving forward at a steady but not spectacular historical rate.

Nothing in the past or likely future of capitalism compares to this, yet the attention devoted to explaining it is paltry. The gap continues to be apparent in the recent work of conventional economic historians. Noting the contrast between the pre–1914, inter-war and long boom periods. Crafts can only lamely say that the boom and 'catch-up is highly contingent on circumstances rather than a general phenomenon' and then have quick recourse to a series of *ad hoc* speculations about changing social capacities.[9]

Theorising on the left has been more systematic, but also encounters serious problems. Explaining the mechanics of the long boom once it was in place is not necessarily difficult. Nor is it difficult to offer an explanation of the much less impressive performance of the world economy since the 1970s. The difficulty is to explain both phases. Unless we have recourse to *ad hoc* factors (and as we shall see some do) we need an approach that can consistently explain the pattern relative success and relative failure over time. Many accounts founder on this problem. Thus Robert Brenner, in a long history of advanced capitalism since 1945, seeks to explain the collapse of the boom in terms of the way increased international competition pulled down the global rate of profit as catch-up occurred. Even if this were a convincing explanation of the end of the boom, however, it leaves unexplained what caused a boom of such length and strength in the first place. Brenner's focus on the centrality of the rate profit as the key determinant of capitalist development focuses on exactly the right issue, but to be effective we need an adequately theorised and consistent historical account not just of its downs but its ups as well.[10] As Michael Kidron put the problem in an important but neglected contemporary analysis:

> High employment, growth and stability explain one another to some extent…each can be seen as the immediate cause of the others, together forming a causal loop, that can be made to revolve in any direction from any point. The loop itself needs to be explained. In the thirties it was one of unemployment-stagnation-instability; now it is one of high employment-growth-stability. The interconnections and sequence are the same. Only the level is different.[11]

With this in mind, let us consider four explanations of the boom remembering that it petered out after three decades.

During the boom, success was conventionally attributed to governments avoiding the errors of 1930s through the application of Keynesian policy in the context of the international Bretton Woods system. Internationally the world economy was gradually opened up, while domestically the state directed, if not controlled, the major economic aggregates. But explanations like this are not convincing. In Keynesian terms private sector investment was high throughout, and therefore did not need deficit budgets. In any case, it seems that most states operated with budgets that were balanced in the periods when we might have expected them to be unbalanced. What demand management there was often had contradictory effects. But the fundamental difficulty with all such explanations is that they cannot cope with the loss of dynamism in the 1970s. If, in whatever form, the magic touch existed in the 1950s and 1960s how was it lost after this? Perhaps the most popular response to this on both right and left is to put the blame on an heroic or evil (depending on your point of view) push from below to increase wages and cut back profits. Brenner and others have extensively documented the deficiencies of this argument as an explanation of the 'fall'.[12] But the problems are no less apparent if we reverse the problem and ask if such an explanation can be turned on its head to adequately explain the origins and length of the boom in the first place—something discussed by Carlo Morelli in his contribution to this work.

One solution to this conundrum is the idea that the rhythm of capitalism was subject to longer Kondratiev cycles, that perhaps lasted up to fifty years, with the twenty-five good years giving way to twenty-five bad ones. This view quickly acquired some popularity across the political spectrum in the late 1970s—perhaps because its apparently neat solution saved the need for serious thought.[13] Kondratiev's own formulation focused largely waves in price movements and was highly speculative. There remain three compelling reasons, however for rejecting the idea of Kondratiev cycles—whichever formulation they are given. First, there is a lack of clarity over how such waves are to be measured (are they global or national, real or monetary phenomena). Second, even if we can agree on what to measure it is not clear that empirically they can be shown to exist at all. The most rigorous study has been undertaken by Solomou, who tested a series of different versions of the idea, only to conclude that 'although the world economy witnessed major long-run discontinuities in growth, these do not belong to as long-wave pattern or a long-wave explanatory framework'.[14]

Third, the key theoretical issue that is too often avoided is the need to identify a clear reason for the existence of long waves. Logically if there is a long cycle in capitalist development then it ought to be possible to theorise endogenous movements in the rate of profit over a longer period. But this has not been satisfactorily done and it remains hard to see how it could be. This is one reason why many long-wave theorists have been attracted to Schumpeter type explanations in terms of an exogenous clustering of new technologies. But it remains difficult to find evidence that such clusterings are real, or that the movement in such variables as technology shouldn't be included as part of the endogenous process of change. Moreover, once we decompose the boom into a frontier effect and a catch-up effect then, as Maddison points out, it remains questionable whether the speed of technological advance was more rapid in the boom.[15]

Rejecting the long-wave hypothesis, Solomou suggested an alternative in the form of *ad hoc* shocks which pushed the world economy onto a different growth path. However a number of difficulties arise with this approach too. First, there is the problem of why such 'shocks' should have a positive or a negative effect: why does the world economy find it easier to adjust in some periods and to respond more vigorously than is the case in other periods? To explain this it is not sufficient just to have regard to the shock itself.

Second, like the Kondratiev cycle approach, the emphasis

on shocks is too simple and neat a solution. Shocks only seem to be identifiable after the event, so that they can appear very much as a *post hoc* rationalisation. As Shaikh points out, the stress on exogenous shocks offers a comforting solution for crisis for those economists who in their hearts hold to the view that capitalism really an essentially stable system capable of harmonious development.[16]

Third, there is the key issue of why the shock effect lasts for so long. Solomou's account of the post-war shock in this respect seems suspiciously lame:

> The post-war boom was founded on transitory variables—the technological gap, flexible labour supplies, flexible and cheap raw material supplies and the dominant leadership of America in 1950. Such a clustering of favourable growth factors in 1950 made possible the most rapid and longest high growth phases in modern economic history.[17]

It is not that factors like this are not important. The issue is whether by themselves they explain the loop or are internal to it. It is not difficult to find factors that should have pushed the world economy onto a lower growth path during the boom; but they did not. It almost seemed as if the boom was being held up by some kind of safety net that was not present to the same extent before 1945, and would not be present to the same extent after 1973. Attention must therefore be shifted away from the 'shock' to an explanation of the generally positive environment that was sustained over such a long period. This leads us to one of the most neglected aspects of the long boom—the arms economy.

The Arms Economy

The possibility that an explanation might be found here has always been at the margins of discussion of the boom, but this is perhaps more a testament to the restricted interests of economists than the real importance of the issue. Sumner

Rosen once suggested that the failure to confront the significance of cold-war related military expenditure was 'the most important abdication of any by the economists.'[18]

The peculiar relationship of orthodox economists to this issue can be traced in the successive editions of the classic economics text of the long boom by Paul Samuelson. When the first edition of his *Economics* was published in 1948 Samuelson, dominated by a sense of the wartime military effort, was happy to set out the arguments for and against the view that there was an inherent tendency towards stagnation in the US economy; but he was nervous about coming to a conclusion on the argument's merits refusing 'to weigh the relative merits, of the stagnationist viewpoint.'[19] The second and third editions (published in 1951 and 1955) kept the discussion of stagnation, but the nervousness gave way to not only an effective rejection of the argument but a celebration of the arms boom:

> The (6–10) years since 1945 proved to be quite the reverse of any gloomy expectations concerning the stagnation of a mature economy. And as long as the tense international situation prevailed, there seemed small reason to fear that there would be too little dollar spending in the United States. It is ironical that the Russians accepted it as an inevitable fact that the post-war capitalistic system must experience a tremendous crisis and collapse. Yet every military move they made had quite the opposite effect ensuring that the capitalist countries would pursue such extensive military expenditures as to make any depression impossible![20]

The whole secular stagnation discussion then disappeared, and by the 8th edition, published in 1970 just as the long boom was about to begin to unravel, Samuelson confidently believed it would continue. Whatever role arms spending had played it was not necessary to the system. 'If there is a political will, our mixed economy can rather easily keep

Consumption + Investment + Government spending up to the level needed for full employment without arms spending.'[21]

To make sense of the real relationship between arms spending and the boom, it will be helpful to sketch the scale of the global arms effort. Table 4 sets out a constant price index of global military expenditures calculated by the Stockholm International Peace Research Institute (hereafter SIPRI) for the first three quarters of this century.

Table 4 World Military Expenditure in Constant US$bn[22]			
1908	9.0	1953	140.9
1913	14.5	1955	127.4
1925	19.3	1960	130.8
1929	21.7	1965	162.2
1935	32.6	1970	209.0
1938	61.6	1975	213.8
1948	64.7		

After the end of the Second World War arms spending quickly fell, and in 1948 in the USA was only 3.2 per cent of output. Then a huge jump took place as the cold war began, reinforced by the Korean War, and spending was subsequently sustained at higher levels. SIPRI studies suggest that on the eve of the First World War military expenditure was some 3–3.5 per cent of global output. In the 1920s its share fell before rising to similar levels in the late 1930s. What crucially held down the military share was the lack of spending by the US state (between 1–2 per cent of output through most of the inter-war years). After 1945 all this changed and in the 1950s the global military burden, supported by the huge American expenditure, was perhaps 10 per cent of output and throughout the boom it averaged 7–8 per cent.[23]

The full scale of the military burden is made clearer by calculations of the US Arms Control and Disarmament Agency, which estimated in 1968 that global military expenditure was three times global health expenditure and 40 per cent more than global education expenditure. In 1962–64 military expenditure in the developed world at 7.8 per cent of output was also 20 times greater than official development aid for the poor countries of the world.[24] An even more fundamental comparison: at the beginning of the 1960s the military burden was the equivalent of 50 per cent of global gross capital formation, and although the ratio fell by the end of the decade the United Nations pointed out that 'it is entirely reasonable to compare fixed investment with military expenditures...for the world as a whole, military expenditure at 6 to 6.5 per cent of world national product—is a about a third as large as fixed capital formation—20 per cent of world national product.'[25]

The impact that such a high level of military expenditure can be argued to have depends on how the crisis mechanism in capitalism is understood.[26] There is what we can call a 'Keynesian effect' on consumption. Contrary to Samuelson's claim that arms expenditure could be easily substituted, it was argued that it is the only politically acceptable form of large-scale Keynesian demand management, since it reinforces rather than challenges the interests of those with power. This argument could be made either in a standard Keynesian form as the Samuelson did in his early discussion, or in some left wing form of an underconsumption argument as did Baran and Sweezy.[27] That military expenditure gave a considerable boost to consumption seems undeniable though military logic meant that governments could not use it to fine tune the economy. Rather, arms expenditure helped to provide a safety net which cushioned the system.

But a second consequence, what we can call 'the Marxist effect' was an even more important part of this safety net. Marx had seen the central contradiction of capitalism not in terms of consumption, but in the inability of the system to sustain a high long-run rate of profit without the operation of countervailing influences. The problems of the inter-war years seemed to confirm that these difficulties were not simply theoretical. Lacking Marx's analytical framework, Keynesian economists were at a loss to explain long variations in the rate of profit (rather than short-run cyclical ones) but they too worried about what they called the declining marginal productivity of capital.[28] No such problems existed after 1945, and some suggested that with military expenditure running at one third to one half the level of capital formation, this was having a fundamental impact on the capital-labour ratio. Military expenditure is a form of luxury production which does not seem to impact on the overall rate of profit in the capitalist system.[29]

But the arms argument has another economic aspect. What we have just called the 'Marxist effect' operates at the level of global capitalism. But the actual rate of profit in any part of the system involves a process of redistribution of surplus value. Those economies with higher military burdens (and less catch up potential) tended to have lower rates of accumulation and inferior rates of technological change as their investment efforts were distorted. This particularly affected the American economy and even more the British economy which was trying to carry a burden of arms spending far out of proportion to its capacity.[30] The asymmetrical military burden therefore created part of the space that allowed for the faster development of those economies which lacked this burden and which had a greater catch-up potential.

This asymmetrical character of the military burden also helps to explain the beginning of the unraveling of the boom. Theorists of the arms economy like Kidron argued that its dynamics were at a partial tangent to the dynamics of capital accumulation. As cold-war tension began to ease and the effects of wars like that in Vietnam began to be played out, the rate of growth in military spending began to decline. At the same time global expansion was increasing the size of the system that needed to be stabilised. The result was a decline in the relative size of the military burden. Detailed global figures are not available, but if we take the NATO countries as an indicator then the military share of output in them fell from 7.7 per cent in 1958 to 6.1 per cent in 1965, 5.8 per cent in 1970; 4.8 per cent in 1975 and 4.4 per cent in 1977.[31]

Although the immediate causes of the end of the boom lay in the break down in 1971 of the Bretton Woods system the long-run result of the decline in the military burden was to gradually lower the safety net that had been supporting the world economy though the fact that it remained in place at a lower level was to help explain how, when instability returned, the problems were not as great as those that had wrecked the world economy in the inter-war years. But alongside this, the disappearance of the boom also eliminated much of the potential for catch-up that had existed in the boom and it is to this aspect that we now turn.

Bringing In Convergence

It was the catch-up effect that gave the boom in Europe its most spectacular features as a group of miracle economies emerged—France, Germany with its *wirtschaftswunder*, Italy with its *miracolo economico* and later Spain. Then in the 1960s the speed of advance of Japan began to be recognised.

The process of catch up involved a rapid switch of resources, particularly from the agricultural sector, into new growth sectors based around more modern industry and ser-vices which incorporated technology from the more advanced countries.

Since these gains were also once and for all it is not sur-prising that over time the convergence effect diminished and growth rates fell. However, if catch up and convergence is necessarily self-limiting within an economy this does not explain why it was not generalised more widely beyond the most advanced countries and this remains one of the most interesting and underexplored issues.

Much conventional economic history, represented in the works of Crafts and his collaborators, has been devoted to explaining the relative differences in the achievements of catch up through an emphasis on what Abramovitz called 'social capability'. Implicitly what this comes to mean is social impediments (or inducements) to market flexibility:

Table 5 Changing Economic Structure in the Long Boom
by % Employment Share[32]

	1913	1950	1960	1973	1984
Agriculture					
UK	11.0	5.1	4.6	2.9	2.6
USA	32.3	13.0	8.2	4.1	3.3
Germany	34.6	22.2	13.8	7.2	5.5
France	37.4	28.5	21.9	11.0	7.6
Netherlands	26.5	13.9	9.5	5.7	4.9
Japan	64.3	48.3	30.2	13.4	8.9
Industry					
UK	44.8	46.5	46.7	41.8	32.4
USA	29.3	33.3	34.3	32.5	28.0
Germany	37.8	34.8	36.3	38.4	32.0
France	33.8	34.8	36.3	38.4	32.0
Netherlands	33.8	40.2	39.2	35.7	26.4
Japan	13.9	22.6	28.5	37.2	34.8
Services					
UK	44.2	48.4	48.7	55.3	65.0
USA	38.4	53.7	57.5	63.4	68.7
Germany	27.6	34.8	38.0	46.2	54.0
France	28.8	36.7	41.8	50.6	60.4
Netherlands	39.7	45.9	51.3	58.6	68.7
Japan	21.8	29.1	41.3	49.4	56.3

Table 6 Estimates of Comparative Levels of Valued Added Per
Hour Worked in Manufacturing[33]

	USA	UK	Germany	France	Japan	Korea	Brazil	India
1950	100	38.2	32.4	38.3	11.8	4.7*	19.1	4.0
1960	100	44.0	58.6	48.0	19.5	7.8	35.6	5.3
1973	100	52.4	79.6	73.3	49.2	11.4	39.8	5.0
1979	100	53.5	95.8	88.7	62.6	14.7	35.9	5.0
1989	100	61.9	83.8	91.0	73.9	18.7	28.4	5.7†

* Estimate for 1953 † Estimate for 1987

the familiar conservative/orthodox economic litany.[34] Obviously an adequate account of differential catch-up from the left would have to recognise that 'social capability' defined in a more acceptable way is a factor. But it is important to appreciate that a key feature of the boom was that within the converging group, catch up was widespread across societies that have been defined in quite different ways in terms of 'social capability'. Over the period 1950–89 it was Japan that experienced the greatest catch-up; then the second most successful state was Italy. While this has led 'social capability' theorists to sing the praises of Japan, few have had the courage to sing the praises of the Italian model as one for emulation![35]

Problems like this lead us to suggest that 'social capability' is as much a consequence as a cause of the catch-up process. and that it is important to focus on real economic factors. Once the boom was underway and creating a healthy and competitive growth climate then a wider dynamic could develop to encourage change. But to understand this we therefore need to focus on development in the boom as a process—something which running ever more sophisticated regressions on limited data is ill-equipped to achieve.

Eastern Bloc Convergence

The cold war also helped to drive forward the economies of the Soviet bloc after 1945. In fact in the Eastern Bloc too the cold war had a double asymmetrical impact. First because the bloc as a whole was much weaker than the NATO group competition with the west was a far more important axis of development than vice versa—the Soviet bloc military industrial complex was proportionately even larger than that in the west and it was the centrepiece of economic planning.

Second, within the bloc Soviet nervousness about the extent of its control meant that it could not share the burden of military competition to the same extent that the US was able to share it in NATO. This is reflected in the different burdens of expenditure carried by other Warsaw Pact mem-

Table 7 Estimates of % of Output Spent in Military Sector by Warsaw Pact[36]

	1955	1965	1970	1975	1980	1985
Bulgaria#	na	na	2.5	2.7	3.0	na
Czechoslovakia*	na	6.0	5.0	4.8	4.7	5.0
GDR#	na	3.2	5.1	5.5	6.1	6.9
Hungary+	na	2.7	2.7	2.4	2.4	3.8
Poland*	na	4.6	4.0	3.5	2.7	4.0
Romania+	na	3.4	2.0	1.7	2.0	1.6
USSR**	na	9.0	10.0	11.0	11.0	12–17?

Measures of output # Net Material Product; * UNI;
+ Gross Domestic Product; ** Gross National Product

bers compared to other NATO members set out in Table 7. As in the west too this enabled the less burdened economies with greater catch-up potential to close the gap somewhat with the Soviet bloc and placed a limit on the USSR's catch-up potential.

But overall what is important is the progress that the Soviet bloc made. In the light of the subsequent development of crisis in the Eastern bloc economies in the 1980s and their collapse in 1989–91, it requires a leap of historical imagination to appreciate its extent.

But this was a period of real advance. If the three decades after 1945 were the golden age of western capitalism, then they were also the golden age of Eastern bloc state capitalism. In the first instance this meant mobilizing resources for growth and sharply increasing the rate of exploitation of workers and peasants, but as the bloc economies boomed it did become possible to increase the standard of living although even though the aspirations of the mass of people were never completely met.[37] But for the rulers of the Eastern bloc what was important was that they had overcome the historical legacy of failure in the region and had now begun to claw back the claim of western capitalism.[38]

Schumpeter had speculated that while state-controlled economies might be less efficient than market ones at any single point in time, in the long run they might prove their superiority. Growth might be the reward for relinquishing choice. In the boom there was no question that the Soviet bloc economies had an impressive capacity to mobilise capital and labour and to gain from moving resources out of lower productivity agriculture into higher productivity industry. Even the most hostile accounts had to admit that the East-West dynamic efficiency gaps appeared to be small and, even if the West proved superior, then so long as the Soviet bloc economies could mobilise more resources they could continue to close the gap.[39] Ironically as late as 1984 one economist measured the scale of British 'crisis' by the fact that in *per capita* output it appeared to have been overtaken by East Germany in 1981.[40] Eastern Europe had its miracle economies, too, which had been basket cases during the inter-war years. In the case of Bulgaria the impeccably orthodox economic historian D.H. Aldcroft could write, as late as 1986, that it 'has been one of the great success stories of the twentieth century, with the highest rate of growth in Europe and a degree of structural change second to none'.[41]

Between East and West was the Yugoslav miracle economy, with one of the fastest rates of growth in the world for much of the 1960s. Comparing Yugoslav performance both with that of its neighbours and its past history. Branko Horvat praised its superiority over both 'West' and 'East'. 'The self-government period appears to be some sort of synthesis of the positive features of the preceding two periods. Employment growth continues to be almost as fast as under central planning. But output expands much faster, so that productivity growth achieves rates beyond anything known before.'[42]

Moreover the fact that growth in Eastern Europe was based on the creation of a self-sustaining industrial core made the approach attractive beyond the advanced world. But even within the advanced world there was appreciation for this aspect of their development. For Hugh Seton-Watson, a leading western cold-war commentator and therefore hardly a friend of the Soviet regimes, there was something not only economically and morally positive to consider in the development pattern on the Soviet side of the cold-war divide in Southern Eastern Europe:

> Great industries have been created...The success is real though, we should not forget first, that there would certainly have been great progress if there had been a mixed economy...Still, on the whole, I believe that they have gained. The sight of the Greek economy, based on mass tourism and vulgarity and with shocking disparities between wealth and poverty, does not make me confident that private enterprise and foreign aid would necessarily have made a very good job of the economies lying to the north.[43]

Ironically one of the most telling testaments to the perceived viability of the Eastern bloc approach to growth was to be made by the World Bank. What appealed to the Bank was the capacity of (repressive) governments to mobilise resources for change, and to guarantee that loans would be repaid. In these terms helping the Eastern bloc was seen as good political sense as the cold war gave way to détente, and good economic sense in view of its past performance and future prospects.[44]

Catch Up and Its Limits

In the event the Eastern bloc suffered even more spectacularly in the 1980s than did the advanced world. But the capacity of the boom to lift the relative position of economies was already problematic elsewhere in the world long before it ended. A crude measure of global inequality is to calculate incomes as a Gini coefficient which measures the spread of inequality on 0 to 1 scale with 0 being absolute equality. One such calculation for states comprising 80 per cent of humanity shows the measure of inequality rising from 0.393 in

1900 to 0.448 in 1938 and 0.530 in 1950. It then fell slightly in the first years of the boom to 0.521 in 1960 before rising to 0.539 in 1970 and a peak of 0.544 in 1980 from which it has fallen slightly, in part because of more recent sustained growth in China and India.[45] The overall pattern for the world economy has therefore been one of long-run 'divergence, big time', as Prichett puts it, and this remains true of the years of the biggest global boom in capitalism's history. It is true that within the wider follower group some did breakaway and begin to sustain what Prichett defines as 'explosive growth' of some 4 per cent per annum for the next decades. But this was true of only 11 out of 108 countries he has examined. The path of the majority was much less impressive and some even experienced implosive meltdowns (of which the crises in the former Soviet bloc are a more recent and extreme example).[46]

We have no space here to offer a serious explanation for this pattern but several comments can be made. The first is that it is important to resist the claim that the poverty of the mass of the world reflects the transfer of wealth from them to the rich. Some such transfers do occur, but the crucial mechanism of development and the boom was the higher rate of profit in the advanced world which enabled the continual re-investment of the surplus created by their better equipped and more exploited workers. But it does not follow from this that we can then support the claim of conventional historians (most recently set out by David Landes), that development is a tribute to the positive social capacities and capabilities of the developed and poverty a testament to the lack of such capacities in the poor.[47] Global capitalism is a structured economic and political system which creates only limited spaces for convergence. If these spaces in past decades have been somewhat wider than was once imagined, they are also much narrower than free market economists have liked to claim. From this it follows that the success of some in the past and the apparent promise of some in the present cannot be a policy guide for the mass of humanity. Convergence is a much more complex and contradictory process than such speculations imply. In a situation where the world economy is more unstable than in the last half century and in which there are major problems of profitability, although some economies may be able to lever their way up, this is unlikely to be repeated on a widespread scale in the foreseeable future. Changing the world to create a more equitable system therefore remains the fundamental solution to the 'convergence' problem now.

11. Socialists and Economic Growth
The Myth of Employers and Union Connivance in Explaining Relative Economic Decline

Carlo Morelli

The existence of a consensus between labour, capital and government has long been the focus of attention for those wishing to explain either the relative economic decline of the British economy or the success of West European capitalism since 1945. Whether in academic or popular accounts, from the political left or right, the degree to which a consensus emerged and was regulated remains a central theme. For Larry Elliott and Dan Atkinson 'connivance between management and unions' protected old methods of working against more modern techniques with the result that British industry became characterised by low productivity, low capital investment and a lack of international competitiveness. Thus the film *I'm Alright Jack* is suggested to symbolise this low productivity consensus in which a strong shop-stewards' organisation, dominated by a Communist Party member played by Peter Sellers, colludes with a conservative management to prevent change.[1] In contrast Will Hutton's influential *The State We're In* identified the European model of collaboration and interdependence between labour, capital and government as the key to the success of Western European capitalism after 1945.[2] Labour's integration within this consensus was of such importance that without it the process of convergence, described in the chapter by Mike Haynes in this book, whereby economies such as the West German first caught up with and subsequently overtook the British economy would have been in doubt. Thus for Hutton 'unions have been important agents in restructuring German industry, using their dominant position in works' councils and their role on supervisory boards to legitimise often painful programmes of job cuts and wage reductions.'[3]

The connection between labour's self-restraint and capital's commitment to high investment became the mechanism for high productivity growth. As Hobsbawm, one of the most influential British socialist historians points out, the growth of the 1950s and 1960s across the industrialised world was a result of a political construct of the left and the right acceptable to all sides. The deal was 'based upon a tacit or explicit consensus between employers and labour organisations to keep labour demands within limits that did not eat into profits, and the future prospects of profits high enough to justify the huge investments without which the spectacular growth of Golden Age labour productivity could not have taken place.'[4]

The explanation for British failure and a comparatively poor post-war productivity record in this era lies in the inability to fully construct the successful productivity consensus which Hobsbawm points to. It is not that a consensus failed to emerge, rather that the consensus within Britain was growth restricting, short-termist and conservative. Employers and trade unions recognised each other but refused to trust each other or embrace change, which would deliver long-term benefits. This itself is explained as a result of a wider failure of the British state to create the mechanisms for modernisation. Thus for Booth, Melling and Dartmann 'to explain Britain's failure, perhaps the key lies in its liberal and reactive state tradition. An effective productivity coalition requires a proactive state to persuade, threaten, or coerce institutions (employers and workers) into a co-operative bargain and to develop the machinery of co-ordination that consolidates such bargains.'[5]

The link between labour and economic growth is thus made in a direct, causal relationship. However, such a direct link is not unproblematic for socialists and indeed leads many to conclusions which are not dissimilar to those of the right. It is hardly surprising that socialist historians should exhibit a predisposition to demonstrating the importance of the working class to capitalism. A sympathy for working people, 'rescuing...from the enormous condescension of posterity' the anonymous, men and women who in challenging the rule of capital made history, has been a project for generations of socialist historians.[6] Nevertheless presenting such an approach over-simplifies the production process within capitalism. All class societies have been based upon the exploitation of the many by the few. Hence relations of production are important issues to be addressed. However it is the dynamic of capital accumulation within capitalism that distinguishes capitalism from other class societies. Individual, and national, capitalist accumulation derives not simply from the exploitation of a working class but also inter-capitalist rivalry and competition.[7]

Explanations of British economic performance based upon the consensus, or otherwise, between workers and employers assumes exploitation and accumulation are the same thing. Similarly it assumes that once a desirable consensus has been achieved, capital accumulation is somehow automatic. It is the absence of an understanding of capitalist accumulation that results in the left adopting a methodology of contracting and bargaining that also forms the basis of the neo-classical approach. In particular the role played by markets in allocating resources, the mechanisms within markets for contracting and finally the emergence within markets for sectional interest groups are shared across the political spectrum. To understand the limitations of adopting these methodologies it is necessary to examine in more detail the neo-classical approach.

Markets and Workers

Classical economics suggests that individuals and firms meet in a market and freely bargain between one another before combining together, in a contract, to exchange the resources each has to offer.[8] So the firm offers wages while the individual offers the ability to work. In combining together both sides gain, the individual a wage to purchase goods and the firm labour power to produce goods which can be sold to other individuals or firms. Starting from this simple assumption economists build elaborate models to explain why one side, or another, in this contract may not fulfil their obligations. Neither side can completely verify the other's honesty prior to entering into the contract. Information is therefore said to be incomplete and a degree of risk is said to enter into the contract. The firm may not fully disclose the conditions of work endured while the labour power provided may be of insufficient intensity to complete the task. In the long-run, explained in economics as a series of repeated games, both parties to the contracts develop institutions which attempt to reduce the degree to which the other side can default on their obligations. So unions, employers organisations and indeed the state mediate contracts. Despite all the possible complexities introduced to explain the diversity of the real world neo-classical economics maintains that two fundamental assumptions still hold in this sea of contracting and bargaining. First the decision to enter into a contract is freely made by both parties and conversely, both sides are equally free to refuse to enter into the contract, and second both sides benefit from the contract, even if the benefit is not evenly shared.

Among socialists the assumption that workers are free to sell their labour power in a capitalist market is an obvious fallacy. In the absence of control over the means of production workers are free to starve rather than free to sell their labour. Marx's expression that workers are in fact 'wage slaves' is a more accurate expression for the position workers find themselves in within a labour market under capitalism. Labour power is therefore extracted through exploitation in this relationship. Indeed neo-classical economics is forced to concede this point but suggests instead that this exploitation is actually at labour's request. Bosses are understood as the 'residual claimant' of surpluses once labour and capital have extracted their share. They are a necessary part of production, whose role is the monitoring of work to prevent shirking by one section of the labour force relative to another.[9] Shirking and wider opportunistic behaviour is thus introduced as part of human nature and the creation of coerced labour is understood to emerge as a solution to the deleterious effects of human nature. Thus Clark maintains that coerced labour under the factory system arose because workers 'were not able to discipline themselves....Whatever the workers themselves thought, they effectively hired the capitalists to discipline and coerce them.'[10] We therefore have the recognition that labour is not freely given but extracted once contracting is complete.

While the assumption that workers are free to sell their labour power may seem an obvious fallacy the assumption that this sale is undertaken within a bargaining environment may seem less so. Within the world of bargaining the demand for labour is assessed by capital within a market environment. The firm recognises its needs and according to the supply and quality of labour provided a price, or wage, is said to be agreed. The market for labour is understood in terms of an open market in which prices, or wages, are openly traded until the bargaining is complete and contracts are agreed. Casualised nineteenth- and early twentieth-century recruitment of dock-workers might be understood as the archetypal example of such a Walrasian market. Similarly George Orwell's account in *Down and Out in Paris and London*, of the recruitment of casual sandwich-board workers displays this point.

> We went at five to an alley-way behind some offices, but there was already a queue of thirty or forty men waiting, and after two hours we were told here was no work for us, they are engaged by the day, or sometimes for three days, never weekly, so they have to wait hours for their job every morning.[11]

The important point to make about the bargain struck is not simply that labour is wage slavery and therefore the price is not freely arrived at but still more importantly the bargain struck is a bargain based upon an unequal access to the means of production. The firm not only controls the means of production but also, importantly, plays a specific intermediary role in realising the value created through labour. In other words workers who refuse to accept wage labour are prevented from establishing themselves as alternative non-exploitative firms for two reasons. First access to resources is removed from the worker. Capitalism's early development was inextricably linked to the physical theft of resources through enclosure, clearance and the redefining and enforcement of private property rights. The victory of market relationships was not simply an evolutionary victory over common rights and moral economy rather it involved violent overthrow and revolution.[12] For an individual worker to refuse to enter into a wage labour relationship they must gain exclusive access to the means of production and in so doing thus become a capitalist.

Second, the results of workers' labour is removed from them through the use of markets as a medium for exchange. The results of human labour become mere commodities valued in terms of their market price, which itself is determined by the combination of rival capitalist firms' abilities to produce similar commodities and the ability to sell these commodities. An understanding of goods value being related to the labour theory of value has no place in this approach. The position the capitalist then occupies, as intermediary, in the exchange process ensures they acquire specialist information unavailable to workers. This intermediary position ensures they develop the personal contacts, contracts and market information necessary to engage in trade. Once this is linked to the ownership of the means of production workers' opportunity to freely bargain is removed. Clear evidence for this can be seen in industries which required low levels of capital investment and employed workers to undertake the role of co-ordinating exchange. Within the eighteenth-century trans-Atlantic shipping industry, clerks were employed to locate trade opportunities between ports. Because this trade was irregular and involved establishing personal contacts, gaining specialist knowledge, it became commonplace for individual clerks to leave their employer and establish themselves as independent capitalist merchants competing with their previous employer. Trans-Atlantic shipping was characterised by atomistic competition with bills of exchange providing credit for the purchase of goods and the combining of individuals into partnerships (typically of 64 persons) to fund the voyage itself. Once the ship returned to port and the goods were sold the bills of exchange were settled, each partner received their share and the partnership dissolved. This atomistically competitive market was broken up when trade became regularised by the 1820s. Now trans-Atlantic trade required a fleet of ships and hence large-scale capital investment, which emerged under the control of a new class of professional shipowners. Commercial information itself also became routinised and easily controlled by the larger firms involved through the employment of resident agents in distant ports. Specialist contracting under these conditions became the preserve of the individual capitalist, or their salaried managers, and competition itself was regulated through shipping conferences, which fixed rates and tonnage in cartel arrangements. Large shipping firms, including Cunard emerged under exactly these circumstances.[13] The bargaining process is itself not independent. If wage labour is more accurately described as 'wage slavery' then the bargaining environment is one in which capital holds a gun to the head of labour during bargaining. Capital and labour come together in a conflicting relationship based upon exploitation and alienation rather than one based upon mutuality and consensus. Contracting in this framework is one in which 'cheating' is not only endemic it is a necessity if either capital or labour is to realise as much of the surplus as possible from the results of the labour process.

Sclerotic Decline

Neo-classical writers have adopted the bargaining framework to explain the alleged failure of the British economy since 1945. Most influentially Mancur Olson's *Rise and Decline of Nations* maintained that societies develop what he termed 'distributional coalitions' over time which essentially usurp surplus through collective action.[14] In Olson's view distributional coalitions include not simply trade unions and employers associations but any form of collective group which interferes with free markets including such groups as the Campaign for Real Ale or even the National Childbirth Trust. Olson maintained that, in an important phrase, in the absence of 'defeat in war, military occupation or revolution' growth would slow as these interest groups emerged and grew resulting in what he termed sclerotic decline. For Olson then it is the liberation of the free market that ensures rapid economic growth. Within the British context this view, has been taken up by the supply-side reform school such as Bean, Broadberry and Crafts. They maintain that the economy became characterised by a lack of commitment and co-ordination such that employers, trade unions and government all pursued short-term goals at the expense of encouraging market mechanisms via supply-side reforms.[15] Management failed to grasp new technologies and new opportunities while trade unions conservatively protected their short-term interests in jobs and wages against prospects of longer-term economic growth and implicit prosperity. The solution presented by this supply-side approach was one of freeing up markets, removing distributional coalitions and introducing wider supply-side reforms. In so doing free market contracting would resolve commitment problems while the price mechanism would resolve co-ordination problems.

For the left, the centrality of exploitation rather than accumulation and the adoption of bargaining and contracting here again leads to similar conclusions, linking institutional stability with economic stagnation.

While Saville argues that it was only in questioning Britain's great power status and defence commitments that an alternative economic strategy could have emerged after 1945, he maintains that it was the continuity of British institutions which acted to stifle new thinking in foreign policy. As Saville suggests the 'stability of the institutional framework at the top level of government worked (to encourage conservatism). Alone among the major powers of Europe during the twentieth century, Britain never experienced either defeat in war or a major upheaval in administrative organisation.'[16] As seen above these distributional coalitions could well unite against change leading to under-performance with an anti-technological bias. Hence Larry Elliott and Dan Atkinson 'connivance between management and unions' in the protection of old methods of working during the long boom. In other areas too these narrow distributional coalitions could lead to under-performance within the British economy. So for Hutton the mindset of city investors and pension funds occurs because of the narrow concerns of the financial sector:

> [the] argument is not that pension funds and insurance companies are intrinsically short-termist and greedy, bleeding British companies dry by their demand for high dividends...it is that there is a complex interaction between the pattern of share ownership, the structure of taxation, the liquidity of the markets and the framework of company law in which every individual actor can behave rationally and even decently, but which still produces the perverse outcome of less investment and output growth than the optimum.[17]

The solution for increasing commitment and co-ordination between labour and capital within these approaches typically lies in the use of government and the state as independent arbitrator and moderniser in the regulation of private business and labour.

A New Post-War Economic History

Challenging this consensus view of British post-war relative economic decline provides important insights into explaining the economic history of both reconversion from war to peace and the long boom.

The uniqueness of the success or failure of reconversion after 1945 has been the centre of debates over Britain's post-war economic record. The Attlee government, alone in Western Europe, is suggested to have allowed for the retrenchment of employer-based sectional distributional coalitions, following the re-introduction of private cartel agreements and government-sponsored trade associations, linked to the continuation of rationing. Similarly trade unions were allowed to defend over-manning and restrictive practices due to a resistance to the return of unemployment.[18] The failure to introduce supply-side reforms including stronger competition policy and challenge trade-union influence is said to have had longer-term welfare implications.

In contrast those sympathetic to the Attlee government point to the macro-economic constraints, the existence of supply-side reform and government concern for productivity through the introduction of the Anglo-American Council of Productivity and support for modernisation from within the trade-union movement.[19] The Attlee government is suggested to have proved highly successful operating as it was against a very difficult background.[20] In contrast to these two views it is possible to suggest that the Attlee government far from being unique to those of Western Europe showed greater similarities than differences. The history of all early post-war Western European countries was one of stabilising conditions for capitalist development. It was not one of freeing up markets and the break-up of distributional coalitions, instead it is one of consolidation of employers' organisations and agreements over competition in order to establish stability in the face of fear from domestic social unrest and, by

1947, concerns over an emerging cold war. At the heart of the Attlee government's concern to create economic stability was the necessity of restraining domestic consumption. Rationing not only continued after the war but was extended to food-stuffs, including bread and potatoes in 1946 and 1947 respectively.[21] While Cairncross, a writer sympathetic to the Attlee government's economic record, disputes the importance of the continuation of rationing, even he admits that personal calorific intake remained below its pre-war level until 1950.[22] Economic policy was summed up under the phrase 'export or die'. Domestic consumption and living standards were held down in order to resolve the crisis derived from sterling balances held abroad. The British economy was financially bankrupt and avoided crisis only by taking dollar loans from the USA and Canada and by the restrictions placed on countries of the Empire which prevented exchange of sterling for dollars. It is Cairncross's contention that the most significant economic legacy of the Attlee government was the holding down of living standards between 1945 and 1951. When decontrol was introduced into the economy it came to private industry first and consumers last, with food rationing finally abolished in 1954. In other areas too the Attlee government proved favourable to capital rather than labour. The nationalisation programme was not only understood by contemporaries as largely 'inevitable' but was also carried out with compensation of £2.6bn, resulting in a series of capital injections into the private sector for further investment.[23] This compensation was paid at a time when the British government's central difficulty in reconversion was an acknowledged shortage of finance. Compensation for nationalisation far exceeded the American loan, negotiated by Keynes, which imposed the conditions of Bretton Woods and convertibility on Britain and was the origin of the establishment of a US hegemony over Western Europe after 1945. By contrast the government took a much tougher line with trade unionists, using troops to break strikes on 18 occasions, introducing two States of Emergency and reviving the Supply and Transport

Organisation whose origin lay in the breaking of the 1926 General Strike.[24] Government was also prepared to use legal prosecution of strike leaders and engage in anti-Communist witch-hunting within the trade unions in order to control the labour movement.[25]

Nationalisation programmes of industries from banking to railways, often requiring large-scale capital investment and integration for national development can be seen throughout Europe. While neo-classical writers have pointed to de-Nazification and deconcentration of West German industry as an example of removing distributional coalitions from business, they have failed to notice the abandonment of this project by 1947. In the face of an emerging cold war, allied policy switched from preventing economic recovery to ensuring West German economic development lay at the heart of plans for a prosperous Europe.[26] Creating economic stability required government intervention and nationalisation along with support for private business in the reconstruction of agreements and cartels limiting competition. Western European governments also sought to limit the impact of communist movements with Marshall Aid explicitly linked to the removal of communist influence within government, particularly in Italy.

Western European recovery from the Second World War was, as Milward has noted, a political rescue of the nation state in which the rescue of one was dependent upon the rescue of all.[27] European integration became a political rather than simply an economic project in which all economies followed a relatively similar pattern.

The Long Boom

While the importance of the similarities between Britain and other Western European economies in the years of reconversion might be disputed most accept that in the long boom that followed Britain, albeit less successfully, adopted the same consensus-based pattern of economic development which emerged throughout West European capitalism. How then are we to explain the long-term relative decline of the British economy from 1951–73?

Here, by contrast with mainstream Keynesian and neo-classical approaches, the important features of the British experience are not the similarities with Western Europe but the differences. First, Britain retained a unique legacy deriving from the fact that its economy was on the frontier of capitalist development at the turn of the twentieth century. Unlike other nations, it was unable to develop utilising the advantages of combined and uneven development, and instead was tied to a range of technologies which were suited to a world of early industrialisation. British capitalism was characterised by export-led heavy industries of the first industrial revolution. Industrial restructuring from textiles, coal, shipbuilding and iron and steel industries into the second industrial revolution such as artificial fibres, electrical engineering, cars and alloy metals was always going to be a slow and painful process.[28] The economy's long-term relative decline therefore derives from its early head-start as the first industrial nation and for the most part requires no explanation.[29]

There are two further factors which influenced British capitalism's development after 1945. First, Britain's legacy of empire with its consequent importance for British trade, combined with Britain's failure to recognise the importance of the emerging European market, have been widely recognised. It was not simply that British firms focused upon slower growing markets, but that firms were not subject to the same competitive pressures. British exports remained in commodity sectors of decreasing importance to importing economies. As late as the 1950s the three largest commodity groups exported were non-electrical machinery, transport equipment and textiles.[30] From the mid-1950s, as cartels gave way to mergers and rationalisation across Europe, British capitalism failed to invest in the industries offering new opportunities in wider consumer mass markets.[31]

This brings us to the second important and neglected aspect of this relative decline; the permanent arms economy.[32] To explain why British capitalism failed to recognise the importance of European markets and failed to recognise the importance of mass markets in consumer goods, we need to understand that the British ruling class still accepted its role as a world power.[33] Britain played a central role in creating and sustaining a pro-western hegemony in the cold war. This role involved military expenditure which inevitably had a major impact on domestic economic development. Of the major western economies, only the US spent more on defence as a proportion of GDP than Britain after 1945.[34] Although defence expenditure in Britain peaked in 1952, following the outbreak of the Korean War, and declined in real terms throughout the 1950s and 1960s, Britain remained a high-spending nation. By 1962, ten years after real expenditure peaked, military orders accounted for around 70 per cent of the aircraft industry's output, 22 per cent of the electronics industry (including at least 35 per cent from the industrial and radio communications sectors) and 23 per cent of shipbuilding.[35] The inter-relation between the importance of public expenditure and the growth of the defence sector has led Edgerton to suggest that the post-war political consensus which emerged after 1945 was constructed around an industrial/military nexus based upon high technology and high defence expenditure.[36] Elsewhere, Freeman maintains that government research and development funding required a 'considerable reorientation' away from military and prestige projects in order to establish a framework conducive to establishing more competitive industries.[37] However, in general the impact of arms expenditure on the British economy and the stabilising effect on world capitalism of a permanent arms economy has largely been ignored among mainstream historians and economists.

Conclusion

The existence of a consensus between labour and capital lies at the heart of the most influential left-wing writing on post-war economic growth. The importance and weakness of this consensus is also understood to be central to explanations of rapid economic growth throughout Western Europe and British relative economic decline respectively. The existence, importance and weakness of this consensus is also shared by those of the right.

This chapter has maintained that to blame the relative failure of the British economy after 1945 on a deal between workers, employers and government is flawed on two counts. First, there is a systematic failure to recognise the role played by accumulation rather than exploitation as the dynamic of capitalist development. This itself may be due to the project of the left being reform within the existing economic order as opposed to revolutionary change. A challenge to the particular form exploitation takes can be accommodated as long as the prospect of future dynamic growth, under the existing conditions for capital accumulation, is maintained. However, a challenge to the process of capitalist accumulation itself leads inevitably to the presentation of an alternative method of economic development. For socialists, economic growth itself is a prospect offering hope and liberation for the mass of the world's population. Yet how can sustained, planned and crisis-free economic growth be achieved without a revolutionary challenge to the mechanisms of capitalist accumulation? Inevitably, an analysis of post-war economic growth which places questions of accumulation at the heart of its explanation leads to a view which recognises the need for revolutionary change.

The second reason for rejecting the consensus hypothesis lies in the fact that the historical record brings the very existence of a consensus into question. To demonstrate a consensus requires ignoring key aspects of the historical evidence. The Attlee government becomes a one-sided monolith, depending upon the left or right view of the consensus hypothesis that is accepted. Either the Attlee government adopted modernising polices under difficult international circumstances and opposition from a domestic employing class, which was highly politicised. In which case the degree to which the Attlee government appeased employer opposition is under-emphasised, and the government's deeply hostile response to independent working-class action is ignored entirely. Or alternatively, the Attlee government entrenched a conservative tripartism which prevented the market pressure supply-side reform would have brought, in which case the ready acceptance of reform and attempted modernisation is equally under-emphasised, while again government's hostility exhibited to independent working-class activity is again ignored.

The historical record demonstrates that a different relationship existed between the Attlee government, labour and capital. It sought to re-establish a stability to economic relationships that the depression had fractured and the Second World War tore apart. As Milward recognised, the nation state required rescuing after 1945.[38] This was a rescue both from itself in reducing the tendency towards war inherent within capitalist accumulation, and a rescue from alternatives to capitalist development deriving from the opposition of the working class to a return to the 1930s. The importance of an analysis rooted in capitalist accumulation goes further than providing an alternative view of the Attlee government. It also provides a unifying theory of the long boom and its subsequent collapse through the recognition played by the permanent arms economy. The long boom was indeed predicated upon a tacit consensus but one based upon cold-war imperialism and its resultant high arms expenditure.

12. The Twentieth Century
An Age of Extremes or an Age of Possibilities?

Chris Harman

'The most terrible century in Western history.' 'A century of wars and massacres.' 'The most violent century in human history'.[1]

The quotes are from one of Britain's best known liberal philosophers, a radical French agronomist and a conservative Nobel prize winner for literature. They are brought together at the beginning of Eric Hobsbawm's history of the world since 1914, which is entitled, *The Age of Extremes*. They sum up a century which has seen bloodletting and barbarity on an immense scale: 20 million dead in the First World War, 40 million dead in the Second World War, 6 million exterminated in the Nazi death camps, 10 million imprisoned, many to die, in Stalin's gulags, 4 million dead in the famine in the Ukraine and Kazakhstan, another 4 million dead in the famine British rule brought to Bengal in the early 1940s, a million killed in the French colonial war in Algeria, 2 million in the US war in Vietnam and Cambodia, countless numbers killed or forced to flee as refugees in the wave of civil wars that swept Africa, the Caucasus, Central America and the Balkans in the 1980s and 1990s. The century began with the barbarity of the Boer War (in which Africans and Boers alike died in British concentration camps) and the Belgian enslavement of the Congo; it ended with the barbarity of ethnic cleansing and aerial bombing in the Balkans and south-east Turkey.

Historians can debate whether the twentieth was more horrible than the fourteenth century in Europe (when the first great crisis of feudalism led to a halving of the population through famine, plague, war and civil war), or than the seventeenth century (when the devastation of the Thirty Years' War reduced the population of central Europe by about one-third). But the absolute level of privation, misery, violence and killing is not the real issue. What is horrifying about the twentieth century is that this was the first century in the history of mankind, or at least since the move from hunter-gathering to agriculture some 10 millennia ago, in which the material means existed to give everyone a better, and hunger and disease free, and more fulfilling life. It was the century of previously unimaginable technological change that opened up the prospect of ending the backbreaking toil that had been the fate of the mass of humanity. Yet the century saw the technology used to terrorise, dehumanise and kill.

People in the 1890s had not imagined it would be like this. A cult of progress dominated much intellectual life and popular opinion and certainly exercised sway over socialist movements of the time. This can be seen by looking at the debate which took place within the German movement over reform and revolution, between Eduard Bernstein, Karl Kautsky and the young Rosa Luxemburg. Bernstein felt able to claim that capitalist society was becoming more peaceful, more crisis-free, more humane, more egalitarian and more democratic:

> In advanced countries we see the privileges of the capitalist bourgeoisie yielding step-by-step to democratic organisations....The common interest gains power as opposed to private interest and the elementary sway of economic forces.[2]

Such a process could come to fruition without the 'dissolution of the modern state system'.[3] All that was necessary was a further spread of parliamentarianism, with socialists embracing a thoroughgoing 'liberalism'[4] and a policy of piecemeal reform within the existing system.

Karl Kautsky, the party's main theorist, denounced Bernstein's argument. Capitalism, he insisted, could not be reformed out of existence; at some point there had to be a 'struggle for power' and a 'social revolution'. But his practical conclusions were not very different to Bernstein's. The socialist revolution would come about, he argued, through the inevitable growth of the party vote, as the working class and the scientific intelligentsia alike saw the need for change.

Both Bernstein and Kautsky shared the optimistic 'scientism' or 'positivism' of the middle-class intelligentsia and believed in the mechanical inevitability of progress. For Bernstein, science, technology and democracy were turning capitalism into socialism in the here and now. Kautsky saw the process as taking place in the future, not the present, but he was just as certain about its mechanical inevitability: throughout history, changes in the forces of production had always, eventually, led to changes in the relations of production, and they would do so now, if people waited patiently. Neither Bernstein nor Kautsky suspected that barbarism was being prepared alongside the prerequisites for socialism.

Rosa Luxemburg's contribution to the debate was the most far-seeing. She insisted that the very processes which Bernstein saw as democratising, civilising and moderating capitalism were leading to a new period of crisis and imperialist conflicts. There is no doubt that the twentieth century vindicated Luxemburg and proved how facile was Bernstein's position and the position of those who have resurrected the notion of inevitable, conflict-free progress since—from Anthony Crosland, John Strachey and Daniel Bell in the 1950s[5] to Francis Fukuyama in the early 1990s. But in the 1890s even Luxemburg could not foresee the horror of the century ahead. There is a tone of the inevitability of socialism in her writings;[6] it was not until she was faced with the mad delirium of the First World War that she returned to a formula of Frederick Engels 'socialism or barbarism'. And by barbarism she did not just mean barbarity, but something more and worse: the destruction of civilisation and culture, as had taken place at the time of the collapse of the Roman Empire in the west.[7]

Recognising the barbarity of the twentieth century is one thing, explaining it another. Not, of course, that everyone is prepared even to recognise it. It hardly fits into the Third Way. I don't believe there is a Barbarity Zone in the Millennium Dome alongside the Spirit Zone and the Money Zone. Nevertheless, the mainstream thinkers quoted earlier have recognised this barbarity, and so does a lot of mainstream history. It is to be found, for instance, in several episodes of the BBC television series *A People's Century*. The problems arise when it comes to integrating the horror into the rest of the picture. It all too easily can appear as a purely irrational aberration, as some inexplicable product of the human psyche, or as the product of deranged individuals such as Mussolini or Hitler in the inter-war years, or of Saddam Hussein and Slobodan Milosevic in the 1990s: the 'great man' theory of history gives way to the 'evil man' theory of history. It can even be seen as the result of the attempt to recast society so as to get rid of its horrors this was the explanation of people like Talmon (in *The Rise of Totalitarian Democracy*) and Popper (in *The Poverty of Historicism* and *The Open Society and its Enemies*) 40 or 50 years ago. More recently it has been the explanation of influential postmodernists, for whom totalitarianism is the product of totalising theories. Rousseau and Marx get the blame for Hitler and Stalin and, presumably, Saddam Hussein and Slobodan Milosevic (such theorists forget, of course, the horror perpetrated by Henry Kissinger and encouraged by Madeleine Albright).

The one approach to history that should be able to explain the twentieth century is Marxism. There have been several important works on aspects of the century inspired by Marxism above all Trotsky on 1905 and 1917, but also lesser writers like Harold Isaacs on the Chinese revolutions of the 1920s, Angelo Tasca (writing under the name Rossi) on the rise of Italian fascism, C.L.R. James on the revolution in Haiti, Broué on the German Revolution of 1918–23 and the Spanish Revolution of 1936, Deutscher's biographies of

Trotsky and Stalin. But there has been an absence of attempts to provide an overview of worldwide developments. This is partly because, as we should never forget, the first generation of twentieth century Marxists usually ended up murdered: Rosa Luxemburg, Trotsky, Bukharin, Andreas Nin, Radek, Volosinov and scores of others; or like Gramsci, driven to premature deaths. It was also to a large extent a product of Stalinism: looking at the present might lead to unpleasant challenges to the party line, and so the best British Marxists looked at the seventeenth, eighteenth and early nineteenth centuries, the best French ones at the heroic years 1789–94.

The one recent exception is Eric Hobsbawm's *The Age of Extremes*. It is probably the most accessible account of the century, providing an overall vision which combines economics, politics, science and art. It is more successful by being more coherent than the BBC's *A People's Century*. It is seductive in its ambition and riveting in its drive. Yet it is also defective in a central way that I did not grasp until I began work on my own book, *A People's History of the World*.

Hobsbawm's book seems to be in the classic Marxist tradition of relating 'base' and 'superstructure', of 'history from below' and 'history from above'. It connects global economic trends of slump and boom, the rise and fall of political movements (its 'extremes'), intellectual fashions, changes in popular culture. In doing so it seems different from recent academic Marxist history, which has dealt simply with particular movements through 'history from below', without connecting them with wider, global trends. This means Hobsbawm conveys something missing from much academic Marxism, a sense of the system's repeated lurches towards barbarism in 1914, 1929, 1933, 1939 and, it is implied at the end, the early twenty-first century.

What is missing, however, is any real notion of an alternative to the threat of barbarism, apart from trying to hold fast to what exists at present. Faced with the First World War, Hobsbawm's conclusion is to bemoan the split in the working-class movement between the openly reformist and revolutionary wings. Faced with the rise of Nazism and fascism in the 1930s, he identifies with the Popular Front coalitions of France and Spain, although they failed miserably in their goal (the Popular Front majority elected to the French National Assembly in 1936 voted Pétain to power in 1940). Faced with the domination of Europe by German Nazism, his alternative lies in an alliance of socialists with British and US capitalism and Russian Stalinism, although the alliance led to Hiroshima, Nagasaki, the cold war, the Korean War, the Algerian War and the Vietnam War. Hobsbawm justifies his position by claiming that the choice was between what in the nineteenth century would have been called 'progress and reaction'.[8] Faced with the horror of the twentieth century, the alternative, was to...move back to the methods of the nineteenth century: the choice between socialism or barbarism becomes 'bourgeois democracy or barbarism'.

Socialism is mentioned through much of the book. But it is the socialism of the Russia (and to a lesser extent China, Vietnam and Cuba) embodied in Stalinism and dying with the events of 1989–91: four revolutions and a long, drawn-out funeral. But the force that classical Marxism saw as the historical protagonist of socialism hardly appears. The Russian Revolution receives a very positive treatment (a welcome contrast to the historical gibberish which has purported to be a history of the revolution since 1989); but the factory workers and the soviets (workers' councils) which were key to it get only passing mention.

The working class is the missing link throughout Hobsbawm's book; it makes an appearance only towards the end to be discussed in terms of lifestyle. There are only four index references in *The Age of Extremes* to trade unions. There are no references to such key expressions of working-class power in the twentieth century as the Spanish CNT, the American CIO, the French CGT, the Central Budapest Workers' Council; the Polish Solidarnosc is mentioned once. From this history you would not know that the occupation of factories was a key turning point in post-First World War Italian history or the sit-ins of June 1936 in French history between the wars. The huge concentrations of workers which characterised much of twentieth-century capitalism are missing: the River Rouge plant in Detroit, Renault Billancourt in Paris, FIAT Mirafiori in Turin, or the Lenin shipyard in Gdansk.

While the previous volume of Hobsbawm's history, *The Age of Imperialism*, the working class did get a chapter, in *The Age of Extremes* it is absent. It is as if Hobsbawm's attitude to the working class is the same as that which Marx says the bourgeoisie has towards history: it has been, but is no more. Hobsbawm wrote of the period leading up to the First World War:

> So far as the core countries of bourgeois society were concerned, what destroyed the stability of the *belle époque* was the situation in Russia, the Hapsburg Empire and the Balkans, and not in western Europe or even Germany. What made the British political situation dangerous on the eve of the war was not the rebellion of the workers, but the division within the ranks of the rulers.[9]

Hobsbawm's approach is to look at the larger picture of politics and economics in terms of bitter rows within ruling classes and between states. But the politics of such rows are not comprehensible without looking at how successful rival rulers are successful in wresting resources from the rest of society, that is, at the struggle to extract a surplus from the exploited classes. The drive of British, French and German capitalisms towards war in 1914 is incomprehensible without looking at this. It is what underlay their rows over spheres of influence, empires, support for client states, and so on. Similarly, you cannot understand why the German ruling class embraced Hitler after his vote had fallen by 2 million in the elections of the autumn of 1932, or why it allowed him to embark on the policies which led to the Second World

War, unless you start with its concern for the surplus.

The century was shaped by throwing ruling-class politics into disarray. Key moments were the syndicalist wave before 1914; the succumbing of workers to war in 1914; the revolutions in Russia 1917 and Germany 1918–1919; the occupation of factories in 1920 and the defeat of Italian workers in the two years after; the defeat of the union drive in steel in the US in 1919 and the collapse of the triple alliance in Britain in 1920; the rise and defeat the anti-colonial movements in Egypt, India, China, Ireland and Morocco in 1919–27; the collapse of the German workers' movement in the face of Nazism in 1933; the upsurge of the workers' movements in France in 1934–36; the rise of the CIO in 1936; the rising against the Francoist *coup* in Spain in July 1936; the containment of movements from below after 1936 opening the way to the Second World War; the resistance movements in Greece, Poland, Italy and, to a lesser extent, France; the containment of such movements after the war; the victories of the anti-colonial movement in India and of the People's Liberation Army in China; the solidification of the cold-war structure with the defeats and splitting of the workers' movements in France, Italy and Greece; the anti-Stalinist risings of 1953 and 1956; the workers' and students' movement of 1968; the anti-Francoist strikes of 1974–76, and the Portuguese Revolution of 1974–75.

Yet most of these events are missing from Hobsbawm's book, as much as from any conventional history of the century. There is not even the sense that, at minimum, class struggle always, at every point, lays down limits within which the system operates. Still less is there any awareness that there were points when workers were close to breaking through. For Hobsbawm, Marx's 'class in itself' rarely makes its presence felt; the 'class for itself', never.

The twentieth century was the century in which capitalism became a global system. There had been a global markets before that. But most of the participants in that market were pre-capitalist ruling classes or small producers controlling their own means of production; it is worth remembering that until the 1940s a huge proportion of the world's population were still subsistence farmers. In 1900, of the world's population of some 1500 million, perhaps 75 million were wage workers; of today's population of 6,000 million, probably more than 2 billion are.

The more wage labour spreads, the more the only source of surplus becomes its exploitation, rather than the extraction of rents and taxes from the peasantry; today there are very few countries in which the majority of national income is produced in agriculture, and a growing portion of agriculture is capitalist agriculture, even in Third World countries. Under these circumstances, success and sometimes even survival for any ruling class depends on reducing labour costs and forcing up productivity. The labour costs which matter are not just those of 'traditional' manual workers, but also of people in occupations that were regarded at the beginning of the century or even in the 1950s as 'middle class': clerical workers of all sorts, technicians, teachers and lecturers, nurses. Work supervision and payment systems that were confined to groups of manual workers a century ago are now being introduced across the board under the guises of 'flexibility', 'payment by results', 'market testing' and so on. There is a homogenisation of conditions and in consequence of lifestyles. Marx in 1843 first referred to workers as 'the universal class'. In fact, it is only at the end of the twentieth century that such a class began to exist worldwide as more than a relatively small proportion of the population.

Under such circumstances, the system is marked, as never before, by the flows of alienated wage labour. Unless these flows are mapped, the logic of the system cannot be seen, nor the logic of conflict between classes within the system. Historians do not see that these flows underlie the contingencies of economic, political and social history; sociologists see the proletarianisation of the working conditions of the salaried middle classes as an embourgeoisement of the lifestyles of the working class. Hobsbawm's history has room for some of the mechanical contrivances used by the system and for the lifestyles of some of the people within it, but no room for the connecting links: the pumping out of surplus value, the distribution of surplus value within the ruling class, the accumulation of surplus value, the waste of surplus value. It therefore has no room for explaining either the centrality of class conflict or the dynamic of class conflict.

This is not just a matter for the past, but also for the future. The collapse of the Eastern bloc and the end of the cold war at the end of the 1980s promised 'an end of history', with a 'New World Order' and a 'peace dividend'. Instead the 1990s witnessed economic collapse in much of the former Eastern bloc, a prolonged recession in Europe and Japan, a rash of civil wars, the aerial bombing of Baghdad and Belgrade, and an economic crisis across East Asia; at the time of writing there is speculation among mainstream economists as to how long the US stock exchange boom can last, and what are the implications for the rest of the world when it collapses. The emergence in major western European countries of fascist parties that used to be regarded as a near joke suggests that the ghosts of the 1930s are far from vanquished.

There are also new threats never imagined in the first half of the century. AIDS, is slashing into life expectancy in wide areas of Africa and threatening to engulf parts of Asia too; yet those who control the world's wealth refuse to release the relatively low level of funds needed to bring it under control. The endless pumping of carbon dioxide and other 'greenhouse' gases into the atmosphere is beginning to radically destabilise the world's climate, threatening both to flood major inhabited areas and to upset the balance of world food supplies; every major government acknowledges the threat; every major government continues with transport, energy and industrial policies which increase the level of greenhouse gases and the danger of a worldwide disaster. Finally, advances in technology continue to be transmuted into increased levels of destructive weaponry; the greatest economic military power, the US, has resumed the search for a

'Star Wars' anti-missile system which will free it from the fear of retaliation if it ever launches a nuclear 'first strike'; a whole range of lesser, medium-size powers are trying to develop their own 'micro' means of mass destruction to threaten each other with and to deter the US (or its nuclear client state, Israel) from one day threatening them with the aerial bombardment used against Baghdad and Belgrade; the result is that the twenty-first century will be a world no longer subject to the horrific deterrent logic of Mutually Assured Destruction. If the twentieth century witnessed recurrent barbarity, barbarism in the full sense of Rosa Luxemburg's use of the term is a very real prospect in the twenty-first century.

Hobsbawm's book comes close to recognising this. He concludes:

> We live in a world captured, rooted and upturned by the titanic economic and techno-scientific process of the development of capitalism, which has dominated for the past two or three centuries. We know that it cannot go on *ad infinitum*. The future cannot be a continuation of the past, and there are signs that we have reached a point of historic crisis. The forces generated by the techno-scientific economy are enough to destroy the environment, that is to say, the material foundations of human life...Our world risks both explosion and implosion. It must change...If humanity is to have a recognisable future, it cannot be by prolonging the past or present...The price of failure, that the alternative to a changed society, is darkness.[10]

But having made the diagnosis, Hobsbawm can offer no cure. His suggestions,[11] amounted to going along with Tony Blair's vision of New Labour, even if he has been critical of Blair since. He can offer no others, because the working class has disappeared from his scheme of things.[12]

Yet the last quarter of the twentieth century saw several major countries shaken by new upsurges of workers, even if workers did not take advantage of their successes to establish new states acting in their own interests. It was the entry of oil workers into struggles which pulled the carpet from under the Shah's regime in Iran in 1979; it was workers who showed how easy it was to puncture the totalitarian pretensions of the late Stalinist states with the Polish movement of 1980–81, and it was workers who dealt a death blow against forces looking towards a repressive solution to the problem of these states with the miners' strikes in the Soviet Union in 1989 and 1991; it was workers who shook the French conservative government, with its record parliamentary majority, in November and December 1995. In none of these cases were workers the major beneficiaries of their own actions: in Iran the gainers were the section of the bourgeoisie around Ayatollah Khomeini; in the Eastern bloc those sections of the old ruling class who jumped ship to embrace the market and their own versions of capitalist democracy; in France the rejuvenated social democracy of Jospin. The power the workers deployed was real enough; so too was their ability to draw in all the other discontented and oppressed groups in society. Their weakness was ideological, a willingness to accept definitions of what should be done provided by some of these other groups, especially the radical intelligentsia and disaffected members of the old ruling class. The result was what may be called 'deflected workers' movements'.

Yet the ideological weakness should not be a surprise. New classes that emerge with changes in production always start by accepting the definitions of society imposed on them by the old order. Their members have never known any other sort of society and take its assumptions for granted. Only as they are driven to struggle by the conditions under which they find themselves do they begin to develop new ways of seeing things, and even then they do not uniformly and immediately reject the old ways. What emerges is what Gramsci called 'contradictory consciousness' or what Lenin, speaking of the Russian working class at the beginning of the twentieth century, called 'trade union consciousness': a defensive challenge to certain aspects of the old society and its ideology, while continuing to accept other aspects. The history of the rise of the bourgeoisie is one of several-hundred years of such contradictory conceptions: on the one hand making wealth in ways very different to the feudal lords and adopting correspondingly new ideas, and on the other wanting to rise within existing society and accepting its old ideas. Such contradictory notions cost the bourgeois dear in many of its early battles to defend itself as society moved into crisis: its deference to the old order led it to suffer devastating setbacks in places like northern Italy, Germany and France in the sixteenth and seventeenth centuries; when it broke through in England in 1649 and France in 1789–94, it was because a minority emerged within the bourgeoisie which was prepared to work with poorer sections of the middle class to impose its will on the rest of its own class as well as on the defenders of the old order.

There is no reason to expect the working class to do what the bourgeoisie never did, and move overnight to a new, pure and a non-contradictory world view. The history of industrial capitalism so far has been of sections of workers moving in this direction, and then suffering defeat and demoralisation. The second quarter of the twentieth century saw defeats on a massive scale: the isolation of the Russian Revolution and rise of Stalinism, the defeat of the German working class and the conquests by Nazism. After the defeat in Germany the most militant workers, desperate for an alternative to Nazism but lacking faith in their own ability to fight successfully, put their faith in Stalinism on the one hand and the 'democratic' bourgeois politicians on the other. This led the great waves of workers struggles, in 1934–36 and in 1943–45 into compromise with the system and to defeat.

An important factor in the second half of the twentieth century was the growth of a new working class—they were the children of peasants, not of previous generations of class-conscious workers and often of peasants living hundreds of miles away. Only a minority of those who occupied the French factories in 1968 were the children of those who had done so in 1936; few of the Spanish workers who took on Francoism in the mid-1970s had more than tenuous links with the revolutionary anarcho-syndicalist and socialist workers of the mid-1930s; virtually none of the Russian miners who were so important in 1989 and 1991 had any connection back the working class of 1917. Every lesson had to be learnt over again; the ideological development of a growing class had to start again, near the beginning.

The beginning is not the end. The workers' movements of the last quarter of the twentieth century, deflected though they were, were also a foretaste of what we should expect from the larger than ever, more universal than ever, working class which enters the new millennium. The most literate, the most cultured, the most homogenous exploited class the world has ever known faces a period every bit as dangerous as Hobsbawm suggests. But Hobsbawm does not see that the dynamics of the system itself will force workers to struggle, and that when they struggle they will have the potential to adopt the new world view necessary to lead humanity as whole away from barbarism and towards socialism. Whether this potential is realised depends upon the degree to which the minority of workers and intellectuals who are already won to the new world view are successful in agitating, organising and educating their fellows.

Notes

The Best of Times, the Worst of Times? The Twentieth Century in Retrospect
Keith Flett and David Renton

1. M. Gilbert, *A History of the Twentieth Century: Volume 1, 1900–1933*, London, 1997; S. Rowbotham, *A Century of Women: The History of Women in Britain and the United States*, London, 1997.
2. *Time*, December 1998; also 'Reflections on the Twentieth Century', *The Economist*, 11–16 September 1999. *Time*'s arguments have trickled down into the academic mainstream, as in T. Smith, *America's Mission: The United States and the Worldwide Struggle for Democracy in the Twentieth Century*, Princeton, 1994.
3. E.J. Hobsbawm, *The Age of Extremes: The Short Twentieth Century 1914–1991*, London, 1994, p.1.
4. C. Denny and V. Brittain, 'UN Attacks Growing Gulf between Rich and Poor', *Guardian*, 13 July 1999.
5. 'The Radical Twentieth Century', *New Internationalist*, January-February 1999; also S. Milne, 'The Twentieth Century: Political Activism', *Guardian*, 14 August 1999.
6. M. Walker, *The Cold War and the Making of the Modern World*, London, 1993, pp.354–5.
7. C. Caufield, *Masters of Illusion: The World Bank and the Poverty of Nations*, Basingstoke, 1997 edn, p.162.
8. S. Rowbotham, op.cit., pp.575–6.
9. Ibid., p.574.
10. E.J. Hobsbawm, *The Age of Extremes*, op.cit., p.8.
11. S. Totten et al., *Century of Genocide: Eyewitness Accounts and*

Critical Views, New York and London, 1997.

12. C. Ponting, *Progress and Barbarism: The World in the Twentieth Century*, London, 1998, p.11.

13. F. Fukuyama, *The End of History and the Last Man*, London, 1992 edn, p.3; H. Arendt, *The Origins of Totalitarianism*, New York and London, 1973 edn, p.vii.

14. C. Ponting, op.cit.; E.J. Hobsbawm, op.cit.; M. Gilbert, op.cit., p.1.

15. Examples of this literature include R.J. Ross and C. Trachte, *Global Capitalism: The New Leviathan*, New York, 1990; and D.A. Smith and J. Böröcz, *A New World Order? Global Transformations in the late Twentieth Century*, Westport and London, 1995.

16. D. Gluckstein, *The Nazis, Capitalism and the Working Class*, London, 1999; there is a similar perspective in D. Renton, *Fascism: Theory and Practice*, London, 1999, pp.30–43.

17. M. Haynes, 'Patterns of Change in Nineteenth Century Europe', unpublished paper, 1998.

18. M. Gilbert, op.cit., Vol.1, p.4.

19. W. Sombart, *Why is there no Socialism in the United States?*, C.T. Husbands (ed.), London, 1976.

20. G. Orwell, *Homage to Catalonia*, Harmondsworth, Penguin, 1966, pp.7–9; C. Barker, 'Poland 1980–1981: The Self-Limiting Revolution', in C. Barker (ed.), *Revolutionary Rehearsals*, London, 1987, pp.169–216.

21. Cited in A. Callinicos, *Theories and Narratives: Reflections on the Philosophy of History*, Cambridge, 1995, p.152.

22. V. Serge, *Memoirs of a Revolutionary 1901–1941*, P. Sedgwick (trans and ed.), Oxford and New York, 1963, p.67, quoted in I. Birchall, below. E.J. Hobsbawm, *The Age of Extremes*, op.cit., p.71.

1. Globalisation in the Twentieth Century
Adrian Budd

1. See K. Ohmae, *The Borderless World*, London, 1990.

2. Gerhard Schröder, 'German economic policy from a European and global perspective', in Dieter Dettke (ed.) *The Challenge of Globalization for Germany's Social Democracy. A Policy Agenda for the 21st Century*, Oxford, 1998, p.11. For a comprehensive

account of one neoliberal modernisation, under a Labour government, of an advanced economy, New Zealand, see Jane Kelsey, *Economic Fundamentalism*, London, 1995.

3. A. Giddens, *The Consequences of Modernity*, Cambridge, 1990, p.64. D. Harvey, *The Condition of Postmodernity*, Oxford, 1989.

4. To say that the processes of globalisation are the product of capitalism is not to present a monocausal argument. See David Held et al., *Global Transformations. Politics, Economics and Culture*, Cambridge, 1999, p.12. Capitalism is not a unity but a differentiated totality of social relations: all economic behaviour is embedded in cultural and political structures and ways of thinking. It is bourgeois social science that reduces these into separate 'specialisms'—economics, culture, politics, etc.

5. P. Hirst and G. Thompson, *Globalization in Question*, Cambridge 1996. For more journalistic accounts see H.-P. Martin and H. Schumann, *The Global Trap*, London, 1997; V. Forrester, *The Economic Horror*, Cambridge, 1999.

6. To take this book as an example. It is written in English, an Indo-European language developed by Germanic peoples with elements from Latin using an alphabet of Phoenician origin. Page numbers are Arabic. The method of printing until recently used movable type developed by the Chinese.

7. Karl Marx and Frederick Engels, 'Manifesto of the Communist Party', in *Karl Marx, Selected Works*, Vol.1, London, 1942, p.209.

8. E.J. Hobsbawm, *The Age of Empire, 1875–1914*, London, 1987, p.13.

9. Ibid., p.50.

10. N. Bukharin, *Imperialism and World Economy*, London, 1987, p.36.

11. E.J. Hobsbawm, op.cit., p.47.

12. M. Chamberlain, *The New Imperialism*, London, 1970, p.22.

13. E.J. Hobsbawm, op.cit., p.66.

14. N. Bukharin, op.cit., p.42.

15. Ibid., p.62.

16. See R. Robertson, 'Social theory, cultural relativity and the problem of globality', in A. King (ed.), *Culture, Globalization and the World System*, London, 1991.

17. B. Anderson, *Imagined Communities: Reflections*. See also E.J.

Hobsbawm, *Nations and nationalism since 1870*, London, 1994.

18. Quoted in N. Bukharin, op.cit., p.109.
19. See E.J. Hobsbawm and T. Ranger (eds), *The Invention of Tradition*, London, especially the chapter by D. Cannadine on the British monarchy.
21. M. Chamberlain, op.cit., p.38.
21. R. Holton, *Globalization and the Nation-State*, London, 1998, p.22. See also M. Mann, 'Nation-states in Europe and other continents: diversifying, developing not dying', *Daedulus*, summer, 1993.
22. J. Holloway, 'Global capital and the National State', in W. Bonefeld and J. Holloway (eds), *Global Capital, National State and the Politics of Money*, London, 1995, p.123.
23. 'Although the benefits and costs of the protective tariff, viewed in their totality, are probably very nearly equal, and theoretically the interests supporting and opposed to the legislation are, therefore, likewise approximately equal, the pressures exerted on Congress are extremely unbalanced'. E. Schattschneider, *Politics, Pressures and the Tariff*, New York 1935, p.285. Quoted in R. Riezman and J. Wilson, 'Politics and trade policy', in J. Banks and E. Hanushek (eds), *Modern Political Economy. Old Topics, New Directions*, Cambridge 1995, p.111. See also H. Milner.
24. L. Trotsky, *The Permanent Revolution and Results and Prospects*, New York, 1969, p.146.
25. See G. Kolko, *The Politics of War. The World and United States Foreign Policy 1943–1945*, New York, 1968.
26. Quoted in S. Ambrose, *Rise to Globalism. American foreign policy, 1938–1980*, London, 1980, p.103.
27. See A. Milward, *The Reconstruction of Western Europe*, London, 1984.
28. W. Ruigrok and R. van Tulder, *The Logic of International Restructuring*, London, 1995, p.125.
29. Although Keynesian demand management took a good deal of the credit for the boom, it was chiefly used to slow expansion down. The key to the boom lies elsewhere. See Michael Haynes's chapter elsewhere in this book.
30. See A. Giddens, op.cit., M. Albrow and E. King (eds), *Globalization, Knowledge and Society*, London, 1990; D.

Harvey, op.cit., Roland Robertson, op.cit., K. Ohmae, op.cit., J. Gray, *False Dawn. The Delusions of Global Capitalism*, London, 1998.

31. Quote in A. Hoogvelt, *Globalisation and the Postcolonial World. The New Political Economy of Development*, London, 1997, p.83. Figures from L. Elliott and C. Denny, *Guardian*, 12 July 1991.

32. P. Hirst and G. Thompson, op.cit., p.68. On third world trade shares see R. Kiely, 'Transnational companies, global capital and the Third World', in R. Kiely and P. Marfleet (eds), *Globalisation and the Third World*, London 1998, pp.49–50.

33. G. Garrett and D. Mitchell, 'Globalization and the welfare state: income transfers in the industrial democracies, 1966–90', unpublished paper presented to the American Political Science Association, 1996, discussed in Holton, op.cit., p.93.

34. See A. Amin and N. Thrift, 'Living in the Global', in A. Amin and N. Thrift (eds), *Globalization, Institutions, and Regional Development in Europe*, Oxford 1994; P. Dicken, M. Forsgren and A. Malmberg, 'Local embeddedness of transnational corporations', in A. Amin and N. Thrift (eds), op.cit., J.H. Dunning, *The Globalization of Business*, London, 1993.

35. See E. Schoenberger, 'Globalization and regionalization: New problems of time, distance and control in the multinational firm' presented to the Association of American Geographers, Miami, 1991.

36. A. Hoogvelt, op.cit., pp.76–7.

37. See A. Hoogvelt, op.cit., pp.69–75.

38. P. Hirst and G. Thompson, op.cit., p.112.

39. W. Ruigrok and R. van Tulder, op.cit., p.156, quoting figures from UNCTAD, *World Investment Report 1993: Transnational Corporations and Integrated International Production*, New York, 1993, p.28.

40. J. Allen, 'Crossing borders: footloose multinationals?', in J. Allen and C. Hamnett (eds), *A Shrinking World?*, Oxford 1995, p.67; P. Hirst and G. Thompson, op.cit., p.115 and p.98.

41. The UN World Investment Report for 1995, *Transnational Corporations and Competitiveness*, pp.192–7 showed that in 1992, 37.2% of US exports and 42.5% of imports were intra-firm.

42. See S. Cohen, 'Geo-economics and America's mistakes', in M. Carnoy (ed.), *The New Global Economy in the Information Age*, London 1993, p.98. Quoted in A. Hoogvelt, op.cit., p.123.

43. 4 June 86–7.

44. *Business Week*, 27 January 1997, cover story 'Two Japans'. My thanks to Pete Green for pointing this out to me.

45. See table pp.170–3.

46. June 1987.

47. For counter-arguments to mine which emphasise local production see K. Moody, *Workers in a Lean World. Unions in the International Economy*, London, 1997, part I; F. Fox Piven and R. Cloward, 'Eras of power', *Monthly Review*, January 1998; E.M. Wood, 'Capitalism, globalization and epochal shifts', *Monthly Review*, February 1997.

48. Quoted in J. McCormick and N. Stone, 'From national champion to global competitor', *Harvard Business Review*, May/June 1990, p.135.

49. A. Giddens, *The Third Way. The Renewal of Social Democracy*, Cambridge, 1998, p.31. Robert Holton, while accepting that the state's role has been reconfigured, rightly argues for its 'continuing robustness', op.cit., p.10.

50. Ibid., p.145.

51. See C. Harman, 'The state and capitalism today', *International Socialism*, 51, 1991.

52. On postwar Japan see M. Itoh, *The World Economic Crisis and Japanese Capitalism*, London, 1990; for a short treatment of the defeats that paved the way for 'Japanisation' see A. Budd, 'The contradictions and crisis of stake-holder capitalism', *Contemporary Politics*, Vol.3, No.2, 1997.

53. J. Petras, 'The Imperial State System', paper presented to the American Political Science Association, Washington DC, referred to in R. Cox, *Approaches to World Order*, Cambridge 1996, p.106. On Europe see S. Andersen and K. Eliassen (eds), *Making Policy in Europe. The Europeification of National Policy-making*, London, 1993.

54. P. Bourdieu, *Acts of Resistance*, Cambridge, 1998.

55. A. Hoogvelt, op.cit., p.169. See also P. Mosley, et al., *Aid and Power*, London, 1991; S. Krasner, *Structural Conflict: The Third World Against Liberalism*, Berkeley, CA, 1995.

56. A. Budd, 'Global Politics: Towards Tripolarism?', *South Bank*

Occasional Papers in Politics, No.2, 1993, p.7.

57. R. Cox, 'Global Perestroika', in R. Miliband and L. Panitch (eds), *New World Order?: Socialist Register*, 1992, London, 1992, p.27.
58. A. Hoogvelt, op.cit., p.164.
59. R. Cox, 'Critical Political Economy', in B. Hettne (ed.), *International Political Economy. Understanding Global Disorder*, London, 1995, p.41.
60. I. Wallerstein, *Utopistics. Or Historical Choices of the Twenty-first Century*, New York, 1998, p.32.
61. A. Hoogvelt, op.cit., p.175. See also W. Reno, 'Markets, war, and the reconfiguartion of political authority in Sierra Leone', *Canadian Journal of African Studies* 29 (2), 1995.
62. *Guardian*, 7 July 1999.
63. Cresson quoted in R. Kiely, op.cit., p.16.
64. On EU limitations on the free movement of people and its associated political project see P. Marfleet, 'Migration and the refugee experience', in R. Kiely and P. Marfleet (eds), op.cit.; G. Delanty, *Inventing Europe: Idea, Identity, Reality*, Basingstoke, 1995.
65. G. Soros, *Soros on Soros*, New York, 1995.
66. N. Bukharin, op.cit., p.87.
67. Quoted in *Financial Times*, 18 September 1993.

2. One Step Forwards, Two Steps Back
Esther Leslie

1. Sometimes the word 'Kultur' in this quotation is translated as 'civilisation'.
2. See W. Benjamin, *One-Way Street and Other Writings*, London, 1979, p.359.
3. Ibid., p.360.
4. Ibid., p.350.
5. Ibid., p.356.
6. Benjamin did not give these 'theses' a title, nor did he necessarily intend them to be published.
7. Walter Benjamin: 'Thesis VII on the Philosophy of History' in *Illuminations*, London, 1992, p.248.
8. Ibid.
9. The physical destruction of this cultural booty was not carried

out wholesale. Some were burnt as a propagandistic gesture, but not all. In 1938 Göring expressed an interest in selling the confiscated and vilified 'cultural-bolshevik' artefacts of the 'Degenerate Art Exhibition' for foreign currency. What Hitler considered 'garbage' was to be converted into gold. Stephanie Barron recounts the story of the auction at the Galerie Fischer in Lucerne where over one-hundred works of 'degenerate' art, described as 'Modern Masters from German Museums', were put up for sale on 30 June 1939. Much of the stock was sold to private collectors in the United States and a small amount went to museums in Liege and Basle. See Stephanie Barron, 'The Galerie Fischer Auction', in *Degenerate Art: the Fate of the Avant-Garde in Nazi Germany*, Los Angeles, 1991. (LACMA exhibition catalogue published in conjunction with 1991 exhibit at Los Angeles County Museum of Art and the Art Institute of Chicago.)

10. See W. Benjamin, *One-Way Street*, op.cit., p.359.
11. See the final section of 'The Work of Art in the Age of Mechanical Reproduction', W. Benjamin, *Illuminations*, op.cit.
12. Quoted in W. Benjamin, *One-Way Street*, op.cit., p.359.
13. See W. Benjamin, *Gesammelte Schriften* (*GS*) VI, Frankfurt, 1991, pp.171, 457–8.
14. This idea is voiced in the collection of notes—known as *The Passagenwerk* (*Arcades Project*)—and written over the last fifteen years of Benjamin's life. See 'Konvolut N., erkenntnistheoretisches, Theorie des Fortschritts' in the *Passagenwerk* (1937–1940) *GS* V, part 1, pp.598–9. In English as Walter Benjamin, *The Arcades Project*, translated by Howard Eiland and Kevin McLaughlin, Cambridge, MA, 1999, p.478.
15. W. Benjamin, *Illuminations*, op.cit., p.250.
16. Ibid., p.251.
17. See 'Konvolut J; Baudelaire' op.cit., p.432.
18. W. Benjamin, *Illuminations*, op.cit., p.250.
19. W. Benjamin, *One-Way Street*, op.cit., p.358.
20. Notes for 'Über den Begriff der Geschichte' *GS* I3, p.1232.
21. Ibid., p.1231.
22. The quotation is taken from *Socialism and the Political Struggle* (1883), quoted at the start of Adam Westoby's *The Evolution of Communism*, Cambridge 1989.

23. See *Marx Engels Werke*, Vol.20, Berlin, 1962 p.146.
24. W. Benjamin: 'Thesis XII on the Philosophy of History', op.cit., p.250.
25. See *GS* 13, p.1226.
26. W. Benjamin, *Illuminations*, London, 1992, pp.251–2.
27. *GS* V1, p.593. 'N' in Gary Smith (ed.), *Benjamin; Philosophy, History, Aesthetics*, Chicago, 1989, p.66.
28. W. Benjamin, *One-Way Street*, op.cit., p.80.
29. Ibid.
30. For a genealogy of the term see Michael Löwy's article 'Rosa Luxemburg's Conception of 'Socialism or Barbarism' in *On Changing the World*, New Jersey, 1993, pp.91–9. For a rebuff of accusations of a productivist bias in Marx and the claim that the derivation of the idea of 'Socialism or Barbarism' is to be found in Marx's 1845–6 writings, see István Mészáros, *The Power of Ideology*, Brighton, 1989, p.34.
31. See F. Jung, *Der Weg nach Unten*, 1961, Hamburg, 1988.
32. See *Bozena Choluj: Deutsche Schriftsteller im Banne der Novemberrevolution 1918*, Wiesbaden, 1991, p.135.
33. From 'Das Stachelschwein', Berlin, 1927, reprinted in Peter Pachnicke and Klaus Honnef (eds), *John Heartfield*, New York, 1992, p.108.
34. See F. Jung, *Die Eroberug der Maschinen*, Berlin, 1923, p.172.
35. F. Jung, op.cit., pp.360–3.

3. Daughters of the Century
Anne Alexander

1. See for example F. Fukuyama, *The Great Disruption*, London, 1999.
2. K. Millet, *Sexual Politics*, London, 1971, p.38.
3. T. Cliff, *Class Struggle and Women's Liberation: 1640 to the Present Day*, London, 1984, p.56.
4. E. Carpenter, *My Days and Dreams*, cited in S. Rowbotham and J. Weeks, *Socialism and the New Life: The Personal and Sexual Politics of Edward Carpenter and Havelock Ellis*, London, 1977, p.27.
5. S. Rowbotham, *Hidden from History: 300 Years of Women's Oppression and the Fight Against It*, London, 1973, p.77.
6. S. Rowbotham, op.cit., p.89.

7. G. Dangerfield, *The Strange Death of Liberal England*, London, 1997 edn, p.311.
8. T. Cliff, op.cit., p.67.
9. Ibid., p.79.
10. Ibid., p.73.
11. Ibid., p.76.
12. C. Rosenberg, *Women and Perestroika*, London, 1987, p.71.
13. L. Trotsky, *History of the Russian Revolution*, London, 1997 edn, p.109.
14. C. Rosenberg, op.cit., p.79.
15. A. Kollontai, *Selected Writings*, London, 1977, pp.14–15.
16. Ibid., p.43.
17. C. Koonz, *Mothers in the Fatherland: Women, the Family and Nazi Politics*, London, 1987, p.22.
18. Ibid., p.36.
19. D. Renton, 'Entartete Musik', *Socialist Review*, March 1997.
20. R. Evans, *Comrades and Sisters: Feminism, Socialism and Pacifism in Europe 1870–1945*, Brighton, 1987, p.170.
21. C. Rosenberg, op.cit., p.88.
22. Ibid., p.95.
23. K. Millett, op.cit., p.174.
24. S. Rowbotham, op.cit., p.3.
25. B. Friedan, *The Feminine Mystique*, quoted in S. Rowbotham, op.cit., p.3.
26. H. Marcuse, *An Essay on Liberation*, London, 1970, p.82.
27. S. Smith, 'Mistaken Identity—or can Identity Politics liberate the oppressed?', *International Socialism Journal*, 62, 1994, pp.3–51.
28. S. Rowbotham, op.cit., p.21.
29. D. Widgery, *Preserving Disorder*, London, 1989, p.109.
30. S. Smith, op.cit., p.9.
31. A. Marwick, *The Sixties: Cultural Revolution in Britain, France, Italy and the United States, c.1958–c.1974*, Oxford, 1998, p.685.
32. The press both at the time and ever since, failed to notice that no bras actually got burnt on the demonstration. The New York Women, who called the protest set up a 'freedom trash can' and invited women to bring along bras, high heels and suspenders to symbolically trash.
33. M.C. Lynn (ed.), *Women's Liberation in the Twentieth Century*

New York, 1975, p.113.
34. S. Smith, op.cit., p.10.
35. Ibid., p.7.
36. Ibid., p.11.
37. *Women's Voice*, January 1975.
38. Ibid.
39. L. German, *Sex, Class and Socialism*, London, 1994 edn, p.182.
40. *Women's Voice*, November 1975.
41. L. German, op.cit., p.178.
42. S. Rowbotham, L. Segal and H. Wainwright, *Beyond the Fragments: Feminism and the Making of Socialism*, London, 1979, p.1.
43. S. Faludi, *Backlash: The Undeclared War against Women*, London, 1992, p.263.
44. S. Rowbotham, L. Segal and H. Wainwright, op.cit., p.6.
45. L. Segal, *Is the Future Female? Troubled Thoughts on Contemporary Feminism*, London, 1987, p.5.
46. Ibid., p.16.
47. Ibid., p.177.
48. Ibid., p.112.
49. Ibid., p.164.
50. S. Lansley, S. Goss and C. Wolmar, *Councils in Conflict: The Rise and Fall of the Municipal Left*, London, 1989, p.144.
51. Faludi, *Backlash*, op.cit.
52. L. German and R. Hoveman, *A Socialist Review*, London, 1998, p.314.
53. L. German, op.cit., p.viii.

4. Reformism at the Polls
Andrew Strouthous

I would like to thank Keith Flett and David Renton for persuading me to write this essay. Rick Halpern, Peter Alexander and David Renton all made very useful comments on an earlier draft. Special thanks to Ian Birchall for his corrections and perceptive comments on the final draft.

1. Werner Sombart, *Why Is There No Socialism In The United States?*, White Plains, 1976 edn, orig.1906.
2. Rick Halpern and Jonathan Morris (eds), *American

Exceptionalism? US Working Class Formation in an International Context, Basingstoke, 1996, p.2.

3. See Seymour Martin Lipset, *American Exceptionalism: A Double Edged Sword*, New York, 1996 for a general exposition of the exceptionalist position.

4. There is a much older historiography which mostly takes the form of unpublished dissertations, many written over 40 or 50 years ago. These include Harry B. Sell, 'The A.F. of L. And The Labor Party Movement of 1918–20', MA thesis, University of Chicago, 1922; Lawrence Rogin, 'Central Labor Bodies and Independent Political Action in New York City: 1918–22', MA thesis, Columbia University, 1931; David Dolnick, 'The Role of Labor in Chicago Politics Since 1919', MA, Chicago University, 1939; Roger Horowitz, 'The Failure of Independent Political Action: The Labor Party of Cook County, 1919–20', Bachelor's Essay, University of Chicago, 1982; David Fickes Simonson, 'The Labor Party Of Cook County, Illinois, 1918–19', MA thesis, University of Chicago, 1959; John Howard Keiser, 'John Fitzpatrick and Progressive Unionism 1915–25', PhD thesis, Northwestern University, 1965; Stanley Shapiro, 'Hand and Brain: The Farmer Labor Party of 1920', PhD thesis, University of California, 1967; Hamilton Cravens, 'A History of The Washington Farmer Labor Party 1918–24', MA thesis, University of Washington, 1962; Jonathan Dembo, *Unions and Politics in Washington State 1885–1935*, New York, 1983.

5. Gwendolyn Mink, *Old Labor and New Immigrants in American Political Development*, Ithaca, 1986, p.18. The old school of labour history's theory that US trade unions restricted themselves to 'job consciousness' is illustrated in J.R. Commons, *History of Labor in the United States*, 4 Vols, New York, 1935–6, and Selig Perlman, *A Theory of the Labor Movement*, New York, 1923. Marc Karson, *American Labor Unions and Politics 1900–18*, Boston, 1958, and G. Mink, op.cit., continue to reinforce this argument up to the present day.

6. Richard White, 'Other Wests', *The West*, Geoffrey C. Ward, London, 1996, p.48; For further debate on exceptionalism, and working-class history see Rick Halpern and Jonathan Morris (eds), *American Exceptionalism?*; Seymour Martin Lipset, *American Exceptionalism*.

7. For a more comprehensive history see A.G. Strouthous, 'A Comparative Study of Independent Working-Class Politics: The American Federation of Labor and Third Party Movement in New York, Chicago, and Seattle, 1918–24', PhD, London University, 1996; Andrew Strouthous, *US Labor and Political Action 1918–24*, London, 2000.

8. Prior to the war the AFL advocated the principle of voluntarism, the belief that workers should improve their conditions through their own economic organisation, and not depend on the state for reform. This anti-statist philosophy argued that state involvement in the industrial field would deprive workers of their rights and constrain the exercising of their economic power.

9. Railroads were 99.1% in favour, but printers gave a 90.8% negative vote. Miners strongly approved 6,310 UMWA members voted overwhelmingly in favour. Of 60 locals participating 48 voted unanimously for, but only one unanimously against. The votes of the six City Central trades' councils stood 85% for and 15% against. *The Intercollegiate Socialist*, Vol.V11, 4, April-May 1919, pp.15–16.

10. The city could challenge London for the title of trade-union capital of the world. Possibly one-third of those members worked in the packing houses, where militant shop committees united the activists of dozens of craft unions. The Chicago Federation of Labor defiantly used sympathy strikes as the touchstone of its success. Montgomery, *Worker's Control*, p.57.

11. See James Weinstein, *The Decline Of Socialism In America*, New York, 1967, ch.4 for full details of the split in the Socialist Party.

12. James P. Cannon, *The First Ten Years of American Communism*, New York, 1973, p.59.

13. *Majority*, 24 April 1920 reported a print run of 5,500. Circulation was spasmodic, increasing to as high as 17,500, during strikes and declining afterwards. *Majority*, 31 July 1920.

14. Ibid., 1 March 1919.

15. Ibid., 5 April 1919, D.F. Simonson, op.cit., pp.74–6.

16. Ibid., p.78.

17. Democratic objections forced Clara Masilotti off the ballot paper, and she ran as a 'write in' candidate. D.F. Simonson, op.cit., pp.69, 81–4; Edward R. Kantowicz, *Polish-American*

Politics in Chicago 1888–1940, Chicago, 1975, p.142.

18. *Majority*, 4 December 1920; E. Kantowicz, op.cit., pp.108, 120, 143.

19. *Congressional Quarterly's Guide to US Elections*, 1976, p.286; Harry B. Sell, 'The A.F. of L. And The Labor Party Movement of 1918–20', MA thesis, University of Chicago, 1922, p.142.

20. *Congressional Quarterly Guide to US Elections*, p.743; Shannon, p.158; John Patrick Buckley, *The New York Irish: Their View of American Foreign Policy 1914–21*, New York, 1976), pp.11, 182–4, *passim*.

21. See A. Strouthous, *US Labor and Political Action*, for a more comprehensive explanation.

22. Ibid.

23. The only major exception to this failure was the Minnesota Farmer-Labor Party which remained successful right in to the 1940s. Richard M. Valelly, *Radicalism in the States Minnesota Farmer-Labor Party and the American Political Economy*, Chicago, 1989.

24. As mentioned in above note the Minnesota FLP remained strong, and in Seattle a sizeable rump of railroad workers continued to support the FLP.

25. Kenneth Campbell MacKay, the major historian of the 1924 La Follette presidential campaign, concentrates on national events and institutions leading him to underestimate the AFL's contribution. Ever since the importance of organised labour's importance to the 1924 campaign has been underestimated. Kenneth Campbell MacKay, *The Progressive Movement of 1924*, New York, 1972 edn, 1947.

26. For detailed evidence see A. Strouthous, *US Labor*; and R. Valelly, op.cit.

27. James P. Cannon described the intervention in the presidential campaign of 1924 as sectarian, op.cit., p.129.

28. See David Milton, *The Politics of US Labour*, London and New York, 1982, for full details of trade unions and politics in the 1930s.

29. Richard White, op.cit., p.48.

5. John Reed and the United States of America
John Newsinger

1. There are a number of biographical studies of John Reed. Of particular interest are Granville Hicks, *John Reed: The Making of a Revolutionary*, New York, 1936; Robert Rosenstone, *Romantic Revolutionary: A Biography of John Reed*, Cambridge, MA, 1976; and Eric Homberger, *John Reed*, Manchester, 1990.
2. For the Paterson strike see Anne Huber Tripp, *The IWW and the Paterson Silk Strike of 1913*, Urbana, IL, 1987, and Steve Gaolin, *The Fragile Bridge: Paterson Silk Strike 1913*, Philadelphia, 1988.
3. Helen C. Camp, *Iron In Her Soul: Elizabeth Gurley Flynn and the American Left*, Washington, 1995, p.50.
4. Philip S. Foner, *History of the Labour Movement in the United States: The Industrial Workers of the World 4*, New York, 1973, p.360.
5. Tripp, op.cit., p.140.
6. John Newsinger (ed.), *Shaking the World: Revolutionary Journalism by John Reed*, London, 1998, p.5.
7. Ibid., xiii.
8. For the IWW see Foner, op.cit., and Melvyn Dubofsky, *We Shall Be All*, Chicago, 1969.
9. J. Newsinger, op.cit., p.229.
10. For the pageant see Martin Green, *New York, 1913: The Armory Show and the Paterson Pageant*, New York, 1988.
11. P. Foner, op cit., pp.362–4.
12. For the Colorado War see George S. McGovern and Leonard F. Gutridge, *The Great Coalfield War*, Boston, 1972 and Priscilla Long, *Where The Sun Never Shines: A History of America's Bloody Coal Industry*, New York, 1987.
13. Philip S. Foner, *History of the Labor Movement in the United States: The AFL in the Progressive Era 5*, New York, 1980, p.202.
14. Ibid., p.207.
15. Reprinted in J. Newsinger, op.cit.
16. Eric Homburger, *American Writers and Radical Politics 1900–39*, London, 1986, p.65.
17. Foner, The AFL in *The Progressive Era*, op.cit., pp.209–10.
18. J. Newsinger, op.cit., pp.221–2.

19. Patricia Cayo Sexton, *The War on Labor and the Left*, Boulder, CO, 1991, p.55.
20. Ibid., pp.80–3. See also chapters 3 and 4 of William E. Forbath, *Law and the Shaping of the American Labor Movement*, Cambridge, MA, 1991.
21. John Reed, *Daughter of the Revolution and Other Stories*, New York, 1927, p.164.
22. Nick Salvatore, *Eugene V. Debs: Citizen and Socialist*, Urbana, IL, 1982, pp.291–301.
23. Julian Jaffe, *Crusade Against Radicalism: New York during the Red Scare 1914–1924*, New York, 1972.
24. *The New York Communist*, 19 April 1919.
25. Philip S. Foner, *History of the Labor Movement in the United States: Post War Struggles 1918–1920*, 8, New York 1988, p.63.
26. Robert K. Murray, *Red Scare: A Study in National Hysteria*, Minneapolis, 1955, p.111.
27. J. Jaffe, op.cit., p.77.
28. J. Newsinger, op.cit., pp.198–201.

6. The Success and Failure of the Comintern
Ian Birchall

1. 'Manifesto of the Communist International to the Proletariat of the Entire World', drafted by Trotsky and adopted by the founding Congress on 6 March 1919. J. Degras (ed.), *The Communist International*, London, 1971, I, 46.
2. P. Broué, *Histoire de l'internationale communiste*, Paris, 1997, p.529.
3. Ibid.
4. *La révolution et la guerre d'Espagne* (with E. Témime), Paris, 1961; *Le parti bolchevique*, Paris, 1963; *Révolution en Allemagne*, Paris, 1971; *Trotsky*, Paris, 1988.
5. P. Broué, op.cit., p.137.
6. *Memoirs of a Revolutionary*, London, 1967. A collection of Serge's writings from Germany in 1923 exists in French, *Notes d'Allemagne*, Montreuil, 1990. An expanded English version will be published by Redwords in 2000.
7. *Lenin's Moscow*, London, 1987. A collection of Rosmer's political journalism is due to appear in *Revolutionary History* 7/4, Autumn 2000.

8. R. Palme Dutt, *The Internationale*, London, 1964, p.212.

9. R. Aron, 'Préface' to B. Lazitch, *Lénine et la IIIe internationale*, Neuchâtel, 1951, p.9.

10. P. Broué, op.cit., p.351.

11. London, 1937.

12. London, 1985. See also P. Frank, *Histoire de l'internationale communiste*, Paris, 1979, II 887.

13. London, 1979.

14. English translation: *The Communist Movement from Comintern to Cominform*, Harmondsworth, 1975.

15. F. Claudin, p.35.

16. Ibid., p.109.

17. Lenin, *Collected Works* XXXIII, Moscow, 1966, pp.431–2.

18. P. Broué, op.cit., p.237.

19. Hallas, pp.105–6.

20. Conditions 4 and 8; J. Degras, op.cit., pp.169–70.

21. See, for example, Jakob Reich ('Comrade Thomas'), 'The First Years of the Communist International', *Revolutionary History* 5/2, 1994.

22. I. Deutscher, 'Record of a Discussion with Heinrich Brandler', *New Left Review*, Sept-Oct 1977, cited T. Cliff, Lenin, Vol.IV, pp.59–60.

23. V. Serge, *Memoirs of a Revolutionary*, op.cit., p.186.

24. V. Serge, *Revolution in Danger*, London, 1997, pp.37–8.

25. See N. Carlin and I. Birchall, 'Kinnock's Favourite Marxist', *International Socialism*, 20, 1983.

26. E.J. Hobsbawm, *The Age of Empire*, London, 1987, pp.108–9.

27. See I. Birchall, 'The Vice-like Hold of Nationalism?', *International Socialism* 78, 1998, pp.133–41.

28. V. Vouïovitch, *L'I.C.J. en lutte contre l'occupation de la Ruhr et la guerre*, Moscow, 1924.

29. Ibid., p.11.

30. M. Philips Price, *Dispatches from the Weimar Republic*, London, 1999, pp.108–9.

31. R. Wohl, *French Communism in the Making*, Stanford, 1966, pp.317–20.

32. P. Broué, op.cit., p.390.

33. J. Maitron and C. Pennetier, *Dictionnaire biographique du mouvement ouvrier français XXV*, Paris, 1985, pp.269–76.

34. *Lenin's Moscow*, pp.169–71, 196–204.

35. See *L'Humanité*, 16 April, 4 May, 9 May 1922.
36. T. Cliff, *Lenin*, Vol.IV, p.17.
37. See, for example, E. Goldmann, *Living my Life*, New York, 1931, II p.765; A. Berkman, *The Bolshevik Myth*, London, 1925, p.143.
38. Makhno's *Memoirs*, cited in *Ni Dieu ni maître*, Lausanne, 1969, p.461.
39. T. Cliff, op.cit., p.27; see Lenin, *Collected Works*, XXX, Moscow, 1965, pp.87–90.
40. P. Broué, op.cit., p.168.
41. *Lenin's Moscow*, pp.94–5.
42. Ibid., p.72.
43. P. Broué, op.cit. p.221.
44. Ibid., pp.225–6; see also D. Fernbach, 'Rosa Luxemburg's Political Heir: An Appreciation of Paul Levi', *New Left Review*, 238, November-December 1999, pp.3–25.
45. P. Broué, *Révolution en Allemagne*, op.cit., p.528.
46. P. Broué, *Histoire*, op.cit., p.225.
47. *Lenin's Moscow*, p.35.
48. P. Broué, *Histoire*, op.cit., pp.309–49.
49. R. Albert (pseudonym of Victor Serge), *Correspondance internationale*, 8 September 1923.
50. Ibid., 27 October 1923.
51. R. Albert, *Clarté*, 1 February 1924; see also *New York Times*, 20 December 1922, and A.C. Sutton, *Wall Street and the Rise of the Nazis*, Sudbury, 1976, pp.91–3.
52. R. Albert, op.cit., 10 November 1923.
53. Ibid., 29 September 1923.
54. Ibid., 27 October 1923.
55. R. Albert, *Clarté*, op.cit., 1 December 1924.
56. Ibid., 1 December 1924.
59. R. Albert, *Correspondance internationale*, op.cit., 10 November 1923.
60. R. Albert, *Clarté*, op.cit., 1 February 1924.
61. Ibid., 15 February 1924.
62. P. Broué, *Histoire*, op.cit., p.315.
63. See Michael Haynes, 'Popular Violence and the Russian Revolution, *Historical Materialism 2*, Summer, 1998, pp.185–213.
64. *Lenin's Moscow*, p.154.

65. P. Broué, *Histoire*, op.cit., p.21.
66. F. Borkenau, *The Communist International*, London, 1938, p.163.
67. V. Serge, *Memoirs of a Revolutionary*, op.cit., p.177.
68. *Rede des Genossen Rosmer*, July 1921, *Bibliothek der Roten Gewerkschaftsinternationale*, Band III, p.10; see also *Lenin's Moscow*, pp.156–8.
69. *La Révolution prolétarienne*, February 1926.
70. Marx and Engels, *Collected Works* XI, London, 1979, p.103 (translation adapted to render *Mensch* as 'human being').
71. *Lenin's Moscow*, p.154.
72. P. Broué, *Histoire*, op.cit., pp.163–7.
73. T. Cliff, *Lenin*, Vol.III, London, 1978, p.7.
74. Hallas, p.101.
75. *Lenin's Moscow*, p.70.
76. Ibid., p.229.
77. V. Serge, *Memoirs of a Revolutionary*, op.cit., p.162.
78. P. Broué, *Histoire*, op.cit., p.241.
79. A. Rosmer, review of A. Rossi, *Les communistes français pendant la drôle de guerre*, *La Révolution prolétarienne*, May 1951, p.189.
80. P. Broué, *Histoire*, op.cit., p.81.
81. T. Cliff, *Lenin*, Vol.IV, op.cit., p.65.
82. P. Broué, *Histoire*, op.cit., p.99.

7. 'Revolutionary Gymnastics' and the Unemployed
Chris Ealham

1. According to one Trotskyist eye-witness, during the first months of the revolution 'the number of organs of workers' power in Spain was proportionally greater than in Russia.' (Gregorio Munis, *Jalones de derrota, promesa de victoria. Crítica y Teoría de la Revolución Española*, Madrid, 1977, p.292.)
2. For the vicissitudes of the revolution see José Peirats, *La CNT en la revolución Española*, Paris, 1971; Burnett Bolloten, *The Spanish Civil War*, Chapel Hill, 1991; and 'The Spanish Civil War: The View from the Left', *Revolutionary History*, 4, 1–2, 1992. On the historiography of the Spanish revolution, see Chris Ealham, 'The Spanish Revolution: 60 Years On', *Tesserae. Journal of Iberian and Latin American Studies* (special

edition on the Spanish Civil War), 2, 2, 1996, pp.209–34.

3. Some of these contradictions are also explored in Chris Ealham, '"From the Summit to the Abyss": The Contradictions of Individualism and Collectivism in Spanish Anarchism', in Paul Preston and Ann Logan MacKenzie (eds), *The Republic Besieged: Civil War in Spain, 1936–1939*, Edinburgh, 1996, pp.135–62. This emphasis on the contradictions of anarchism is a corrective to the views of those historians who argue that Spanish libertarianism was eminently rational in its anti-capitalist resistance and that it failed simply because of the ferocity of state repression (see note 10).

4. E.J. Hobsbawm, *Primitive Rebels. Studies in Archaic Forms of Social Movement in the 19th and 20th Centuries*, Manchester, 1959, pp.74–92.

5. Jon Amsdem, 'Spanish Anarchism and the Stages Theory of History', *Radical History Review*, 6, 1978, pp.66–75.

6. Hobsbawm's approach to the development of social protest movements has much in common with 'Modernisation' theorists and their assumption that industrialisation leads to an incremental modernisation and institutionalisation of social conflicts. 'Modernisation' theorists normally point to the supposed replacement of insurrectionary forms of protest by more peaceful forms of bargaining to support their argument.

7. Charles Tilly, *From Mobilisation to Revolution*, Reading, MA, 1978, ch.6.

8. Temma Kaplan, *The Anarchists of Andalusia*, Princeton, NJ, 1977; Anna Monjo Omedes, 'La CNT durant la II República a Barcelona: líders, militants, afiliats', unpublished doctoral thesis, University of Barcelona, 1993; Eulàlia Vega i Massana, 'La Confederació Nacional del Treball i els Sindicats d'Oposició a Catalunya i el País Valencià (1930–1936)', unpublished doctoral thesis, University of Barcelona, 1986.

9. The most extensive study of the evolution of labour unions in Spain is Benjamin Martin, *The Agony of Modernization. Labor and Industrialization in Spain*, Ithaca, 1990.

10. Kaplan, *The Anarchists*; Clara E. Lida, *Anarquismo y Revolución en la España del siglo XIX*, Madrid, 1972; and Jerome Mintz, *The Anarchists of Casas Viejas*, Chicago, 1982.

11. For instance, the leading FAI newspaper argued that 'it is from the fields, from the countryside, where the revolutionary pha-

lanxes will embark on their mission to end the hegemony of the cities [the] centre of state power, the focal-point of capitalist forces [which] corrupts or suffocates protest movements...we do not need the cities to make the revolution.' (*Tierra y Libertad*, 1 April 1932.) The tensions within the anarchist movement between the advocates of rural and urban revolution underline the movement's crisis of modernity during the 1930s. See Xavier Paniagua, *La sociedad libertaria. Agrarismo e industrialización en el anarquismo español (1930–1939)*, Barcelona, 1982.

12. See Eve Rosenhaft, *Beating the Fascists? The German Communists and Political Violence, 1929–1933*, Cambridge, 1983.

13. In January 1936 unemployment stood at 5.6% in Catalonia, Spain's most industrial region, which compared favourably to Britain (15–20%) and Germany (25–35%). (Albert Balcells, *Crisis económica y agitación social en Cataluña de 1930 a 1936*, Barcelona, 1971, p.8.) This difference reflected the limited integration of the Spanish economy within the world economic system.

14. The average wage of Spanish workers was twice as low as that of German workers, while the food price index was markedly higher in Spain. This meant that the distance between the semi- and unskilled working class and the unemployed was not that great. Thus, in 1931, when perhaps as few as 4% of the Barcelona working class was unemployed, the CNT estimated that as many as 200,000 workers—some 20% of the total population of the Catalan capital—lived below the poverty line. (*Solidaridad Obrera*, 26 April 1931.)

15. For more details see Chris Ealham, 'Policing the Recession: Unemployment, Social Protest and Law-and-Order in Barcelona, 1930–1936', unpublished doctoral thesis, University of London, 1996.

16. During the June 1931 elections Catalan republicans promised that helping the unemployed was 'one of the most imposing problems that the Republic has been presented with.' (*L'Opinió*, 13–26 June 1931.)

17. These republican myths prospered due to the combination of political autocracy, electoral fraud and physical repression that characterised the Restoration monarchy (1875–1923) and the

Primo de Rivera dictatorship (1922–30). That said, we must also bear in mind that the anti-political anarchists did not offer a coherent revolutionary alternative to republicanism.

18. In February 1933, nearly two years after the birth of the Republic, only 2.4% of the unemployed received any kind of state benefit, and this expired after a fixed period. (Balcells, *Crisis económica*, p.127.)

19. See, for instance, the Law for the Defence of the Republic, which was modelled on the repressive laws of the Weimar Republic and which allowed for the use of martial law and paramilitary policing in defence of the social order. During 1931–33 social democrats were at the forefront of this repressive offensive that included anti-vagrancy legislation and internment without trial in order to remove unemployed organisers and worker-activists from the streets.

20. The most influential liberal analysis is Gabriel Jackson, *The Spanish Republic and the Civil War*, Princeton, 1965.

21. These were the dissident communists of the *Bloc Obrer i Camperol* (BOC—the Worker-Peasant Bloc) who later formed the bulk of the *Partido Obrero de Unificación Marxista* (POUM—the Workers' Party of Marxist Unification). The BOC split from the Stalinist *Partido Comunista de España* (PCE—Communist Party of Spain) over its 'united front from below' policy, through which the pro-Moscow party sought to split the CNT. The dissident communists rejected this strategy, claiming that it could only weaken class organisation. The best study of the BOC is Andrew Durgan, *BOC, 1930–1936. El Bloque Obrero y Campesino*, Barcelona, 1996.

22. Juan Gómez Casas, *Historia del anarcosindicalismo español*, Madrid, 1968, p.166.

23. These conflicts ranged from partial strikes affecting specific workshops across to general strikes that paralysed entire industries. For the most part, these conflicts were defensive in nature and sought to regain lost working conditions. See Vega i Massana, 'La Confederació'.

24. For factory occupations, see *La Vanguardia*, 16 July, 23 August 1931. At the height of the labour unrest the BOC called on the CNT to 'take power'. (La Batalla, 30 July and 3 September 1931.)

25. One activist described his duties as arranging 'hospital visits' for

'scabs'. Although these union activities were not without physical risk, importantly for the unemployed, they were also remunerated, with militants being paid at approximately the daily wage rate for semi-skilled manual labours. (Enrique Martín, *Recuerdos de un militante de la CNT*, Barcelona, 1979, pp.91–2.)

26. It would be more correct to say that this was a protest by the unemployed and the low-paid: for the jobless, it meant liberation from the burden of rent payments; for the low-paid, it promised an immediate material gain without the hardships of an industrial stoppage. See Nick Rider, 'The practice of direct action: the Barcelona rent strike of 1931', in David Goodway (ed.), *For Anarchism. History, Theory and Practice*, London, 1989, pp.79–105.

27. During the period of post-war inflation anarchists participated in rent protests, believing that they could lay the basis for proletarian unity. (Ángeles González Fernández, *Utopía y realidad. Anarquismo, anarcosindicalismo y organizaciones obreras. Sevilla, 1900–1923*, Seville, 1996, pp.351–6.)

28. It is difficult to assess the number of strikers with any precision, although it has been suggested that the best measure of the strike was the fierce denunciations of the landlords. (Rider, 'The practice of direct action', in Goodway (ed.), p.95.)

29. Interview with Juan Giménez Arenas, a former CNT and FAI activist, November 1997.

30. Given that Malatesta was guilty of ignoring the repressive capacity of the nineteenth-century state, the oversight of the FAI was all the greater, notwithstanding the relative backwardness of the Spanish state.

31. Rafael Vidiella, 'Psicología del anarquismo español', *Leviatán*, May 1934, pp.50–8.

32. It is then something of an irony that the anarchists put so much energy into rent strikes, which have been dubbed 'collective consumption trade unionism'. (Manuel Castells, *The City and the Grassroots. A Cross-Cultural Theory of Urban Social Movements*, London, 1983.)

33. According to *Solidaridad Obrera*, 6–8 May 1936, CNT membership stood at around 600,000, which meant that approximately half of the 1.2 million members of 1932 had deserted its unions. Of the workers who left the CNT, around one-quar-

ter (some 150,000) joined rival unions; the remaining workers were apparently demobilised and unorganised. Only the introduction of compulsory union membership in Catalonia during the first weeks of the civil war enabled the CNT to re-gain the strength it enjoyed in 1931–32.

34. The term was borrowed from Malatesta. *Minutes of the Plenum of the Barcelona CNT Local Federation*, 24 October 1931.

35. In the words of one of the main architects of the 'revolutionary gymnastics', these mobilisations would 'overcome the complex of fear towards repressive state forces and the army through the systematisation of insurrectionary actions, the implementation of revolutionary gymnastics'. (Juan García Oliver, *El eco de los pasos*, Barcelona, 1978, p.115.)

36. Unemployed direct action provided the source for many of the moral panics in 1930s Spain.

37. This process is fully explored in Ealham, 'Policing the Recession'.

38. Anarchist-led unions called for the jobless to storm workplaces and demand work (*Solidaridad Obrera*, 12–17 May 1931).

39. I am referring here to the 'occasional' armed robbery of the unemployed and not the 'professional' criminality of those who always lived from crime, even in times of full employment.

40. Armed robbery was a major funding mechanism for the FAI during the thirties, with the monies generated from attacks on banks and pay-rolls financing arms and explosives as well as the everyday activities of the CNT unions, particularly the prisoners' welfare committee and the action groups. See Chris Ealham, 'Anarchism and Illegality in Barcelona, 1931–1937', *Contemporary European History*, 4, 2, 1995, pp.133–51. This practice was not exclusively anarchist; for instances of armed robbery by German communist defence squads, see Rosenhaft, *Beating the Fascists?*, p.126.

41. According to one anarchist veteran and resident of the proletarian ghetto in l'Hospitalet, plans to open a new police station in his neighbourhood were shelved following repeated bomb attacks on the building site. It seems that this campaign of armed obstruction to the extension of state power enjoyed widespread support from within the local community. (Interview with Juan Giménez Arenas, November 1997.)

42. Monjo Omedes, 'La CNT...', Ch.8.

43. Joan Peiró, *Ideas sobre sindicalismo y anarquismo*, Madrid, 1979, pp.124–7.
44. Chris Ealham, 'La lluita pel carrer, els vendedors ambulants durant la II República', *L'Avenç. Revista d'Història*, November 1998, No.230, pp.21–6.
45. This is not to suggest that the struggle for the latter might not lead to the former, but it does show that the relation between the two was not as simple as the anarchists postulated.
46. During the January 1933 uprising, which is famous for the harsh repression in Andalusia, the anarchists of Casas Viejas entered the field of battle when the rising had already been extinguished elsewhere in Spain, with the result that the government simply redeployed security forces to quell the last isolated pocket of the rebellion. See Mintz, *The Anarchists*, passim.
47. Take for instance the plan for National Industrial Federations, which sought to modernise trade union structures and bring greater national coordination. Although accepted as the blueprint for the organisation of the CNT at the May 1931 National Congress in Madrid, the opposition of the radical anarchists ensured that this organisational model existed on paper only.
48. This is an example of 'the spatialities of counter-hegemonic cultural practices'. (Michael Keith and Stephen Pile, 'Introduction: The Politics of Place', in Keith and Pile (eds), *Place and the Politics of Identity*, London, 1993, p.6.)
49. Frederic Jameson, *Postmodernism, or the Cultural Logic of Late Capitalism*, London, 1991, p.413.
50. That this is not simply a case of damning anarchists for being anarchists is proven by the identical criticisms of foreign anarchists, who bemoaned the CNT's absence of any organisational mechanisms for channelling the upsurge of the masses and its lack of any coherent anarcho-syndicalist strategy designed to articulate the collective force of its base. See, for example, Helmut Rüdiger, *Ensayo crítico sobre la revolución española*, Buenos Aires, 1940.
51. *Tierra y Libertad*, 11 July 1931.
52. *Unidad Sindical*, 31 March and 21 April 1932.
53. In June 1932 the PCE established a Comité para la Reconstrucción de la CNT (Committee for the Reconstruction

of the CNT), which, despite its name, aimed to split the CNT. Although it claimed to have 280,000 members at the time of its creation, the actual figure probably never exceeded 46,000, its influence remaining limited to Sevilla in the south and areas on the north coast, such as Asturias and the Basque Country.

54. Víctor Alba, *La Alianza Obrera. Historia y análisis de una táctica de unidad en España*, Madrid, 1977.

55. For a contemporary account of the Asturian events, see Narcís Molins i Fabregà, La revolución proletaria de Asturias, Madrid, 1977 (2nd edition). Among the best later accounts are Paul Preston, 'Spain's October Revolution and the Rightist Grasp for Power', *Journal of Contemporary History*, 10, 4, 1975, pp. 555–78 and David Ruiz, *Insurrección defensiva y revolución obrera. El octubre español de 1934*, Barcelona, 1988.

56. The same can also be said of their anarcho-syndicalist rivals who, despite their collectivism, possessed a similarly defensive and anti-political orientation.

57. The most important and influential examples of anti-Soviet anarchist literature, both of which are based on short visits to the USSR, are Ángel Pestaña, *Setenta días en Rusia: lo que yo ví*, Barcelona, 1924 and Vicente Pérez Combina, *Un militante de la CNT en Rusia*, Barcelona, 1932.

58. To quote Marx, 'Every class struggle is a political struggle'.

59. According to one commentator, 'During the crisis of 1936, the CNT found itself caught in a cul-de-sac as far as the definition of its political strategy was concerned.' (Antonio Elorza, 'Notas sobre cultura y revolución en el anarcosindicalismo español, 1934–1936', in José Luis García Delgado (ed.), *La II República española. Bienio rectificador y Frente Popular, 1934–1936*, Madrid, 1988, p.175.)

60. Take, for instance, the response of the anarchist leadership to the moves by Catalan republicans and Stalinists to isolate the POUM during the winter of 1936. Instead of rallying to the defence of fellow revolutionaries, the anarchist hierarchy allowed the POUM to be hounded from the Catalan government in return for an increase in CNT-FAI representation.

61. The classic English eye-witness account of the 'May Days' is George Orwell's, *Homage to Catalonia*, London, 1938. For a suggestive reinterpretation, see Helen Graham '"Against the State": A Genealogy of the Barcelona May Days (1937)',

European History Quarterly, 29, 4, 1999, pp.485–542.

62. According to the programme of the Amigos de Durruti, 'The CNT was utterly devoid of revolutionary theory. We did not possess a concrete programme. We had no idea where we were going' (Los Amigos de Durruti, *Hacia la nueva revolución*, Barcelona, 1937, p.15). See also the excellent study by Agustín Guillamón, *The Friends of Durruti Group, 1937–1939*, Edinburgh, 1996.

63. In the view of Guillamón, the real significance of the Amigos 'lies in its attempt, emanating from within the ranks of the libertarian movement itself (in 1937) to constitute a revolutionary vanguard' (Ibid., p.1).

64. A group of Italian anarchists exiled in Barcelona issued an impassioned call to their Spanish comrades, warning of the dangers of élitism and calling for an appraisal of past defeats of the revolutionary left, both at home and abroad (*Tierra y Libertad*, 8 August, 12 September 1931). There is no evidence that this plea was acted upon.

65. It would be grossly unfair to blame all of this on the anarchists given the obvious contribution of domestic and international reactionaries, the western democracies and the perfidious role of Spanish republicanism and the international communist movement.

8. Recent Trends in the Historiography of Italian Fascism
Tobias Abse

1. The book translated as *Three Faces of Fascism*, New York, 1965, was originally entitled *Der Faschismus in Seiner Epoche*, Munich, 1963.

2. Zeev Sternhell's attempt to locate the origins of fascism in France before 1914, and to some extent before 1900—see, in particular, *The Birth of Fascist Ideology*, Princeton, 1994—is unconvincing. Whilst some strands of thought that were incorporated into fascist ideology can be traced back to the period before 1914, fascism as a mass movement is impossible to envisage without the experience of both the war itself and the Russian Revolution of 1917 which was a direct product of the war.

3. London, 1998.

4. Ernst Nolte, *Der europaische Burgerkrieg*, Frankfurt, 1987. A number of Nolte's shorter pieces in the same vein have been translated into English—see *Forever in the Shadow of Hitler?*, New Jersey, 1993.

5. François Furet, *The Passing of an Illusion: The Idea of Communism in the Twentieth Century*, Chicago, 1999.

6. Obviously there have been some major works on Italian Fascism produced over the last decade which take their distance from such trends. See, in particular, Perry Willson, *The Clockwork Factory: Women and Work in Fascist Italy*, Oxford, 1993, Philip Morgan, *Italian Fascism 1919–1945*, London, 1995 and Richard Bosworth, *The Italian Dictatorship: Problems and Perspectives in the Interpretation of Mussolini and Fascism*, London, 1998.

7. The American culturalist Jeffrey T. Schnapp has identified himself with 'scholarship inspired by the pioneering work of scholars such as Ernst Nolte, George Mosse and Renzo De Felice'—'Fascinating Fascism', *Journal of Contemporary History*, Vol.31, No.2, April 1996, p.237. Given Nolte's reputation in 1996, linked to the *Historikerstreit* rather than the early comparativist work on generic fascism, Schnapp has placed himself in an ambiguous position and it may be no accident that even a postmodernist culturalist like Mabel Berezin seemed remarkably eager to distance herself from his recent work in her review of *Staging Fascism: Journal of Modern Italian Studies*, Vol.3, No.3, Fall 1998, pp.335–7.

8. See *Journal of Contemporary History*, Vol.31, No.2, April 1996 'Special Issue: The Aesthetics of Fascism', pp.235–418.

9. *Il culto del littorio: la sacralizzazione della politica nell'Italia fascista, Bari, 1993*, translated as *The Sacralization of Politics in Fascist Italy*, Cambridge, MA., 1996.

10. Mabel Berezin, *Making the Fascist Self: The Political Culture of Interwar Italy*, Ithaca and London, 1997 and Simonetta Falasca-Zamponi, *Fascist Spectacle: The Aesthetics of Power in Mussolini's Italy*, Berkeley, 1997.

11. George L. Mosse, *The Nationalization of the Masses: Political Symbolism and Mass Movements from the Napoleonic Wars through the Third Reich*, New York, 1975.

12. Mosse's own observation—'it is astounding that before Emilio Gentile's path-breaking *Il culto del littorio* published in 1993,

we had no comprehensive analysis of Italian Fascism as a political religion with its own liturgy'—George Mosse, 'Fascist Aesthetics and Society: Some Considerations', *Journal of Contemporary History*, Vol.31, No.2, April 1996, p.246 would suggest that the American veteran endorsed my assessment.

13. Jeffrey T. Schnapp, *Staging Fascism: 18BL and the Theater of Masses for Masses*, Stanford, CA, 1996.

14. Marla Stone, *The Patron State: Culture and Politics in Fascist Italy*, Princeton, 1998.

15. Jeffrey T. Schnapp, '18BL: Fascist Mass Spectacle', *Representations* 43 (Summer 1993), pp.89–125.

16. Marla Stone, *The Patron State: Culture and Politics in Fascist Italy*, Princeton, 1998.

17. Dante Germino, *The Italian Fascist Party in Power: A Study in Totalitarian Rule*, Minneapolis, 1959.

18. Edward R. Tannenbaum, *Fascism in Italy: Society and Culture, 1922–1945*, London, 1973, Victoria De Grazia, *The Culture of Consent: Mass Organization of Leisure in Fascist Italy*, Cambridge, 1981, and Tracy H. Koon, *Believe, Obey, Fight: Political Socialization of Youth in Fascist Italy, 1922–1943*, Chapel Hill and London, 1985.

19. Richard Bosworth, *The Italian Dictatorship*, p.27.

20. One who has is Professor Macgregor Knox of the LSE whose critique 'The Fascist regime, its foreign policy and its wars: an anti-anti-Fascist orthodoxy', *Contemporary European History*, 1995, Vol.4, No.3, pp.347–65, presents a devastating, detailed and cogently argued case for the prosecution, attacking De Felice on his home ground, the archives, as only a genuinely empirical military and diplomatic historian could. Denis Mack Smith has recently delivered a paper 'Fascism and historiography from De Felice' at St. Antony's College, Oxford, on 24 May 1999, attacking De Felice from a similar standpoint.

21. Turin, 1974.

22. Renzo De Felice, *Mussolini il Duce*, Vol.1, p.642.

23. Ibid., *Gli anni del consenso, 1929–1936*, Turin, 1974, p.54.

24. 'Tutti si aspettavano che il duce cadesse…Dialogo fra Giorgio Amendola e Renzo De Felice', *L'Espresso*, 20, 15 December 1974.

25. Bari, 1975.

26. Richard Bosworth, *The Italian Dictatorship*, p.122.

27. New Brunswick, N.J., 1977.

28. This was first made apparent in Denis Mack Smith, *Italy: A Modern History*, Ann Arbor, 1959.

29. *Times Literary Supplement*, 3824, 31 October 1975, pp.1278–80. De Felice's description of the conquest of Ethiopia as Mussolini's 'political masterpiece and greatest success' was according to Mack Smith 'worse than shocking, it is nonsense'. More generally, Mack Smith felt that it was 'hard to avoid the impression that Mussolini has been given the benefit of too many doubts'.

30. London, 1976.

31. London, 1981.

32. Rosaria Quartararo, *Roma tra Londra e Berlino: la politica estera fascista dal 1931 al 1941*, Rome, 1980.

33. Renzo De Felice, *Mussolini l'alleato 1940–1945*, Vol.1, *L'Italia in guerra 1940–1943* (2 vols), Turin, 1990.

34. Renzo De Felice, *Rosso e Nero*, Milan, 1995.

35. *Alleanza Nazionale*, the allegedly post-fascist successor party to the *Movimento Sociale Italiano*, whose neo-fascism was never disputed.

36. *Repubblica Sociale Italiana*, Italian Social Republic, Mussolini's puppet regime in northern Italy in 1943–45, popularly called the Republic of Salò, after its capital.

37. It is hard to know how seriously to take this eulogy of Churchill given the unfounded allegations against the British prime minister that De Felice makes elsewhere in *Rosso e Nero*, which I will deal with in due course. De Felice had earlier shown a great hostility to Churchill as Mack Smith noted in *The Times Literary Supplement* in 1975—Mack Smith summarising De Felice's view of Mussolini wrote 'we are informed, for example, that he was not cruel (also, incidentally, that he lacked the cold fanaticism of Winston Churchill)'. In reply to a question from me in the discussion following his Oxford talk on 24 May 1999, Mack Smith expressed the view that De Felice during the two decades he had known him had displayed a consistent animosity to Churchill and, to a lesser extent, the British in general.

38. It was assumed the final volume of the biography would attempt to back it up. There was nothing in the unfinished posthumous volume that touched on the issue nor have any

papers or notes been produced by De Felice's widow or pupils to substantiate the claim.

39. Benito Mussolini, interview with the journalist Gian Gaetano Cabella, director of *Popolo di Alessandria*, 20 April 1945, printed in the *Testamento politico di Mussolini*, Rome, 1948. Extract translated by Roger Griffin under title 'What Might have Been: Axis Europe' in Roger Griffin (ed.), *Fascism*, Oxford, 1995, pp.89–90. It included such sentiments as 'I was not bluffing when I declared that the Fascist idea will be the idea of the twentieth century...History will vindicate me.'

40. For details of Borghese's postwar career, see Franco Ferraresi, *Threats to Democracy: The Radical Right in Italy after the War*, Princeton, 1996, especially pp.117–24 which detail the *coup* attempt.

41. Ernesto Galli della Loggia, *La morte della patria: la crisi dell'idea della nazione tra Resistenza, antifascismo e Repubblica*, Bari, 1996.

42. 'In Italy, it seemed the right has won the historians' quarrel' was Bosworth's judgement—Richard Bosworth, *Explaining Auschwitz and Hiroshima: History Writing and the Second World War 1945–1990*, London, 1994, p.140.

9. Woodrow Wilson is Amongst Us
Barry Pavier

1. See my forthcoming work *South Asia in the era of capitalism 1600–2000*, London, 2000.

2. David Washbrook: 'After the Mutiny: from Queen to Queen-Empress', *History Today*, 47 (9), September 1997, pp.10–15.

3. Thus Hindu grammarians invented Hindi in the late nineteenth century by excising Arabic and Farsi loan words from the colloquial language Hindustani, and replaced them with terms derived from Sanskrit. This means that the only difference between Urdue and Hindi is approximately 10% of the vocabulary. One route out of this situation was suggested by the Congress dissident Subhas Chandra Bose: the state language should be Hindustani (spoken by people on a comprehensive geographical spread) in the Roman script, which would do away with the problem of a religiously identified script.

4. R.J. Moore, 'Jinnah and the Pakistan demand', in Mushirul

Hasan (ed.), India's Partition, Delhi, 1993, p.170.
5. Maulana Abul Kalam Azad, Presidential address to the Congress, Ramgarh, December 1940, in Mushirul Hasan, op.cit., pp.67–8.
6. See crucially his speech of 4 February 1931.

10.The Long Boom and the Advanced World 1945–73
Michael Haynes

1. J. Robinson, *The Problem of Full Employment*, London, Workers' Educational Association, 1949, p.10.
2. For brief a survey of the history of output measurement see B. van Ark, 'Towards European historical national accounts', *Scandinavian Economic History Review*, Vol.xliii, No.1, 1995, pp.3–16.
4. A. Maddison, *Monitoring the World Economy*, Paris, 1995, p.19.
5. A. Maddison, *Dynamic Forces in Capitalist Development*, Oxford, 1991, pp.49–50.
6. A. Botho and G. Tonioli, 'The assessment: the twentieth century—achievements, failures, lessons', *Oxford Review of Economic Policy*, Vol.15, No.4, winter 1999, p.10.
7. M. Haynes, 'The European Union and its periphery: inclusion and exclusion', forthcoming in W. Bonefeld (ed.), *The Politics of European Integration: Monetary Union and Class*, London, 2000.
8. Calculated from A. Maddison, *Monitoring*, op.cit.
9. N.F.R. Crafts, 'The golden age of economic growth in western Europe, 1950–1973', *Economic History Review*, Vol.xlviii, No.3, August 1995, pp.439. See also N.F.R. Crafts, and G. Tonioli (eds), *Economic Growth in Europe Since 1945*, Cambridge, 1996; N.F.R. Crafts, 'Macroeconomic policies in historical perspective' in M. Mackintosh et al., *Economics and Changing Economies*, Open University-Thomson, 1996. B. van Ark and N. Crafts (eds), *Quantitative Aspects of Post-war European Economic Growth*, Cambridge, 1996. G. Toniolo, 'Europe's golden age, 1950–1973: speculations form a long-run perspective', *Economic History Review*, Vol.ii, No.2, 1998, pp.252–67.
10. R. Brenner, 'Uneven development and the long downturn: the advanced capitalist economies from boom to stagnation,

1950–1998', *New Left Review*, No.229, May–June 1998. For a discussion of Brenner's account see the contributions in *Historical Materialism*, nos.4 and 5, 1999.

11. M. Kidron, *Western Capitalism Since the War*, Harmondsworth, 1970, pp.12–13.

12. R. Brenner, op.cit.

13. For a Marxist approach see E. Mandel, *Late Capitalism*, London, 1975 and his, *Long Waves of Capitalist Development. The Marxist Interpretation*, Cambridge, 1986. For a recent non-Marxist account built around the idea of Kondratiev cycles see R. Lloyd-Jones and M. Lewis, *British Industrial Capitalism Since the Industrial Revolution*, London, 1998.

14. S. Solomou, *Phases of Economic Growth 1850–1973. Kondratiev Waves and Kuznets Swings*, Cambridge, 1987, p.169. See also S. Solomou, *Economic Cycles: Long Cycles and Business cycles since 1870*, Manchester, 1998.

15. See A. Maddison's exercise in conventional growth accounting, 'Growth and slowdown in advanced capitalist economies: techniques of quantitative assessment', *Journal of Economic Literature*, Vol.XXV, No.2, June 1987, passim.

16. A. Shaikh, *Crisis Theories in Economic Thought, Thames Papers in Political Economy*, London, 1977, p.3.

17. S. Solomou, op.cit., p.167.

18. S. Rosen, 'Keynes and the Gadflies' in T. Rosack (ed.), *The Dissenting Academy*, Harmondsworth, 1968.

19. P. Samuelson, *Economics*, New York, First edn, 1948, p.423.

20. Ibid., Third edn, 1955, p.348.

21. Ibid., Eighth edn, 1970, p.803.

22. SIPRI, *Armaments and Disarmament in a Nuclear Age*, Stockholm, 1976, p.12.

23. SIPRI, *Yearbook of World Armaments and Disarmament 1968–69*, Stockholm, Almqvist and Wicksell, 1969 (hereafter *Yearbook...*), p.27.

24. SIPRI, ibid., p.108.

25. M. Kidron, op.cit., p.49; *United Nations, Economic and Social Consequences of the Arms Race and of Military Expenditure*, Geneva, 1972, p.21.

26. For a good discussion of this see A. Shaikh, op.cit.

27. P. Baran and P. Sweezy, *Monopoly Capital*, Harmondsworth, 1968.

28. For this aspect of the weakness of the Keynesian discussion of profit see P. Sweezy, 'Keynesian economics: the first quarter century' in his *Modern Capitalism and Other Essays*, New York, 1972.
29. The detailed theory behind this can be found elsewhere, see the discussion and references in M. Kidron, op.cit., pp.54–6; C. Harman, *Explaining the Crisis: A Marxist Reappraisal*, London, 1984, passim.
30. See Carlo Morelli's contribution to this volume. K. Smith, *The British Economic Crisis*, Harmondsworth, 1984 has a good discussion of why the negative technological impact of military spending weighed more heavily on the British economy. He is rather less persuaded of the investment effect than we are.
31. I have calculated this data from the 1979 SIPRI *Yearbook*. They are presented as a guide rather than an exact measure because of valuation difficulties extensively discussed in the SIPRI handbooks.
32. A. Maddison, 'Growth and slowdown', op.cit., p.684.
33. N.F.R. Crafts, 'Macro-economic policies', op.cit., p.689.
34. 'Social capability [for catch up] depends on more than the content of education and the organization of firms…it is a question of the obstacles to change raised by vested interests, established positions and customary relations among forms and between employers and employees' M. Abramovitz, 'Catching-up, forging ahead and falling behind', *Journal of Economic History*, Vol.46, June 1986, p.389.
35. From 1860s to 1890s Italian output may have grown at 0.5% per annum. In the *boom Giolittiano* 1895–1913 it grew 2.16% per annum, between 1913–50, 0.73%—half the G7 average for that period. See N. Rossi and G. Tonioli, 'Catch-up or falling behind? Italy's economic growth, 1895–47', *Economic History Review*, Vol.XLV, No.3, 1992, pp.537–63.
36. International Institute of Strategic Affairs, *The Military Balance 1987–1988*, London, 1987. There are enormous controversies about the size of the Soviet bloc military effort and especially that of the USSR. These figures are offered as a reasonable approximation. We should also note that the inconsistency of output measures means that it is strictly illegitimate to compare military shares but the difference is not so great as to affect the point we wish to make.

37. See C. Harman, *Class Struggles in Eastern Europe, 1945–1983*, London, 1988 for an historical account of the class conflicts that resulted in the former Soviet bloc.
38. M. Haynes and R. Hasan, 'State and market in the Eastern European transition', *Journal of European Economic History*, Vol.27 No.3, winter 1998, pp.609–44.
39. See, for example, the measurement attempts of Bela Belassa and the discussion they provoked, B. Belassa, 'The dynamic efficiency of the Soviet economy', *American Economic Review*, Vol.LIV, No.3, May 1964; pp.490–505, 517–20; B. Belassa and T.J. Bertrand, 'Growth performance of Eastern European economies and comparable Western European countries', *American Economic Review*, Vol.LX, No.2, May 1970, pp.314–25.
40. K. Smith, op.cit., p.55. This comment remained unammended in the 1989 edition.
41. See his introduction to J. Lampe, *The Bulgarian Economy in the Twentieth Century*, London, 1986, p.8.
42. See Horvat's comment on Belassa and Betrand's 1970 paper, op.cit., p.323.
43. H. Seton-Watson, *The 'Sick Heart' of Modern Europe. The Problem of the Danubian Lands*, Seattle, 1975, p.59. On the wider problems of south-western Europe see G. Tortella, 'Patterns of economic retardation and recovery in south-western Europe in the nineteenth and twentieth centuries', *Economic History Review*, Vol.XLVII, No.1, 1994, pp.1–21.
44. K. Danaher (ed.), *50 Years is Enough: A Case Against the World Bank and the International Monetary Fund*, South End Press, 1994, p.10.
45. Boltho and Tonioli, op.cit., p.7. Their calculation weights states by population.
46. L. Prichett, 'Divergence, big time', *Journal of Economic Perspectives*, Vol.11, No.3, summer, 1997, pp.3–17.
47. D. Landes, *The Wealth and Poverty of Nations. Why Some are so Rich and Some so Poor*, London, 1998.

11. Socialists and Economic Growth
Carlo Morelli

1. L. Elliott and D. Atkinson, *The Age of Insecurity*, London, 1998, p.36.

2. W. Hutton, *The State We're In*, London, 1995, pp.262–8.
3. Ibid., p.265.
4. E.J. Hobsbawm, *The Age of Extremes: The Short Twentieth Century 1914–1991*, London, 1994, p.282.
5. A. Booth, J. Melling and C. Dartmann, 'Institutions and economic growth: The politics of productivity in West Germany, Sweden and the United Kingdom 1945–55', *Journal of Economic History*, No.2, Vol.57, 1997, p.436.
6. E.P. Thompson, *The Making of the English Working Class*, Middlesex, 1980, p.12.
7. For a fuller discussion of capitalist accumulation see C. Harman, *Explaining the Crisis*, London, 1984, and C. Harman, *Economics of the Madhouse: capitalism and the market today*, London, 1995.
8. Readers should be aware that a market in this context does not necessarily mean a physical meeting of the parties involved. Rather it is any environment where exchange can take place, including the postal, telephone or the internet systems.
9. D.S. Landes, 'What do bosses really do?', *Journal of Economic History*, No.3, 1986 and A. Alchian and H. Demsetz, 'Production, information costs and economic organisation', *American Economic Review*, Vol.62, 1972.
10. G. Clark, 'Factory discipline', *Journal of Economic History*, Vol.54, No.1, 1994, p.131.
11. George Orwell, *Down and Out in Paris and London*, 1974, p.159.
12. Again this is conceded by neo-classical school, see D.C. North, *Structure and Change in Economic History*, New York, 1981, p.208–9.
13. G. Boyce, *Information, Mediation and Institutional Development: the rise of large-scale enterprise in British shipping 1870–1919*, Manchester, 1995.
14. M. Olson, *The Rise and Decline of Nations*, New York, 1982.
15. C. Bean and N. Crafts, 'British economic growth since 1945: relative economic decline... and renaissance' in N.F.R. Crafts and G. Toniolo (eds), *Economic Growth in Europe Since 1945*, Cambridge, 1996, pp.131–72 and S.N. Broadberry and N.F.R. Crafts, 'British economic policy and performance in the early post-war period', *Business History*, Vol.38, No.4, 1996, pp.65–91.

16. J. Saville, *Politics of Continuity: British foreign policy and the Labour Government 1945–6*, 1993, p.4 and pp.149–75.

17. W. Hutton, *The State to Come*, London, 1997, p.44.

18. See R.J. Flanagan, D.W. Soskice and L. Ulman, *Unionism, Economic Stabilisation and Incomes Policy: The European experience*, Washington D.C. 1983, and S.N. Broadberry, 'Unemployment', in N.F.R. Crafts and N. Woodward (eds), *The British Economy Since 1945*, Oxford, 1991, p.212–35.

19. J. Tomlinson and N. Tiratsoo, *Industrial Efficiency and State Intervention 1939–51*, London, 1993.

20. A. Cairncross, *The Years of Recovery: British economic policy 1945–51*, London, 1985.

21. Ibid., pp.334–5.

22. Ibid., pp.31–2.

23. T. Gourvish, 'The rise and (fall?) of state-owned enterprise', in T. Gourvish and A. O'Day, *Britain Since 1945*, Hampshire, 1991, p.115 and Cairncross, op.cit., p.466.

24. G. Ellen, 'Labour and strike breaking 1945–51', *International Socialism Journal*, Vol.2, No.24, 1984, pp.45–73.

25. J.D. Smith, *The Attlee and Churchill Administrations and Industrial Unrest 1945–55: A study in consensus*, London, 1990, pp.9–32.

26. See M.L. Djelic, *Exporting the American Model: the post-war transformation of European business*, Oxford, 1998, pp.81–6.

27. A.S. Milward, The European Rescue of the Nation State, London, 1992, and A.S. Milward, *The Reconstruction of Western Europe 1945–51*, London, 1984.

28. See B.W.E. Alford, 'New for old? British industry between the wars', in R. Floud and D. McCloskey (eds), *The Economic History of Britain since 1700, Vol.2: 1860 to the 1970s*, Cambridge, 1981, pp.308–31.

29. See B. Supple, 'Fear of failing: economic history and the decline of Britain', *Economic History Review*, Vol.XLVII, No.3, 1994, pp.441–58 and R. Pope, *The British Economy since 1914: A study in decline?*, London, 1998, p.15.

30. J. Foreman-Peck, 'Trade and the Balance of Payments', in Crafts and Woodward (eds), op.cit., table 5.2.

31. K. Williams, 'BMC/BLMC/BL—A misunderstood failure' in K. Williams, J. Wiliams and D. Thomas, *Why are the British Bad at Manufacturing?*, London, 1983, pp.248–9.

32. The following discussion focuses upon the impact of the permanent arms economy on the British economy. See T. Cliff, *State Capitalism in Russia*, 1974 and P. Binns, 'The New Cold War', *International Socialism Journal*, No.19, 1983, for the development of the ideas behind the permanent arms economy and Mike Haynes chapter in this volume for details of the general importance of the permanent arms economy to the long boom.
33. J. Saville, op.cit., pp.10–80.
34. R. Middleton, *Government Versus the Market*, Cheltenham 1996, table 12.15.
35. Economist Intelligence Unit, *Economic Effects of Disarmament*, London, 1963, p.49 and p.82 and C.J. Morelli, 'British government expenditure 1948–1963: What does a sectoral Input-Output analysis tell us?', University of Dundee, Economic Discussion Series, No.82, 1997.
36. D.E.H. Edgerton, 'Liberal militarism and the British state', *New Left Review*, No.185, 1991.
37. C. Freeman, 'Government policy', in E. Pavitt (ed.), *Technical Innovation and British Economic Performance*, London, 1980, pp.310–35.
38. Milward, *European Rescue*.

12. The Twentieth Century
Chris Harman

1. I. Berlin, R. Dumont and W. Golding, quoted at the beginning of E.J. Hobsbawm, *The Age of Extremes*, London, 1994, p.1.
2. E. Bernstein, *Evolutionary Socialism*, London, 1909, p.xi.
3. Ibid., p.159.
4. Ibid., p.160.
5. See A. Crosland, *The Future of Socialism*, London, 1956; J. Strachey, *Contemporary Capitalism*, London, 1956; D. Bell, *The End of Ideology*, Illinois, 1960.
6. See especially the various editions of her 1898 pamphlet *Reform or Revolution*.
7. See the various editions of her *Junius* pamphlet.
8. E.J. Hobsbawm, *The Age of Extremes*, op.cit., p.144.
9. E.J. Hobsbawm, *The Age of Imperialism*, London, 1989, p.109.

10. E.J. Hobsbawm, *The Age of Extremes*, op.cit., pp.584–5.
11. In articles in the *Guardian*. See, for instance, 20 June 1996.
12. He has insisted, for instance in TV interviews, that while Marx was right about the crisis prone nature of capitalism, he was wrong about the working class.

Index

Abd-el-Krim, 123
Abortion, 63
Adorno, Gretel, 42
Africa, 3, 10, 16, 17, 32
AIDS, 229
Alleanza Nazionale (AN), 157,
    168–9, 170
America, United States of, 1–2, 6,
    10–11, 16, 18, 20–1, 25–6,
    57–8, 66, 69, 80–116, 157,
    183, 187, 192–4, 229;
    American century, 2, 10–11;
    American exceptionalism,
    10–11, 80–2, 98–9, 109,
    115–16
American Federation of Labor
    (AFL), 10, 80–3, 85, 93–5,
    104; American Socialist Party,
    84–6, 90–4, 96–8, 111–16
Anarchists, 81, 133–55
Anderson, Benedict, 19
Arendt, Hannah, 7
Armenia, 6
Arms expenditure, 193–6, 199
Art, 33–53, 157, 164
Asia, 10
Atkinson, Dan, 204, 212
Attlee, Clement, 6, 213–15,
    218–19
Australia, 17

Bangladesh, 6

Barcelona, 11, 135, 138–40
Barker, Colin, 11
Battleship Potemkin, 49
Benjamin, Walter, 11, 33–53;
    Annales Project, 38, 44; *One-
    Way Street*, 44; 'Theses on the
    Philosophy of History', 35, 37,
    40
Berezin, Mabel, 159–60, 162
Besant, Annie, 175–6
Blair, Tony, 30, 181, 230
Blanqui, Auguste, 36
Bolsheviks, 84, 89, 99, 110–16,
    129–30, 161
Boom, Post-war, 5, 20–2,
    183–203, 205, 215–17
Bourdieu, Pierre, 28
Brecht, Bertolt, 51, 65
Bretton Woods, 21, 32, 189, 196
Britain, 4, 6, 10, 16, 18, 20, 24,
    135, 157, 172–6, 185, 187,
    196–203
Broué, Pierre, 12, 118–19, 223
Budapest uprising, 11
Bukharin, Nikolai, 16, 18, 29, 32,
    125, 184, 224
Bund für Mutterschutz, 61, 65
Burning of Books, 53

Callaghan, James, 22, 28
Cambodia, 6
Canada, 17

Cannon, James P., 85
Carmichael, Stokeley, 70
Carnegie, Andrew, 109–10
Carpenter, Edward, 58
Chicago, 82, 84–7, 93, 96–8;
    Federation of Labor, 84, 86–7,
    94
China, 16, 28, 172, 202, 225, 227
Churchill, Winston, 169–70
Citicorp, 23
Civil Rights movement, 67–8
Claudin, Fernando, 120, 122–4
Cliff, Tony, 119–20, 131–2
Cohen, Stephen, 25
Cold War, 3, 5, 67, 118–19, 195,
    217
Communism, 12, 19, 32, 34, 38,
    42, 44, 46–8, 52, 81, 84–5,
    112–32, 149, 166, 18;
    Communist International
    (Comintern), 12, 19, 47, 84,
    117–32; American, 84–5,
    112–16; British, 118; French,
    123, 130; German, 34, 38, 42,
    46–8, 52, 121, 126–9
*Confederación Nacional del
    Trabajo* (CNT), 133–55, 225
Conference for Progressive
    Political Action, 94–8
Congo, 4
Congress, Indian National, 175,
    178, 181
Consensus between labour and
    capital, 218–19
Convergence, economic, 184–5,
    187, 196–203
Copper, 50
Cox, Robert, 30
Crash, Wall Street, 52
Cresson, Edith, 30
Cultural history, 156–8

Daily Express, 19
Daily Mail, 19

Darwinism, 41
De Felice, Renzo, 7, 157–60, 164,
    166–71
De Gaulle, General, 21
Debs, Eugene, 91, 111
Debt, Third World, 29
Decline, economic, 204–19
Democrats, 81, 87, 92–4
Dialectics, 33
DNA, 5
Duncan, James, 89–90
Duncker, Hermann, 38
Dworkin, Andrea, 76

Eastern Europe, 184–7, 199–201
Eastman, Max, 99, 107
Einstein, Albert, 5
Electricity, 48, 50–1
Elliot, Larry, 204, 212
Engels, Frederick, 15, 35, 38, 40,
    222, *Anti-Dühring*, 40
Erotica, 34
Eskimos, 48
Ethiopia, 3, 4
Expressionism, 50

Falange, 143
Falasca-Zamponi, Simonetta, 159,
    162–3,
Faludi, Susan, 75, 77
Farmer Labor Party, 87, 89-90, 95
Fascism, 36, 38, 41–2, 52, 65, 67,
    127–8, 156–75, 220, 223, 225,
    232
Fashoda incident, 18
Federación Anarquista Ibérica
    (FAI), 133–55
Fini, Gianfranco, 161, 168–9, 170
Firestone, Shulamith, 56, 70
First World War, 12, 19, 39, 62,
    102, 110, 117, 122, 175, 177,
    220
Fitzpatrick, John, 86–7, 94
Foner, Philip, 104, 106

France, 4, 6, 11, 13, 16, 18, 23, 124, 131, 157, 172, 196
Franco, General, 12, 22, 133
Frick, Henry, 109–11
Friedan, Betty, 68
Friends of Durruti, 153–4
Frontier, economic, 187–91, 216
Fuchs, Eduard, 34, 38
Fukuyama, 7, 222
Futurism, 49

Gandhi, Mahatma, 176
General Agreement on Tariffs and Trade (GATT), 21
Genocide, century of, 6–7, 220
Gentile, Emilio, 158–60
German Youth Movement, 40
Germany, 4, 7, 9–10, 16–20, 33–53, 113, 117, 121, 126–9, 135, 196, 200, 215
Giddens, Anthony, 14, 27
Gilbert, Martin, 1, 8
Globalisation, 14–32
Gluckstein, Donny, 9
Gold, 51
Gomez, Alain, 27
Gramsci, Antonio, 224, 232
Greater London Council, 76
Greece, 23, 201
Greenham Common, 76
Griffin, Roger, 158–9
Gurley Flynn, Elizabeth, 57, 99–100

Harvey, David, 14
Haywood, Big Bill, 99–102, 104, 111
Heartfield, John, 45, 49
Hilferding, Rudolf, 17, 224
Hill, Joe, 108
Hirst, Paul, 14, 23–7
Historical materialism, 33–5
Historical pessimism, 8, 220–1,
Hitler, Adolf, 117, 127–8, 223,

226, 227; Hitler-Stalin pact, 42, 52
Hobsbawm, Eric J., 5, 8, 12, 15, 122, 134, 156, 205, 220–33; *The Age of Extremes*, 224–30
Hobson, J. A., 16
Holloway, John, 19
Holocaust, 7, 9, 11, 32, 65, 117, 156–7, 169, 220
Homosexuality, 63, 69, 75, 78
Honda, 26
Hoogvelt, Ankie
Humanité, 124, 131
Hutton, Will, 204–5

I'm Alright Jack, 204
Incest, 53
India, 7, 172–82, 202
Indonesia, 30
Intercollegiate Socialist, 83
International Monetary Fund, 21
International Workers of the World (IWW), 57, 81, 89, 99–104, 107–11
Iran, 11, 172, 230
Iraq, 32, 220
Ireland, 92, 173, 175, 178
Italy, 18, 30, 156–75, 196, 198; Italian Socialist Party, 30

Japan, 10, 16, 20–1, 24, 26, 28, 186, 196, 198
Jinnah, M. A., 177–9
Journal of Contemporary History, 158–9, 167
Jung, Franz, 45–53; *Conquest of the Machines*, 45–8

Keynes, John Maynard, 22, 31, 183, Keynesianism, 189, Keynesian effect, 194
Kidron, Mike, 188–9
Kollontai, Alexandra, 63, 64
Kondratiev waves, 189–91

Korea, 29, 193, 220, 225
Kurdistan, 32

La Follette, Robert, 94–8
Labour Party, 67, 81–2
Labour power, 208–11,
Labour, spread of, 227–9, 232
Lacis, Asja, 44
Laos, 6
Larkin, James, 59
Lenin, Vladimir, 1, 8, 12, 16, 46, 113, 119–20, 125, 132, *Left-wing Communism*, 125
Levi, Paul, 125–6
Liberia, 3
Liebknecht, Karl, 39, 43, 46, 65, 127
London Socialist Historians' Group, 12, 32
Ludlow Massacre, 105–7
Lukács, Georg, 44, 121
Luxemburg, Rosa, 8, 12, 43–4, 46, 52, 61, 65, 127, 221–2, 224, 230

MacDonald, Ramsay, 11
Mack Smith, Denis, 167–8
Malaysia, 30
Marcuse, Hebert, 69
Market theory, 206–10
Marshall Aid, 21, 215
Marx, Karl, 5, 9, 15, 35, 38, 48, 43, 130, 195, 207, 223, 229; *Critique of the Gotha Programme*, 38; *The Communist Manifesto*, 15
Marxism, 33–5, 44, 49, 52, 57, 118–19; dissident, 119
Marxist effect, 194–5
Mehring, Franz, 34
Millet, Kate, 56, 66
Mitterrand, François, 28
Mosse, George, 159–60, 164
Motherhood, 65, 66

Muslim League, 177–82
Mussolini, Benito, 12, 159, 163, 166–71, 222

Nationalism, 172–82
Neue Zeit, Die, 35
New Internationalist, 3
New Jersey, 99–100
New Majority, 86
New World Order, 2, 229
New York, 82–5, 90–4, 96–8, 103, 112–14; *Communist*, 112–14
Nolte, Ernst, 7, 156–7, 169

Orwell, George, 11, 107, 208

Pakistan, 7, 176–82
Palestine, 173, 178
Pankhurst, 59, 60
Paris Commune, 37, 109
Paterson strike 101–4
Permanent Arms Economy, 183, 188–9, 193–6
Petras, James, 28
Philippines, 30
Pinkerton detectives, 110–11
Piscator, Ernst, 51
Poland, 11
Polanyi, Karl, 31
Police, Spanish, 144–5
Ponting, Clive, 7, 8
Pornography, 76
Portugal, 4, 23, 133–6, 172; Portuguese revolution, 11, 227
Progress, 5–6, 8, 11, 33–53, 222; *and* retreat, 8, 220, 230; century of, 5–6, 11, 33
Prohibition, 90
Proletariat, 36; 'Proletarian shopping trips', 143

Rape, 76
Reed, John, 11, 99–106; *Ten Days*

That Shook the World, 99,
111–16
Republicans, 81, 95
Revisionism, 158, 166–71
Revolution, as brake on history, 40
Robertson, Roland, 18
Rosie the Riveter, 67
Rosmer, Alfred, 12, 118, 125,
130–1, 137
Rowbotham, Sheila, 1, 4, 58–9,
67, 74–5
Ruhr crisis, 122–3
Russia, 6–7, 10–12, 18, 20, 29,
32, 42, 62–4, 66, 113, 116–32,
184, 199–201, 230, 232;
Russian Revolution, 62–3,
117–33, 225
Rwanda, 6

Saint-Denis, 123
Samuelson, Paul, 192–4
Saville, John, 10, 212
Schneiderman, 91–2
Schröder, Gerhard, 14
Seattle, 32, 82–5, 88–90, 96–8;
Central Labor Council, 83,
88–90; *Union Record*, 88
Second World War, 20, 117, 133,
168, 220, 226
Segal, Lynne, 74–5
Serge, Victor, 12, 118, 121, 125,
127–30
Shipping, trans-Atlantic, 209–10
Sinclair, Upton, 101
Social Democracy, 5–6, 12, 34,
38–9, 41, 43, 52, 60, 117, 119,
126; American, 80–98; and
Second International, 117;
German 38–9, 41, 43, 52, 60,
117, 119, 126
Social fascism, theory of, 117, 119
Socialist history, 9
Solidarity, role of in Polish revolu-
tion, 11, 225

Somalia, 4
Sombart, Werner, 80
Sony, 26
Soros, George, 31
South Africa, 17
South Asia, 172–82
South-west Africa, 6
Soviet Union, 7, 29, 32; see also
Russia
Spain, 11, 117, 122, 133–55, 198,
225; Spanish Second republic,
136, 138–9
Spartacist uprising, 43, 45
Spice Girls, 76
Stalin, Joseph, 2, 12, 42, 66, 116,
223–4; Stalinism, 117–32, 184,
224, 225, 227
State capitalism, 18–20, 26–8,
200, 211–12
Stöcker, Helen, 61, 65
Stone, Marla, 163–4
Suffragettes, 58–9

Taiwan, 29
Tanzania, 23
Tariffs, 17–18, 21
Taxi drivers, 143
Technology, 5–6, 39
Thailand, 30
Thatcher, Margaret, 22
Third World, 29, 184
Thompson, Grahame, 14, 23–7
Time, 1, 2
Tobin Tax, 31
Totalitarianism, 7–8
Totten, Samuel, 6
Toyota, 26
Trade unionism, 80–98
Triadisation, 23–4
Trotsky, Leon, 20, 62–3, 118–19,
125, 223–4
Trotskyism, 118, 148–9

Ukraine, 6

Ultra-leftism, 125
Unemployed, 133–55
United front, tactic of, 124
United Hebrew Trades, 90–1
United Nations, 31

Valentino, Modestino, 101–2
Value, law of, 17
Versailles, Treaty of, 32
Vietnam, 6, 29, 67–8, 191, 220, 225
Violence; 106–11, 115–16, 142–6; by American bosses, 106–11, 115–16

Wainwright, Hilary, 74–5
Wallerstein, Immanuel, 30
Washington 87–90; State

Federation of Labor, 88–90
Weber, Alfred, 36
Weber, Max, 36
Weill, Kurt, 52
White, Richard, 81, 98
Wilson, Woodrow, 93, 107, 172, 177, 182
Women, 3, 4, 54–79; century of, 3, 4, 54; in women's movement, 54–79, Women's Trade Union League, 93
Workers' councils, 11
World Trade Organisation, 32

Zetkin, Clara, 61
Zhenotdel, 63, 66
Zinoviev, Grigory, 12, 46, 119–21, 129–30